WORSHIP through the CHRISTIAN YEAR

All-age resources for the three-year lectionary

YEAR B

edited by Diana Murrie and Hamish Bruce

Contributors:
Gill Ambrose
Mary Binks
Donald Dowling
Martin Green
Alison Harris
Pam Jones
Kevin Parkes
Steve Pearce
Betty Pedley
Judith Sadler

The National Society
*Leading Education
with a Christian Purpose*
Church House Publishing

National Society/Church House Publishing
Church House
Great Smith Street
London SW1P 3NZ

ISBN 0 7151 4927 X

Published 1999 by the National Society (Church of England) for Promoting Religious Education and
Church House Publishing

Cover design by Leigh Hurlock

Printed in England by Biddles Ltd, Guildford and King's Lynn

Contents

Worship through the Christian Year has been compiled to help those who design all-age learning and worship

Appendix A

Collects and Post Communion Prayers: Ordinary Time (Before Lent)

Appendix B

Collects and Post Communion Prayers: Ordinary Time (After Trinity and Before Advent)

Acknowledgements

The publisher gratefully acknowledges permission to reproduce copyright material in this book. Every effort has been made to trace and contact copyright holders. If there are any inadvertent omissions we apologise to those concerned and will ensure that a suitable acknowledgement is made at the next reprint.

Collects and post communion prayers

C = Collect; PC = Post communion prayer

The Archbishops' Council: pp. 16-17 (C and PC), 51 (PC); 54 (C), 57 (PC), 58 (C), 60 (C), 63 (PC), 118 (C), 122 (C), 126 (C), 131 (C: Third Sunday after Trinity), 133 (C: Ninth Sunday after Trinity), 134 (C: Thirteenth and Fourteenth Sundays after Trinity), 135 (PC: Sixteenth Sunday after Trinity; C: Seventeenth Sunday after Trinity), 136 (C: Eighteenth Sunday after Trinity), from *The Alternative Service Book 1980*; pp. 64 (C), 130 (PC: Second Sunday after Trinity), 132 (PC: Seventh Sunday after Trinity), from *Lent, Holy Week, Easter, 1984 and 1986*; pp. 9 (PC), 12 (C), 21 (PC), 25 (PC), 29 (PC), 121 (PC), 130 (PC: First Sunday after Trinity), from *The Promise of His Glory*, 1991; pp. 133 (PC: Ninth Sunday after Trinity), 136 (PC: Nineteenth Sunday after Trinity), from *Patterns for Worship*, 1995; pp. 40 (C), 55 (PC), 128 (C: Fifth Sunday before Lent), from *The Prayer Book as Proposed in 1928*; pp. 23 (PC), 129 (PC: Third Sunday before Lent), 136 (C: Twentieth Sunday after Trinity); 137 (PC: Twenty-First Sunday after Trinity), by the Liturgical Commission.

Cambridge University Press: pp. 6 (C), 8 (C), 10 (C), 14 (C), 19 (PC), 20 (C), 30 (C), 42 (C), 44 (C),45 (PC), 47 (PC), 52 (C), 56 (C), 62 (C), 66 (C), 68 (C), 70 (C), 116 (C), 120 (C), 124 (C), 127 (PC), 128 (C and PC: Fourth Sunday before Lent), 129 (C), 130 (C: First and Second Sundays after Trinity), 131 (C: Fourth and Fifth Sundays after Trinity; PC: Fifth Sunday after Trinity), 132 (C: Sixth, Seventh and Eighth Sundays after Trinity), 133 (C: Tenth and Eleventh Sundays after Trinity), 134 (C: Twelfth Sunday after Trinity), 135 (C: Sixteenth Sunday after Trinity; PC: Fifteenth and Seventeenth Sundays after Trinity), 136 (C: Nineteenth Sunday after Trinity), 137 (C: Twenty-first Sunday and Last Sunday after Trinity). Extracts adapted from *The Book of Common Prayer* (1662), the rights in which are vested in the Crown, are reproduced by permission of the Crownís Patentee, Cambridge University Press.

Cassell plc: pp. 9 (PC), 28 (C), 39 (PC), 134 (PC: Thirteenth Sunday after Trinity), 135 (C: Fifteenth Sunday after Trinity), 136 (PC: Twentieth Sunday after Trinity), from David Silk (ed.), *Prayers for Use at the Alternative Services*, 1980; revised 1986; pp. 125 (PC: Second Sunday before Advent), 133 (PC: Eleventh Sunday after Trinity), from C. L. MacDonnell, *After Communion*, 1985. Copyright © Mowbray, an imprint of Cassell.

Church of the Province of Southern Africa: pp. 24 (C), 26 (C), 50 (C), 123 (PC), from *An Anglican Prayer Book*, 1989. Copyright © Provincial Trustees of the Church of the Province of Southern Africa.

Episcopal Church of the USA: p. 46 (C), from The Book of Common Prayer according to the use of the Episcopal Church of the USA, 1979. The ECUSA Prayer Book is not subject to copyright.

General Synod of the Anglican Church of Canada: pp. 15 (PC), 27 (PC), 41 (PC), 59 (PC), 65 (PC), 67 (PC), 69 (PC), 117 (PC), 128 (PC: Fifth Sunday before Lent), 131 (PC: Fourth Sunday after Trinity), 132 (PC: Sixth Sunday after Trinity), 134 (PC: Twelfth and Fourteenth Sundays after Trinity), 137 (PC: Last Sunday after Trinity), based on (or excerpted from) *The Book of Alternative Services of the Anglican Church of Canada*, copyright © 1985. Used with permission.

General Synod of the Church of Ireland: p. 53 (PC), from *Alternative Prayer Book*, 1984; pp. 18 (C), 61 (PC) from *Collects and Post-Communion Prayers*, 1995. Reproduced with permission.

Hodder & Stoughton Limited: p. 13 (PC), from Frank Colquhoun (ed.), Parish Prayers, 1967. Reproduced by permission of the publisher.

International Commission on English in the Liturgy: pp. 31 (PC), 136 (PC: Eighteenth Sunday after Trinity), from the English translation of The Roman Missal, © 1973, International Committee on English in the Liturgy, Inc. All rights reserved.

Janet Morley and SPCK: p. 131 (PC: Third Sunday after Trinity) from *All Desires Known*, SPCK, 1992.

Oxford University Press: pp. 22 (C), 38 (C), 71 (PC), from The Book of Common Worship of the Church of South India.

The Very Reverend Michael Perham: pp. 48—9 (C and PC), from Michael Perham (ed.), Enriching the Christian Year, SPCK/Alcuin Club, 1993.

The Right Reverend Kenneth Stevenson: 133 (PC: Tenth Sunday after Trinity).

Westcott House, Cambridge: pp. 11 (PC), 43 (PC), 119 (PC).

Other prayers and intercessions

The Archbishops' Council: 'We pray for God's faithfulness to be known in our world' (p. 35), 'We pray to Jesus who is present with us to eternity' (p. 113) and 'We pray that Christ may be seen in the life of the Church' (p. 119) from *Patterns for Worship*, Church House Publishing, 1995; 'Thanks be to God, who gives us the victory' (p. 51) and 'We stand with Christ in his suffering' (p. 53) adapted from *Lent, Holy Week, Easter*, Church House Publishing/SPCK, 1986; 'God of glory, whose radiance shines from the face of Christ' (p. 23) from *Common Worship: Initiation Services*, Church House Publishing, 1998. 'As we kneel with the shepherds before the new born Christ child' (p. 15) from *The Promise of His Glory*, Church House Publishing, 1991.

Edmund Banyard: 'Lord, we bring you our love' (p. 29) from *Turn but a Stone*, NCEC, 1992.

Charlotte Dyer: 'Dear Lord, I would like to talk' (p. 109) from *Pocket Prayers for Children*, National Society/Church House Publishing, 1999.

St George's, Oakdale: 'Lord Jesus, Light of the world, born in David's city. . .' (p.7), 'Lord Jesus, Light of the world, John told. . .' (p. 11), and 'Lord Jesus, Light of the world, blessed is Gabriel. . .' (p. 13) from *The Promise of His Glory*, Mowbray/Church House Publishing, 1991.

Arthur Gray: 'O Christ, the Master Carpenter' (p. 123), copyright © Arthur Gray, from *The Iona Community Worship Book*, Wild Goose Publications, The Iona Community, Glasgow, 1991.

The Right Reverend Christopher Herbert: 'Holy and loving God' (p. 33), 'Lord, you are love' (p. 43), 'Lord, you are our hope and strength' and 'Give us big hearts, dear God' (p. 47), 'I know, O God, that wherever I travel' (p. 105), 'Lord Jesus, You suffered so much pain and cruelty on the cross' (p. 111) from Christopher Herbert (comp.), *Pocket Prayers for Children*, National Society/Church House Publishing, 1999.

Andrew Hood: Dear God, Thank you for the people who invented medicines' (p. 107) from *Pocket Prayers for Children*, National Society/Church House Publishing, 1999.

International Consultation on English Texts (ICET): 'You are God and we praise you' (p. 127) from the Te Deum, *The Alternative Service Book 1980* copyright © 1970, 1971, 1975, ICET.

Kate McIlhagga: 'Merciful God, for the things we have done that we regret' (p. 45), copyright © Kate McIlhagga, from *The Pattern of Our Days*, ed. Kathy Galloway, Wild Goose Publications, The Iona Community, Glasgow, 1996.

Christine Odell: 'Lord, as we grow older' (p. 31) from Donald Hilton (ed.), *The Word in the World*, NCEC, 1997.

Mrs B Perry / Jubilate Hymns: 'We pray for God's grace' (p. 37) from *Patterns for Worship*, Church House Publishing, 1995: Prayers/intercessions: Michael Perry © Mrs B Perry / Jubilate Hymns.

The lectionary

The Consultation on Common Texts: *The Revised Common Lectionary* is copyright © The Consultation on Common Texts 1992. The Church of England adaptations to the Principal Service lectionary are copyright © The Archbishops' Council, as are the Second and Third Service lectionaries.

Introduction

– both clergy and laity – to explore and implement the varied opportunities offered by the newly authorized three-year lectionary.

For each Sunday there is a brief summary of the Old Testament, New Testament and Gospel readings, ideas for a talk or sermon, group and/or congregational activities, ideas for prayers and intercessions, stories and other resources, suggestions for songs and hymns, and the appropriate collect and post communion prayer.

The aim of the book is to stimulate an individual, creative approach. It could be that the ideas suggested here may inspire something totally different yet appropriate for your church. This is to be welcomed and encouraged. Only those working with real people in a real church can effectively identify what will, or will not be, successful in their 'patch'.

Using the three-year lectionary

The new three-year lectionary authorized for use in the Church of England from Advent 1997 onwards is closely based on the Revised Common Lectionary that is already used by a number of other Churches throughout the world. Readings are provided for every Sunday and Holy Day in the Christian year.

Year A This focuses on the Gospel of Matthew. During Advent, the Old Testament reading is from Isaiah, illuminating the Gospel readings about the coming of Christ, and the second readings come from Romans and 1 Corinthians. From Ash Wednesday to Pentecost, while Matthew remains the focus, there are some of the traditional readings from John's Gospel, during the last three Sundays of Lent and the Easter season.

Year B This focuses on the Gospel of Mark. During Advent, the New Testament readings come mainly from the two letters to the Corinthians, while from Ash Wednesday to Pentecost the New Testament readings are a semi-continuous reading from 1 John. The first readings come from Acts during the Easter season in Year B.

Year C This focuses on the Gospel of Luke, again with readings from John coming in during the Ash Wednesday to Pentecost season. After Easter, there are semi-continuous readings from Revelation. After Pentecost, Jeremiah figures largely in the Old Testament reading, with semi-continuous selections from Galatians, Colossians, 1 & 2 Timothy, and 2 Thessalonians.

As in the other years, the final Sundays after Pentecost focus on the Second Coming and the reign of Christ.

If you are unfamiliar with the three-year lectionary, it is worth carefully reading the Notes section of *The Christian Year: Calendar, Lectionary and Collects* (p. 36), CHP, 1997. This outlines a number of points that you should bear in mind as you plan the Sunday service. These are summarized below:

- When there are only two readings at the Principal Service and that service is Holy Communion, the second reading is always the Gospel reading.

- In the choice of readings other than the Gospel reading, the minister should ensure that, in any year, a balance is maintained between readings from the Old and New Testaments and that, where a particular biblical book is appointed to be read over several weeks, the choice ensures that this continuity of one book is not lost.

- Verses in brackets may be included or omitted, as desired.

Worship through the Christian Year comprises three volumes of resource material to match Years A, B and C of the lectionary.

Church Year (Advent to Advent)	Lectionary Year
1999/2000	B
2000/2001	C
2001/2002	A
2002/2003	B
2003/2004	C
2004/2005	A
2005/2006	B
2006/2007	C
2007/2008	A
2008/2009	B
2009/2010	C

The seasons of the Christian year
Advent

The Christian year traditionally begins on the First Sunday of Advent, four weeks before Christmas. The three-year lectionary returns to this pattern rather than the ASB model which begins the year on the Ninth Sunday before Christmas.

Christmas

Material has been provided for the Christmas Day service itself and for the two Sundays after Christmas.

Epiphany

This season includes material for the Epiphany (which can also be celebrated on the Second Sunday of Christmas) and for the four Sundays of Epiphany, as well as for the service celebrating the Presentation of Christ in the Temple (Candlemas) that is celebrated either on 2 February or on the Sunday falling between 28 January and 3 February.

Ordinary Time (Before Lent)

There are two periods of 'ordinary time' in the new calendar, the first being relatively short, lasting from the Presentation of Christ until Shrove Tuesday. There is no seasonal emphasis in this period. Greater flexibility is given in this period to the worship leader. As is stated in the Notes to *The Christian Year: Calendar, Lectionary and Collects*: 'During Ordinary Time . . . authorized lectionary provision remains the norm but, after due consultation with the Parochial Church Council, the minister may, from time to time, depart from the lectionary provision for pastoral reasons or preaching or teaching purposes.'

The Sunday (lectionary) provisions in this shorter period of Ordinary Time are: Proper 1, Proper 2, Proper 3, The Second Sunday before Lent and The Sunday next before Lent. The first three are used for Sundays that fall in a specific period of time: Proper 1 for Sundays between 3 and 9 February inclusive, Proper 2 for Sundays between 10 and 16 February inclusive and Proper 3 for Sundays between 17 and 23 February inclusive. As the date of Easter obviously changes each year, these Propers similarly chop and change. For instance, if Easter is earlier than usual, you might only use Proper 1 and 2. This may seem confusing and it is recommended that you refer to the specific annual guides that are being published, such as *Advent 1999 – Advent 2000* (Church House Publishing, 1999).

To further complicate the issue, the collects during Ordinary Time are not linked with specific calendar dates, like the lectionary readings, but to the Sunday title. So in this period of Ordinary Time the collects are for the Fifth, Fourth, Third, Second and the Sunday Next before Lent. For ease of use, we have grouped all of the collects and post communion prayers for Ordinary Time at the back of the book in Appendix A (see pp. 128-9). Again, you will need to refer to the specific annual lectionaries to place the readings and collects together. We have provided a simple chart to show which collects and post communion prayers you should use for these services for the next three Year B lectionary years.

Lent

This period includes the five Sundays of Lent and Palm Sunday. Mothering Sunday can be celebrated in preference to the provision for the Fourth Sunday of Lent and we have concentrated on this festival in *Worship through the Christian Year*.

Easter

This season runs from Easter Day, through the Second to Seventh Sundays of Easter and culminates in Pentecost. If the Old Testament reading is used during the Sundays in Eastertide, the reading from Acts must be used as the second reading.

Ordinary Time (After Trinity)

This is a lengthy period of Ordinary Time which runs from Trinity Sunday, through Propers 4–25, ending with Bible Sunday and the Dedication Festival. As in the first period of Ordinary Time, the collects and lectionary readings do not have the same name. All dates cited are inclusive. We have again placed all the collects for this period at the end of the book (see Appendix B on p. 130).

During this period, alternative Old Testament readings are given. Those under the heading 'Continuous' offer semi-continuous reading of Old Testament texts but allow the Old Testament reading to stand independently of the other readings. Those under the heading 'Related' relate the Old Testament reading to the Gospel reading. It is not recommended that you move from week to week from one column to another. One column should be followed for the whole sequence of Sundays after Trinity.

Ordinary Time (Before Advent)

This short period rounds off the Christian Year. It begins with All Saints' Day and ends with the festival of Christ the King.

Resources

Many churches that have already spent large amounts of money on resources for children's work and all-age activities may be concerned about having to purchase a whole range of new resources to complement the new lectionary. The approach in *Worship through the Christian Year* has been to recommend books and other resources that you may already possess.

The following list is divided into core books which are referred to in a number of sessions and others which are referred to only occasionally. It may be a helpful guide to building up a library of resource material for use by all the leaders in your church. To save unnecessary repetition, only the titles of the core books are cited in each session and for this reason the core books are listed alphabetically by title, rather than by author.

Core books and resources

All Aboard!, Steve Pearce and Diana Murrie, NCEC, 1996

Building New Bridges, Claire Gibb, NS/CHP, 1996

Children and Holy Communion, Steve Pearce and Diana Murrie, NS/CHP, 1997

The Christian Year: Calendar, Lectionary and Collects, 1997

Church Family Worship, Michael Perry (ed.), Hodder & Stoughton, 1986

A Church for All Ages: A Practical Approach to All-age Worship, Peter Graystone and Eileen Turner, Scripture Union, 1993

The Discovery Wheel, Gillian Ambrose, Andrew Gear and David Green, NS/CHP, 1994

Festive Allsorts, Nicola Currie, NS/CHP, 1994

In the beginning: An Old Testament Activity Book, Nicola Currie and Jean Thomson, NS/CHP, 1995

Instant Inspirations, Zoë Crutchley and Veronica Parnell, BRF, 1998

Lent, Holy Week, Easter, CUP/SPCK/CHP, 1984 and 1986

The Pattern of Our Days, Kathy Galloway (ed.), Wild Goose Publications, 1996

Patterns for Worship, CHP, 1995

Pick and Mix, Margaret Dean (ed.), NS/CHP, 1992

The Promise of His Glory, Mowbray/CHP, 1991

Reign Dance, Martin J. Nicholls, URC, 1997

Seasons, Saints and Sticky Tape, Nicola Currie and Jean Thomson, NS/CHP, 1992

Seasons and Saints for the Christian Year, Nicola Currie, NS/CHP, 1998

Together for Festivals, Hamish Bruce and Pam Macnaughton (eds), NS/CHP, 1994

Together with Children subscription magazine, NS/CHP

Under Fives – Alive!, Jane Farley, Eileen Goddard and Judy Jarvis, NS/CHP, 1997

Other useful resources
Drama

Anita Haigh, *Rap, Rhyme and Reason*, Scripture Union, 1996

Derek Haylock, *Plays for All Seasons*, NS/CHP, 1997

Derek Haylock, *Plays on the Word*, NS/CHP, 1993

Dave Hopwood, *Acting Up*, NS/CHP, 1995

Dave Hopwood, *A Fistful of Sketches*, NS/CHP, 1996

Dave Hopwood, *Playing Up*, NS/CHP, 1998

Ruth Tiller, *Keeping the Feast: Seasonal Dramas For All-Age Worship*, Kevin Mayhew, 1995

Dave and Lynn Hopwood, *Telling Tales*, CPAS, 1997

Dave and Lynn Hopwood, *Telling more Tales*, CPAS, 1998

Bible resources

Pat Alexander, *Young Puffin Book of Bible Stories*, Puffin, 1988

Arthur Baker, *Palm Tree Bible*, Palm Tree Press, 1992

Selina Hastings (ed.), *The Children's Illustrated Bible*, Dorling Kindersley, 1994

Robin Sharples, *Livewires Live,* BRF, 1998

Storybooks and poetry

Jim Dainty, *Mudge, Gill and Steve*, NS/CHP, 1997

Lynda Neilands, *50 Five-Minute Stories,* Kingsway, 1996

General resource books

Mary Batchelor, *The Lion Christmas Book*, Lion, 1986

Christopher Herbert, *Prayers for Children*, NS/CHP, 1993

Christopher Herbert, *Pocket Prayers for Children*, NS/CHP, 1999

Gordon and Ronni Lamont, *Children Aloud!*, NS/CHP, 1997

Sue Relf, *100 Instant Children's Talks*, Kingsway, 1994

Susan Sayers, *Focus the Word*, Kevin Mayhew, 1989

Susan Sayers, *More Things to Do in Children's Worship*, Kevin Mayhew, 1996

Katie Thompson, *The Complete Children's Liturgy Book*, Kevin Mayhew, 1995

How to use this book

 ## Lectionary readings

These are the readings set for the Principal Service in Year B and provide the main ideas and thrust for the Sunday worship. The principle on which the lectionary is constructed is that the readings speak for themselves, without a stated theme. This may mean that those compiling services come up with different thematic material. That is perfectly acceptable. What is offered here are resources which tend to follow one trend or idea in the readings; these will need adjusting and selecting according to the readings and main idea which those planning the worship decide to emphasize. The following sections will have to be adapted accordingly but this should not be difficult for anyone used to designing all-age learning and worship.

 ## Talk/address/ sermon

These are designed as starting points, arising from the collect and readings. They can be used to prepare material for use in church, or for other occasions such as a school assembly. Further suggestions can be gleaned from looking at the Congregational/group activities section, as can ideas for visual aids to illustrate the talk or sermon. These can be prepared in advance, perhaps by the children and young people of the church, particularly if you have a mid-week group. It will involve them more fully in mainstream Sunday worship. But, as pointed out above, feel free to interpret or develop the readings in the way most appropriate to your situation. It would be helpful to look at the Stories and other resources section for further ideas.

 ## Congregational/ group activities

These are suggestions for activities that develop from the readings and collect. It is important that if work is produced by groups outside the main worship, the rest of the church should have the opportunity to see the results at some point. No indication has been given here as to which activities are suitable for different age groups. It is left entirely to the leaders to decide what would be appropriate. If your church has yet to experience all-age congregational activities, now could be the time to try!

 ## Prayers/ intercessions

Again, these are designed to inspire creativity and originality. It is important that anything produced in the Congregational/group activities section which could be used here should be, and that those leading these activities should be made aware of this.

 ## Stories and other resources

Resources already in use for ASB activities can be used effectively with the new three-year lectionary, even session-dated material. The core books in the Resources section have been widely used by children's work leaders across the dioceses. If you do not have any, or many of them, do consult your Diocesan Children's Work Adviser about them, or inspect them in your local bookshop. It might be interesting for you to note when you last purchased a new resource book!

 ## Music

Each church tends to have its own unique mixture of songs, taken from a diverse range of music books. We have chosen a selection of songs, choruses and modern hymns, alongside familiar traditional hymns, that will help you to focus upon the lectionary readings. Again, it must be stressed that these are only *suggested* songs and hymns and do not provide a complete or definitive list. Please see p. 5 for a list of music books and their abbreviations.

 ## Drama

In recent years, a number of excellent drama books have been published. We have given a few suggestions for appropriate sketches for some of the Sundays in the Christian year. Although the sketches need to be rehearsed in advance, the end result is certainly worth any extra effort.

Collects and post communion prayers

These are the set prayers for the relevant Sunday and can also be used in non-eucharistic worship. The collect for each Sunday is used on the following weekdays, except where other provision is made. *The Christian Year: Calendar, Lectionary and Collects* provides further collects for saints' days throughout the year.

Music book abbreviations

BBP   *Big Blue Planet*, Stainer & Bell and Methodist Church Division of Education and Youth, 1995

CP   *Come and Praise*, Vols 1 and 2, BBC Books, 1978

FG   Peter Churchill, *Feeling Good!*, NS/CHP, 1994

HAMNS   *Hymns Ancient and Modern New Standard*, Hymns Ancient and Modern Limited, 1983

HON   *Hymns Old and New: New Anglican Edition*, Kevin Mayhew, 1996

HTC   *Hymns for Today's Church*, Hodder & Stoughton, 1982

JP   *Junior Praise*, Marshall Pickering, 1986

JU   *Jump Up If You're Wearing Red*, NS/CHP, 1996

KSHF   *Songs and Hymns of Fellowship*: *Integrated Music Edition*, Kingsway, 1987

MP   *Mission Praise*, Marshall Pickering, 1992

SHP   *Spring Harvest Praise 1997*, Spring Harvest, 1997

The First Sunday of Advent

 ## Readings

Isaiah 64.1-9

Yahweh, the living God, is awesome in his anger. Reference is made to his dealings with Israel in earlier days. A sharp contrast is made between those who love God and those who disobey him. The Lord is referred to as 'the Potter' and the people as 'the clay'.

1 Corinthians 1.3-9

Paul gives thanks for the Christians in Corinth and he writes to assure them that the one who has already done great things in them will be faithful to them until he returns.

Mark 13.24-37

Jesus is speaking about the end of time. He uses the imagery of the fig tree in bloom to illustrate his point about discerning when a time or season is near. He tells people to be always alert and on their guard like servants who are left in charge of their master's house in his absence.

Collect

Almighty God,
give us grace to cast away the works of darkness
and to put on the armour of light,
now in the time of this mortal life,
in which your Son Jesus Christ
    came to us in great humility;
that on the last day,
when he shall come again in his glorious majesty
    to judge the living and the dead,
we may rise to the life immortal;
through him who is alive and reigns with you,
in the unity of the Holy Spirit,
one God, now and for ever.

 ## Talk/address/ sermon

Using the potter/clay imagery of the Isaiah reading, start with a ball of clay and demonstrate how that same ball can be made into different shapes. We, made in the image of God, can be responsible for distorting ourselves into all kinds of shapes which are contrary to our Maker's intention. Relate the earlier ways in which God dealt with the people of Israel and the way in which he deals with us now through sending Jesus.

The faithfulness of God referred to by Paul in his letter to the Corinthians can be linked to past, present and future. God was utterly faithful to his promise never to leave his people (such as Noah) and so the opportunity for the new start they needed came through sending Jesus. At Advent, we prepare to celebrate his coming in the past, his being among us in the present and we also think about his promise to come again – in the future. God is faithful and he will keep that promise to return.

When the fig tree is in bloom, we know the season of the year. Use different examples of everyday situations which help us, through observation, to discern the time of year – when things are ready to come to blossom and to fruition (this is not always so easy in our climate!), such as:

> snow drops – winter
>
> daffodils – spring
>
> roses – summer

Advent is the time of year when we think about Jesus' Second Coming. We should not ignore this season but use it to help us to prepare for the day when Jesus will return.

 ## Congregational/ group activities

- Have a large traffic light drawn and displayed with 'Stop! Get ready! Go!' written on it. Liken these instructions to our Advent journey.

Stop: to pray, to think, to listen, to repent.

Get ready: to welcome Jesus into our homes and lives, etc.

Go: and witness for him this Advent and Christmas time.

Provide a task each week of Advent to fit with each of the three colours (red, amber and green). It is helpful if they are printed on card.

- A simple traffic light card (with no wording) could be coloured appropriately by the people and made into an unusual Christmas tree decoration. One idea for an ongoing Advent activity might be to give the people a different decoration for their Christmas tree each week. These are designed to attract attention and give people reason to ask why such an item is hanging on the tree. This would be an opportunity to explain that Advent is a time to Stop and pray/Get ready for Jesus' coming again/and a time to Go and introduce him to others this Christmas.

- Give people the opportunity to mould shapes using clay as they reflect on the words:

  You are the potter, I am the clay
  Make me and mould me in your own way.

- Invite people in groups to discuss what they think their Advent prayer should be this year. After a time for discussion, write them out. There will be lots of different prayers around the groups. Encourage people to offer their Advent prayer every time they open a window on an Advent calendar or use an Advent candle. If none of these things are used, set aside a specific time each day for the offering of this prayer.

- You might want to assemble the Advent wreath as a congregational activity and then light the first candle using suitable words such as those given below under the Prayers/intercessions section.

 ## Prayers/ intercessions

Use the following prayer when lighting the first candle on the Advent wreath:

  Lord Jesus, Light of the world,
  born in David's city of Bethlehem,
  born like him to be a king:
  Be born in our hearts this Christmastide,
  be king of our lives today.

  The Promise of His Glory (p. 137)

Alternatively, use the words on pp. 115–17 of *Prayers for the People* when lighting the Advent wreath.

Stories and other resources

'An illustrated Advent talk: how did God get people ready? Are we ready?', in *Making the Most of Christmas*, CPAS, 1992

Lynda Neilands, Story no. 46: 'Gone for good', in *50 Five Minute Stories'*, Kingsway, 1996

Susan Sayers, All-age talks on: judgement (48, 116), Advent (107, 114), hope (94), being watchful (114)' in *100 Talks for All Age Worship*, Kevin Mayhew, 1997

Stuart Thomas, 'Ideas for all age services on Advent Sunday', in *Come to the Feast: Book 1*, Kevin Mayhew, 1997

Advent sections, in Joan Chapman, *Children Celebrate!* (Marshall Pickering, 1994), *Seasons, Saints and Sticky Tape* and *The Discovery Wheel*

Michael Perry, Patrick Goodland and Angela Griffiths, *Prayers for the People*, Marshall Pickering, 1992

The Promise of His Glory, pp. 136–7

 ## Drama

Dave Hopwood, 'No Room' and 'If Christ returned in the middle of Christmas', in *Stage Right* (obtainable from Dave Hopwood, 40 Walton Road, Woking, Surrey GU21 5DL)

'Message received, but not understood', in Derek Haylock, *Plays for all Seasons,* NS/CHP, 1997

 ## Music

Soon and very soon (JP 221)

Make way, make way (JP 427)

Let us sing and praise God for all that he has done (JU, p. 16)

Come, Lord Jesus (SHP 38)

O Lord, all the world belongs to you (HON 378)

Come, thou long-expected Jesus (HAMNS 31, HON 98, HTC 52)

Earth was waiting, spent and restless (HTC 54)

O come, O come, Emmanuel (HAMNS 26, HON 358, HTC 66)

The advent of our king (HAMNS 25)

Post communion prayer

O Lord our God,
  make us watchful and keep us faithful
  as we await the coming of your Son our Lord;
  that, when he shall appear,
  he may not find us sleeping in sin
  but active in his service
  and joyful in his praise;
  through Jesus Christ our Lord.

The Second Sunday of Advent

 ## Readings

Isaiah 40.1-11

Israel is in exile in Babylonia and the exile has lasted for a long time. The people of Israel are in distress but the prophet promises that Yahweh is about to free them once more. As he urges them to believe this promise he uses imagery of withering grass set against that of the flourishing Word of God and the shepherd with his flock.

2 Peter 3.8-15a

Time is meaningless in the ways of the Lord – 'a day is like a thousand years and a thousand years like a day'. Peter warns people that when the Lord returns he will come like a thief – when they are least expecting him. He calls them to be holy and godly as they await the Second Coming so that they will be found blameless.

Mark 1.1-8

Mark quotes words from Isaiah chapter 40 (see Old Testament reading) and links them to the coming and the preaching of John the Baptist. John calls people to repentance and then baptizes in the River Jordan those who respond. He tells of one who will follow him who will be greater.

Collect

O Lord, raise up, we pray, your power
and come among us,
and with great might succour us;
that whereas, through our sins and wickedness
we are grievously hindered
in running the race that is set before us,
your bountiful grace and mercy
may speedily help and deliver us;
through Jesus Christ your Son our Lord,
to whom with you and the Holy Spirit,
be honour and glory, now and for ever.

 ## Talk/address/sermon

Place around the church large pictures of sheep each bearing a short phrase describing the quality of a shepherd – some good qualities and some not so good. Invite children to go around the church to collect the sheep and then the children, with help from the congregation, can sort the sheep into the two types of qualities of shepherd – good and bad. Pick up the pictures of all the good qualities. Link these to words in the Old Testament reading and to the nature of the promised Messiah.

Use the B.P. motto associated with the Scout movement (B.P. = Baden Powell and also Be Prepared). Think about applying 'B.P.' to a lot of different situations. How do we prepare for going into hospital, going on holiday, moving house, etc? What happens if we are totally unprepared for such situations? Why are we encouraged to be ready for Jesus' Second Coming? What happens if we are not?

John the Baptist called people to repentance – turning round, changing the direction of their ways. The call to us as individuals and as a church is to repent. Where do we feel in our personal lives, the life of the Church, the nation and the world there is a real call to repent? Invite people to use the challenge of this reading as part of their preparation for Christmas.

Prepare the way of the Lord . . . Link the Old Testament reading and the message of John the Baptist. Ask how we prepare our lives for Christmas. What has to be cleared out of the way in order to make a straight path? This could be illustrated by a simple obstacle course set up in the church. Each obstacle could be named as something which blocks the way to our welcoming and receiving Christ again at Christmas. The removal of the obstacles could link into the prayers of penitence.

 ## Congregational/group activities

*   At the beginning of the service when everyone is appropriately still, without any kind of warning or announcement play the music 'Prepare ye the way of the Lord' from the musical *Godspell* (music and lyrics by Stephen Schwartz). This is particularly powerful if it can be played through a public address system which fills the church with sound.

- Divide the congregation into groups and invite them to put the following objects into the centre of each group: a leather belt, a piece of rough, heavy cloth, a small dish with a spoonful of honey on it, a container of water. Use these objects in conjunction with the prayer suggested below or with other suitable words of meditation.

- In groups during the service, cut out the shape of a large water drop, or you can have them pre-prepared to give out in the service. This water drop is attached to a thread and people are invited to hang it on their Christmas tree. 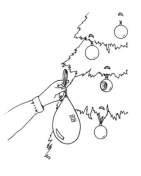 Each week in Advent, it is suggested that they are offered a different symbol of their journey through Advent. The water drop is a symbol of baptism and of John the Baptist's message of repentance.

Prayers/ intercessions

Heavenly Father, you sent your servant John to prepare the way for the coming of Your Son, Jesus Christ.

Today we remember the boldness and clarity of his message. Help us to live in penitence and in faith experiencing the joy of sins forgiven. Help us to help others to seek your forgiveness too.

Lord, in your mercy . . . hear our prayer.

John wore clothes that were tough but uncomfortable. Help us to remember that speaking out for you requires a resilience and toughness because it is not easy or comfortable. Give us the toughness and courage we need to proclaim your message and help to prepare the way for your coming.

Lord, in your mercy . . . hear our prayer.

John was sustained by the simple but good things which you provided. Help us to be nourished in body, mind and spirit by the simplest of your gifts which we so often overlook and ignore. Fill us with a contentment and appreciation that is a witness to your peace.

Lord, in your mercy . . . hear our prayer.

John baptized with water but told that you would baptize with the Holy Spirit. Help us to live out our lives as the baptized people of God and fill us with your Holy Spirit so that we too may help to prepare the way for your coming among us again this Christmastime.

Lord, in your mercy . . . hear our prayer.

Use one of the prayers in *The Promise of His Glory* (on pp. 137–8) as you light the second candle on the Advent wreath.

Stories and other resources

Brian Ogden, 'Dawn the fawn – being lost and found', in *Aunt Emily's African Animals*, Scripture Union, 1997

Lynda Neilands, Stories 10 and 21, in *50 Five Minute Stories*, Kingsway, 1996

'Baptism, forgiveness, incarnation', in *Pick and Mix*

Drama

Jane Phillips, 'Are you ready for Christmas?', in *Together for Festivals*

'Preparing for Christmas', in *Making the Most of Christmas*, CPAS, 1992

Music

Make way, make way (JP 427)

When the Lord in glory comes (JP 280)

God whose love is everywhere (JP 353)

Wait for the Lord (HON 528)

See, your Saviour comes (SHP 116)

Come and see the shining hope (MP 86)

Soon and very soon we are going to see the King (JP 221).

Hail to the Lord's anointed (HAMNS 142, HON 193, HTC 190, KSHF 146)

Hark, a thrilling voice is sounding (HAMNS 24, HON 196, HTC 192)

Hills of the north, rejoice (HAMNS 470, HON 209)

O God, our help in ages past (HAMNS 99, HON 366, HTC 37)

Ye servants of the Lord (HAMNS 150, HON 566, HTC 598)

Post communion prayer

Father in heaven,
who sent your Son to redeem the world
and will send him again to be our judge:
give us grace so to imitate him
    in the humility and purity of his first coming
that, when he comes again,
we may be ready to greet him
with joyful love and firm faith;
through Jesus Christ our Lord.

The Third Sunday of Advent

 ## Readings

Isaiah 61.1-4,8-11

Yahweh shows great kindness and mercy to his people. He is going to restore them to their former glory. Isaiah is telling the people of Israel that God will save them from all their troubles. He describes a glorious future with the ruined cities rebuilt. God's people will become the nation of priests which he always intended them to be.

1 Thessalonians 5.16-24

Paul urges the people of Thessalonica to be joyful, prayerful and thankful at all times. They are to live in the power of the Spirit, upholding good and avoiding evil so that they will be found blameless when Jesus returns.

John 1.6-8,19-28

God sent John as a witness to the light that had come into the world. John has to justify who he is. Many enquirers link him with the prophets of old. He explains that he is preparing the way for the one who will follow him.

Collect

> O Lord Jesus Christ,
> who at your first coming sent your messenger
> to prepare your way before you:
> grant that the ministers and stewards of your mysteries
> may likewise so prepare and make ready your way
> by turning the hearts of the disobedient
>   to the wisdom of the just,
> that at your second coming to judge the world
> we may be found an acceptable people in your sight;
> for you are alive and reign with the Father
> in the unity of the Holy Spirit,
> one God, now and for ever.

 ## Talk/address/sermon

Through the prophecy of Isaiah, God pledges himself in tender, unswerving and enduring love to his people. In peace and security the foundations are laid for a new city. The gates are open to anybody who responds to God's invitation. The New Testament translates Isaiah's concept into spiritual and unusual terms (cf. Romans 9-11, Galatians 3, Revelation 21). What does this say to us about our relationship with Christ whose coming we prepare to celebrate very soon?

The second reading is anticipating the Second Coming of Jesus. Paul teaches the Thessalonians about the lifestyle which is required of them as they await Jesus' return. Because we tend not to think of the Second Coming with the same imminence as Paul did, have we lost the punch in our response to that as reflected in lifestyle?

John the Baptist was at the heart of the Gospel last week also. Do a 'This is your life' approach to telling the story of John the Baptist.

 ## Congregational/group activities

- Take each of the key phrases from the Old Testament reading about the good news to the poor/bind up the broken hearted/freedom for the captives, etc. Print each in large letters on a poster mounted on stiff card and attached to a stick. These promises can be paraded around the church in procession among the people as the words of a song such as 'We are marching in the light of God' are sung.

- Arrange for different parts of the church to represent the different times in John the Baptist's life of which we have some knowledge. Each group prepares from Bible references a one-minute presentation on their part of his life story.

- Continue with the theme of giving people a simple tree decoration throughout this season of Advent to put on their tree. This week's decoration is an unusual one and should invite questions from people who see it – make or give people an arrow. This is a symbol of the way in which the message of the prophets and John the Baptist pointed the way to Jesus.

- All of the Advent themes help us to point to Jesus. Divide the congregation into four groups. Ask them to design a banner/poster, with some of the following phrases on them:

  The Advent hope points the way to Jesus.
  Prophets point the way to Jesus.
  John the Baptist points the way to Jesus.
  Gabriel points the way to Jesus.

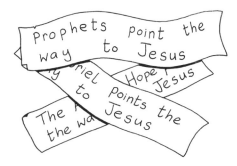

- Light the third candle on the Advent wreath using suitable words, such as those in the Prayers/intercessions section below.

Prayers/intercessions

Jesus, you came to be good news for the poor

(*Hold up the manger or a large picture of it*)

Silence

We pray for them
Jesus you came to be good news for the sad
We pray for them
Jesus you came to be good news for the sick
We pray for them
Jesus you came to be good news for . . .
We pray for them
Jesus you came to be good news for everyone.
We pray for them

In between each sentence and 'We pray for them', someone comes to the front with a symbol or large picture and holds it there in the silence.

Use the following prayer as you light the third candle on the Advent wreath:

Lord Jesus, Light of the world,
John told the people to prepare,
for you were near.
As Christmas grows closer day by day,
help us to be ready to welcome you now.
The Promise of His Glory (p. 139)

Stories and other resources

Lynda Neilands, Stories about forgiveness (10, 21), freedom (16), hope (3), kingdom values (45), repentance (13), return of Christ (46), in *50 Five Minute Stories*, Kingsway, 1996

Lesley and Neil Pinchbeck, Games about the story of John the Baptist, Games 21, 79 and 91, in *Theme Games*, Scripture Union, 1993.

Stuart Thomas, 'Outlines for Third Sunday of Advent', in *Come to the Feast: Book 1*, Kevin Mayhew, 1997

Donald Hilton (ed.), *Seasons and Celebrations*, NCEC, 1996

The Promise of His Glory (p. 139)

Drama

Anita Haigh, 'The weather report', in *Oh No, Not the Nativity!*, Scripture Union, 1998

Music

We are marching in the light of God (JU, p. 34)

How lovely on the mountains (JP 84)

Mighty in victory (JP 430)

Come, Lord Jesus, come (JU, p. 88)

For Mary, mother of our Lord (HON 136)

Lord may we see (MP 438)

God is working his purpose out (HON 172, HTC 191, KSHF 134)

I will sing, I will sing a song (HTC S15)

Jesus shall reign where'er the sun (HAMNS 143, HON 277, HTC 516, KSHF 289)

Soldiers of Christ, arise (HAMNS 219, HON 449, HTC 533, KSHF 483)

Post communion prayer

We give you thanks, O Lord, for these heavenly gifts;
kindle in us the fire of your Spirit
that when your Christ comes again
we may shine as lights before his face;
who is alive and reigns now and for ever.

The Fourth Sunday of Advent

 ## Readings

2 Samuel 7.1-11,16

In the early years of David's reign, he questions whether it is right that he should be a king living in a palace made of cedarwood whilst the Ark of God remains in a tent. He consults the prophet Nathan who tells him that God has never dwelt in one place. Instead, he has always been with his people in their travels. This incident is part of the story of the transition of Israel from an alliance of tribes to a monarchy (the House of David).

Romans 16.25-27

In these words, Paul links the prophecies which pointed the way to the coming of Jesus with the Word made flesh – the person and work of Jesus. He praises God for the wonder of the good news which he is able to proclaim and to share.

Luke 1.26-38

The Angel Gabriel appears to the Virgin Mary at her home in Nazareth. She is told that she is to be the mother of a baby called Jesus. Mary is troubled by this message but is reassured by the angel. Mary is obedient to the Lord God's call upon her. She is also told of her cousin Elizabeth's pregnancy.

Collect

God our redeemer,
who prepared the Blessed Virgin Mary
to be the mother of your Son:
grant that, as she looked for this coming as our
    saviour,
so we may be ready to greet him
when he comes again as our judge;
who is alive and reigns with you,
in the unity of the Holy Spirit,
one God, now and forever.

 ## Talk/address/ sermon

Prepare two people in advance to provide a simple mime taking the roles of the Angel Gabriel and the Virgin Mary. This mime is offered as the words of the Gospel are read. Use this to talk about Mary's obedience, her willingness to say 'yes' and to be the servant of the Lord, but ensuring that the obedience is not made to sound easy; it was very costly. What did it/could it have cost Mary?

Develop the 'Getting ready' theme (see the material for the Second Sunday of Advent). Mary has to get ready to be the mother of Jesus. We have to get ready for the coming of Jesus again this Christmastime. What do the latter stages of this 'getting ready' involve us in this year?

Have a person dressed as a town crier who comes to the front of the church to proclaim (from a scroll) the good news that a baby is going to be born. Who is he? Where will he be born? When?

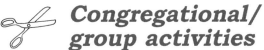 ## Congregational/ group activities

- Give every member of the congregation a card with the word YES printed in bold outline. Give everyone time to think about what God is asking of them this Christmastime. Ask them to write or draw on the reverse of the card, or within the lines of the letters if big enough, all the things that they feel able to say 'Yes' to God to (forgiveness of . . ., generosity to . . ., hospitality this Christmas, etc.).

- Use the carol 'The angel Gabriel from heav'n came'. It can be listened to on tape if there is not a choir or group to sing it. Ask people in advance to prepare a dance, taking the parts of the Angel Gabriel and the Virgin Mary.

- Prepare the stable scene in the church. This may be the small-model size or a life-size adaptation in a corner of the church. Prepare the straw, the manger, etc. and leave it ready for the arrival of Mary and Joseph and the infant Christ on Christmas Eve and Christmas Day.

- The emphasis of Gabriel's message was on the child, not on Mary. Invite people to list all the names or descriptions associated with the infant Christ (King of Kings, Lord of Lords, Saviour, Emmanuel, etc.). Cut out a large silhouette of a baby in a manger. Cut this into about eight pieces. As each name is offered, write it onto one of the pieces. When all the pieces are labelled, re-assemble the pieces to put together a word picture of the baby promised to Mary by the Angel Gabriel.

- Give everyone in the congregation a small, simple cut-out of an angel. These can be made in groups at the time of the service or be pre-prepared if necessary. This is to be taken home and hung on the Christmas tree.

- Light the fourth candle on the Advent wreath using the words written out in the Prayers/intercessions section below.

Prayers/ intercessions

Heavenly Father, we rejoice as we remember the obedience of the young woman, Mary, chosen to be the Mother of Jesus. Mary when called to be your servant said 'Yes'.
Give to us the faith and the courage, the obedience and hope to be able to respond to your call.

When you ask for our time, help us to say
Yes, I am the Lord's servant!

When you ask for our enthusiasm and conviction, help us to say
Yes, I am the Lord's servant!

When you ask for our generosity and sacrifice help us, knowing the cost, to say
Yes, I am the Lord's servant!

When you ask for our penitence and faith help us to say
Yes, I am the Lord's servant! Amen.

Use the following prayer as you light the fourth Advent candle on the Advent wreath:

Lord Jesus, Light of the world,
blessed is Gabriel who brought good news
blessed is Mary your mother and ours.
Bless your Church preparing for Christmas;
and bless us your children who long for your coming.

The Promise of His Glory (p. 139)

Stories and other resources

Bob Hartman, 'The surprise', in *Star of Wonder – Christmas Stories and Poems for Children*, compiled by Pat Alexander, Lion, 1996.

Section on the Blessed Virgin Mary, in *Seasons and Saints for the Christian Year*

Sections on Incarnation, Obedience and Promises, in *Pick and Mix*

The Advent section, in *The Promise of His Glory*

Drama

Dave Hopwood, 'The News – the promises of Jesus', in *Hitting Home* (obtainable from Dave Hopwood, 40 Walton Road, Woking, Surrey GU21 5DL)

Alistair Kennedy, 'The director of music', in *Oh No, Not the Nativity!*, Scripture Union, 1998

Dave and Lynn Hopwood, 'Mary and the angel', in *Telling Tales*, CPAS, 1997

Music

Jesus, how lovely You are (JP 133)

Amazing grace (HON 27, HTC 28, KSHF 10)

Come all you good people (HTC 80)

Sing we the King (MP 602)

Soon and very soon (MP 605)

Hark the glad sound! The Saviour comes (HAMNS 30, HON 198, HTC 193)

The angel Gabriel from heaven came (HON 471)

Post communion prayer

Heavenly Father,
who chose the Blessed Virgin Mary
to be the mother of the promised saviour:
fill us your servants with your grace,
that in all things we may embrace your holy will
and with her rejoice in your salvation;
through Jesus Christ our Lord.

Christmas Day

25 December

 ### Readings (set II)

Isaiah 62.6-12

Yahweh is a living God who is kind and merciful to his people. He restores their comfort but it is clearly stated that it is necessary to practise righteousness if a person is to share in the coming salvation.

Titus 3.4-7

When God sent his Son Jesus to live on earth, he sent a saviour, not because of anything we have deserved, but because he had mercy on us. We are only saved by the Grace of God and it is through that grace that we have the hope of eternal life.

Luke 2.[1-7]8-20

A census takes Mary and Joseph to the town of Bethlehem. While they are there, Mary gives birth to her firstborn son. She lays him in a manger because there is no room for them to stay in an inn. Shepherds in nearby fields are visited by angels who tell them of the birth of a saviour. The shepherds go to visit the baby and they tell Mary what the angels have said to them.

Alternatively one of the following sets of reading may be used:

Set I	Set III
Isaiah 9.2-7	Isaiah 52.7-10
Titus 2.11-14	Hebrews 1.1-4[5 -12]
Luke 2.1-14[15-20]	John 1.1-14
See *Worship through the Christian Year:* Year A	See *Worship through the Christian Year:* Year C

Collect

Almighty God,
you have given us your only-begotten Son
to take our nature upon him
and as at this time to be born of a pure virgin:
grant that we, who have been born again
and made your children by adoption and grace,
may daily be renewed by your Holy Spirit;
through Jesus Christ your Son our Lord,
who is alive and reigns with you,
in the unity of the Holy Spirit,
one God, now and for ever.

 ### Talk/address/ sermon

Make up your own Christmas crackers (kits for making crackers are very easily obtained in the shops in the weeks leading up to Christmas). In the crackers, put small pieces of paper bearing a Christmas message or text, stickers, badges, etc. The crackers can be pulled as part of the celebration on Christmas morning and the messages and text which are discovered can be woven together to build up a Christmas talk.

Provide a real or pretend Christmas/birthday cake with candles. Light the candles and sing Happy Birthday to Jesus. This is particularly meaningful if the birthday cake candles which re-light are used. These help to symbolize the truth that no amount of darkness can extinguish the Light of Christ.

Cut up a large piece of card into about ten pieces to make a jigsaw with one piece clearly occupying a central position. Invite people to call out different aspects of what have been their preparations for Christmas (wrapping presents, writing cards, making mince pies, etc.) Write one of these things on each of the pieces of the jigsaw. Get people to come out and assemble the pieces. One piece is missing. On this piece, have a picture of the baby Jesus. Complete the picture puzzle, put the heart into Christmas – Jesus – and talk about the true meaning of the Christmas celebrations.

Many Christmas gifts come in pieces and need assembling. Sometimes we get confused and need help when trying to make sense of the instructions in order to put things together. Sometimes the message of Christmas is heard, or only remembered, in pieces. Let's assemble all the pieces of the story so that we hear it afresh and are able to worship the one who came as a baby in a manger.

 ### Congregational/ group activities

- Light the central candle in the Advent wreath. Invite each member of the congregation to hold a small hand candle. The first candle is lit from the central candle in the wreath and the light passed around the Church. As this is taking place, the congregation and/or choir sing 'The Light of Christ has come into the world'.

- Give people a Polo mint or other sweet which can be threaded onto a string and invite them to hang it on their Christmas tree in a prominent position! This can be used in conjunction with one of the Talk/address/sermon ideas on making a jigsaw, or the idea can stand independently. When visitors to a home question the unusual tree decoration people are able to explain that for so many people Christmas is all sweet and sugary on the outside, but that it has a hole in the middle. People are encouraged to ask the enquirers if there is any 'heart' to their own Christmas?

- Use the relevant sections from Handel's Messiah to tell parts of the Christmas story. As the music is played, pictures could be projected onto an overhead projector screen or a video could be used.

- Print out the Gospel reading from 'The Dramatised Bible' and give everyone in the congregation a copy. Divide the whole congregation into parts so that everybody has a part to play in the re-telling of the Christmas story.

- Invite people to bring along a wrapped present which they are willing to unwrap in front of the congregation. Ask people to guess what might be inside. After two or three presents have been unwrapped produce one which says on the label 'To the congregation at St _____ and for the whole world'. Invite some children to help to open the parcel. Inside is a small manger with the baby Jesus in the straw.

 Prayers/ intercessions

As we kneel with the shepherds before the newborn Christ child, we open our hearts in penitence and faith:

You, Lord, were born for our salvation.

Lord, have mercy.

Lord, have mercy.

You came as Saviour to bring wholeness and peace.

Christ, have mercy.

Christ, have mercy.

You came to bring light into the darkness of our lives.

Lord, have mercy.

Lord, have mercy.

May Almighty God, who sent his Son into the world to save sinners, bring you his pardon and peace, now and for ever. **Amen.**

The Promise of His Glory

Stories and other resources.

Lynda Neilands, Story no. 6: 'Snowdrop's first Christmas' and Story no. 7: 'Red giant and white dwarf', in *50 Five Minute Stories*, Kingsway, 1996

Michael Botting (ed.), *Prayers for all the Family* (pp. 113–14), Kingsway, 1993

Michael Perry, *The Dramatised Bible*, Marshall Pickering/Bible Society, 1989

The Christmas section, in *Together for Festivals*

Kimberley Rinehart, *The Greatest Gift of All,* An Inspirational Press Book for Children, A division of BBS Publishing Co., 1987

Jan Peters, *The Little Christ Child and the Spiders*, Macdonald Children's Books, 1988.

 Drama

Dave Hopwood, 'Silent night and the first day of Christmas', in *A Fistful of Sketches,* NS/CHP, 1996

Michael Botting (ed.), Dramas 11–16, in *Drama for all the Family,* Kingsway, 1993

Susan Sayers, *Not Another Carol Service*, Kevin Mayhew, 1997.

 Music

All the traditional carols are obvious choices for a Christmas Day service.

Born in the night (JP 313)

Christmas is a time to love (JP 321)

Long ago there was born (JP 418)

Christmas, Christmas (CP 122)

Rise up, shepherd (CP 116)

A great and mighty wonder (HAMNS 43, HON 2, HTC 49)

Infant holy, infant lowly (HON 251, HTC 86)

See him lying on a bed of straw (HON 440, HTC 91)

Post Communion

God our Father,
whose Word has come among us
in the Holy Child of Bethlehem:
may the light of faith illumine our hearts
and shine in our words and deeds;
through him who is Christ the Lord.

The First Sunday of Christmas

Readings

Isaiah 61.10–62.3

The prophet Isaiah declares that the day is coming when God will be able to rejoice and delight in his people; a day to long for, pray for and to prepare for.

Galatians 4.4-7

Paul is explaining the purpose of the Law (the Law operated as a temporary restraint until the promise made to Abraham was fulfilled in the Coming of Christ). By faith in Christ, all are God's children. We are his heirs.

Luke 2.15-21

Having heard the message of the angels, the shepherds decide to go to Bethlehem to see for themselves what the angels had spoken about. The shepherds find Mary, Joseph and the baby. They speak of what the angels said and Mary remembers what the shepherds tell her. On the eighth day, Jesus is taken to be circumcised and he is officially given the name which Gabriel had given the baby when he spoke to Mary.

Collect

Almighty God,
who wonderfully created us in your own image
and yet more wonderfully restored us
through your Son Jesus Christ:
grant that, as he came to share in our humanity,
so we may share the life of his divinity;
who is alive and reigns with you,
in the unity of the Holy Spirit,
one God, now and for ever.

Talk/address/ sermon

This is the day which the Lord has made
we will rejoice and be glad in it . . .

Link these familiar words to the Old Testament reading. What were the qualities of the day about which Isaiah spoke when he said God would rejoice and delight in his people? How is the fulfilment of this prophecy linked to the Coming of Jesus? How does it relate to our life as a Church today?

Explain what it means to be an heir (heir to the throne, heir to an estate, heir to a fortune, etc.). Discuss the implications of this and relate it to the utterly amazing fact that we are heirs to the kingdom of God. How? Who says so? Why? How do we react to this?

Take the part of the shepherd. Reflect on your experiences of visiting the stable and observing Mary's reactions to your words. 'I'll never forget the night when . . .'

Congregational/ group activities

- The shepherds visit the stable. If there is a stable scene in the church (either small or large), use this or create one. Create another area in the church to represent the hillside where the shepherds encountered the angels. Dress a few people of all ages as shepherds. They will lead all the congregation in a procession. Everyone will travel by a roundabout route from the hillside to the stable to worship the baby. Prayers can be offered on the hillside and in the stable. Perhaps music could be played on the journey.

- Show pictures (slides or on an overhead projector) of the hillside near Bethlehem where the shepherds looked after their sheep. Show pictures of the stable scene. Use the pictures for simple reflection as if these were pictures from your photograph album. Talk about them as if you and a few members of the congregation had been there.

- Give material for children to make simple crowns.

This adds to the festive feel of this season. The crowns could bear the message 'Jesus, King of Glory, Truth and Love'. These might be used in preparation for an Epiphany party. Alternatively, give people some shiny stars to wave about on strings, elastic or sticks. Similar messages about Christ might be stuck on to these.

Prayers/ intercessions

Use the following prayer of thanksgiving:

God, our Father, we listen again to the story of Christmas, and we are glad that Jesus has come to be our saviour and our friend.

We hear how Mary laid her baby in a manger. Jesus has come:

Thank you, Father

We hear how the angels sang over the Bethlehem hills: 'Glory to God; peace for the world'. Jesus has come:

Thank you, Father

We hear how the shepherds hurried to see that what the angel said was true. Jesus has come:

Thank you, Father

You may omit this part of the prayer if used before Epiphany.

We hear how the wise men came to bring their worship and their precious gifts. Jesus has come:

Thank you, Father

Stories and other resources

Christmas chapter, in *Seasons and Saints for the Christian Year*

Incarnation section, in *Pick and Mix*

Angela Elwell Hunt, 'The singing shepherd', in *Star of Wonder – Christmas Stories and Poems for Children*, compiled by Pat Alexander, Lion, 1996

Robin Sharples, 'Jesus is coming and Jesus is born', in *Livewires Live,* BRF, 1998

David Kossof, 'I was there!', in *Star of Wonder – Christmas Stories and Poems for Children*, compiled by Pat Alexander, Lion, 1996

Paddie Devon, *The Grumpy Shepherd*, Scripture Union, 1995

Mary Batchelor, *The Lion Prayer Collection*, Lion, 1992

Michael Perry, Patrick Goodland and Angela Griffiths, *Prayers for the People*, Marshall Pickering, 1992

Drama

Dave and Lynn Hopwood, 'The Nativity', in *Telling Tales*, CPAS, 1997

Peter Comaish, 'In the picture', in Pam Macnaughton and Hamish Bruce (eds), *Together through the Bible*, NS/CHP, 1998

Music

See, to us a Child is born (JP 452)

A special star (JP 305)

When our God came to earth (HON 552)

Jesus, Jesus here I am (JU, p. 96)

The Virgin Mary (CP 121)

Who came to Mary? Angel Gabriel (BBP 30)

Go tell it on the mountain (HON 165)

Love came down at Christmas (HON 320, HTC 62)

See, amid the winter's snow (HON 439, HTC 90)

Post communion prayer

Heavenly Father,
whose blessed Son shared at Nazareth
   the life of an earthly home:
help your Church to live as one family,
united in love and obedience,
and bring us all at last to our home in heaven;
through Jesus Christ our Lord.

The Second Sunday of Christmas

 ## Readings

Note: these readings are the same as in Years A and C and so additional ideas (i.e. resource material) can be found in *Worship through the Christian Year: Year A* and *Worship through the Christian Year: Year C*.

Jeremiah 31.7-14

Jeremiah speaks of a new covenant that will replace the old one made at Sinai, which the children of Israel had broken. This time God is going to remake his people from within, giving the power to do his will. He is talking about the actual return from exile, but in the long term he looks forward to the new covenant.

or

Ecclesiasticus 24.1-12

Wisdom is of God. It has taken root in God's chosen people. The God of eternity, present in creation is present with us now.

Ephesians 1.3-14

Paul describes what God has done for us in the gift of Christ. We have been chosen, so that we may become holy and be the realization of God's plan for his people.

John 1.[1-9],10-18

During Advent the readings concerning John have been pointing the way to the one who would follow. In this beautiful passage of Scripture Jesus himself is revealed as the one who was present in creation but who is now present on earth to light the way to God, for those who choose to see it.

Collect

Almighty God,
in the birth of your Son
you have poured on us the new light of your incarnate Word,
and shown us the fullness of your love:
help us to walk in his light and dwell in his love
that we may know the fullness of his joy;
who is alive and reigns with you,
in the unity of the Holy Spirit,
one God, now and for ever.

 ## Talk/address/ sermon

The Coming of Christ to live on earth, born as a baby in Bethlehem, changed the world. Try to involve people in putting together the 'Who? What? Why? When? Where?' of the incarnation.

Who came to live on earth?
What difference did/does his coming make?
Why did God send Jesus?
When did he come?
Where is he now? etc.

'The Light shines in the darkness. The darkness has not understood it'. 'The Word was in the world. The world did not recognize him'. Link these powerful sayings to the condition of our world and communities and to their need for God. Discuss how these words influence our prayers and desires for the New Year and coming millennium.

 ## Congregational/ group activities

- Make a banner or very large wall hanging-type poster with the words boldly presented – 'The Light shines in the darkness'. Cut out in advance a number of small candles. At an appropriate moment in the service, each person is asked to take one of the small candles and stick it onto the large banner. This is a symbol of the part that each one of us has to play in taking the Light of Christ out into the darkness of the world.

- Give each person a small cardboard candle to display in a prominent place in their home during the New Year and its coming months. Use the words from the baptism service:

  Shine as a light in the world
  To the glory of God the Father

  for people to say to each other as they exchange candles during a re-commissioning service at the beginning of the New Year. The people, in effect, commission each other for their work and witness. The candles can be exchanged many times over.

- After warning people in advance, make the church as dark as possible. Light a candle or use a torch. Show how far the effect of the light stretches. Take the light into dark corners of the church. Explain that the only way of chasing away darkness is by replacing it with light. Put posters in different parts of the church representing places or situations of darkness. The light is taken to each of the identified parts of the church and prayers offered asking for light to come to this particular kind of the world's darkness.

- What is the nature of the light which Jesus brings into the world? In groups, brainstorm ideas. Give each group a poster-size piece of paper with a candle drawn on it. Write the group's ideas about different kinds of light onto long strips of paper. Stick these in position around the candle flame to represent the rays of light radiating from the source.

- Organize a Christingle Service. Develop the symbolism of the Christingle to link with today's themes of the God in creation, present in the person of Jesus, Light of the world (link the use of the orange, sweets, red band and candle). Use the symbolism of the Christingle to link the way in which the money raised from the services is a contemporary example of the way the work of the Children's Society can bring light into the darkness of those children's lives that have been disadvantaged.

 ## Prayers/ intercessions

Each year there are prayers which use the light imagery produced by the Children's Society for use at Christingle Services. Link them with the theme the Light of the World and the work of the society shining as a light into the darkness of many children's lives.

Alternatively, use the prayers from one of the following sources:

'Prayers for use in the Christmas season', in Michael Perry, Patrick Goodland and Angela Griffiths, *Prayers for the People*, Marshall Pickering, 1992 (pp. 125–30)

'Responsive prayers for use at Christmas', in *Patterns for Worship* (pp. 67–9)

 ## Stories and other resources

Sue Relf, 'The Light of the World', in *100 Instant Children's Talks*, Kingsway, 1994

Leslie Francis and Nicola Slee, *Lights – Teddy Horsley Celebrates Christmas*, NCEC, 1985

Bob Hartman, 'A night the stars danced', in *Star of Wonder – Christmas Stories and Poems for Children*, compiled by Pat Alexander, Lion, 1996

Joan Chapman, The chapter on Christingle, in *Children Celebrate!*, Marshall Pickering, 1994

Drama

Glynis Heatherington, 'The Light of the World', in *Tale of Two Houseplants and Other Plays*, Mothers' Union, 1991

Derek Haylock, 'Light of the World', in *Plays on the Word*, NS/CHP, 1993

 ## Music

Born in the night (JP 313)

Girls and boys, leave your toys (JP 344)

It was on a starry night (JP 396)

Keep a light in your eyes for the children of the world (BBP 24)

Alleluia (HON 23)

Alleluia, alleluia (BBP 43)

As I went riding by (CP 120)

Child in the Manger (HON 75, MP 71)

You laid aside Your majesty (MP 795)

Angel-voices ever singing (HAMNS 163, HON 33, HTC 307)

Jesus, hope of every nation (HTC 58)

Praise be to Christ in whom we see (HTC 220)

To us a child of royal birth (HAMNS 45, HTC 64)

Post communion prayer

All praise to you,
almighty God and heavenly King,
who sent your Son into the world
to take our nature upon him
and to be born of a pure virgin:
grant that, as we are born again in him,
so he may continually dwell in us
and reign on earth as he reigns in heaven,
now and for ever.

The Epiphany

January 6th

In any year when there is a Second Sunday of Christmas, the Epiphany may also be celebrated on this Sunday.

As the readings are the same for Years A and C, please refer to the other books in the *Worship through the Christian Year* series for further ideas.

 ### Readings

Isaiah 60.1-6

A new manifestation of God's redeeming glory is shown here. The light of God's glory will dispel the darkness that covers the earth and will gather nations to his light.

Ephesians 3.1-12

Although Paul is writing from prison, he is able to write with confidence about the 'unsearchable riches of Christ'. For it is through all that Christ has accomplished that we can now approach God with freedom and confidence.

Matthew 2.1-12

The Magi travel from the east to find the one born king of the Jews. King Herod is determined to find out who this might be in order to destroy any threat to his own authority. The Magi follow the star to the house where Jesus, now a child, lives. They offer gifts of gold, incense and myrrh. Warned in a dream not to return to Herod, they go back home by a different route.

Collect

> O God,
> who by the leading of a star
> manifested your only Son to the peoples of the earth:
> mercifully grant that we,
> who know you now by faith,
> may at last behold your glory face to face;
> through Jesus Christ your Son our Lord,
> who is alive and reigns with you,
> in the unity of the Holy Spirit,
> one God, now and for ever.

 ### Talk/address/ sermon

The star guided the wise men towards the baby Jesus. We use many different kinds of light ourselves to help us to see during dark evenings. Which do you use? Show an assortment of lights (light bulb, bike light, candle, lantern, etc.). Discuss how these are used and for what purpose.

Each of these lights has a special purpose. We have been looking at a different kind of light today – the light of Christ. What is special about the light of Christ?

It is a *revealing* light. The Gospel reading tells us that Christ reveals God to us. Because he is God's own Son, he can show us what God is like.

It is a *saving* light. Just as a lighthouse saves the ships from being shipwrecked on the rocks hidden in the darkness, Christ saves us from all that is wrong and brings us back to God.

It is a *guiding* light. Just as a bike light or lantern shows us the right path forward, so Christ is our guide throughout life to show us the way we should live.

 ### Congregational/ group activities

- Cut out enough card stars for each member of your group or congregation. Ask each person to write or draw pictures of people, nations or events that they want to pray for. Use these as candleholders for the prayer activity.

- Wrap up three prizes in small boxes, labelled Gold, Frankincense and Myrrh. Hide these in the church building. Separate the congregation/children into three groups and give them instructions to follow in order to find their treasure box.

- Collect as many postcards, pictures or stamps that depict the Epiphany story as you can find. Ask the group to select which, for them, is closest to the accounts in the Bible. What do they add or omit from the Bible story of the wise men? Why do they do this? What else can we learn from these different perspectives on the story?

- Nicola Currie's book, *Seasons and Saints for the Christian Year* gives a seasonal twist to some familiar games. The rules will be familiar to children, but will also have a strong link to the Epiphany story (such as 'Collect a camel', 'Crossing the Euphrates' and 'Journey list').

Prayers/ intercessions

Give out candles to each person. When they have finished drawing and writing on their candle holders (see activity above), ask the adults and children at the end of each row of seats or pews to come to the the front and light their candles from the altar. They then go back to their seats and 'pass on' the light to the person sitting next to them. Ensure that there are enough adults strategically placed to supervise the younger children during this activity. Sing 'The light of Christ' during the lighting of the candles. Allow a time of silence as the congregation pray for the people and events on their candles.

Use the following response after each confession:

> Jesus, light of the world
> **shine in our darkness**

Lord Jesus Christ, we confess our sins before you.

Forgive us, we pray, for the times we shun your light and prefer to hide in the darkness of our hearts . . .

Forgive us, we pray for the times we do not stand up for your truth but hide in the darkness . . .

Forgive us, we pray, for our own selfishness and greed . . .

Forgive us, we pray, for the harmful things we do and say to others . . .

Forgive us, we pray, that we live by the light of our own eyes and not by your light of truth . . .

Use the following blessing at the end of the service:

God sends us out in the light of Christ
to bring light into our world of darkness.
May the light of Christ so shine in our hearts
that we might bring his light to others.
And the blessing of God almighty,
the Father, the Son, and the Holy Spirit,
be among you and remain with you always.
Amen.

Stories and other resources

'The story of the Epiphany tree', in *It's a Very Special Day*, NCEC, 1998

'The wise men and the flight into Egypt', in *Instant Inspirations*

The Epiphany sections, in *Seasons and Saints for the Christian Year* and *Together for Festivals*

Drama

Katherine Musson, 'The story of the fourth wise man', in *Together for Festivals*

Dave Hopwood, 'Light and dark – a responsive sermon', in *Playing Up*, NS/CHP, 1998

 ## Music

Unto us a boy is born! (JP 263)

Within our darkest night (HON 562)

A special star, a special star (BBP 37)

Baboushka (Come in, my royal masters) (CP 115)

We are marching in the light of God (JU, p. 34)

Lord the light of your love (HON 317, MP 445)

He made the stars to shine (JP 76)

Christ is the world's true light (HON 78)

The light of Christ (MP 652)

As with gladness (HAMNS 51, HON 41, HTC 99, MP 39)

Wise men, they came to look for wisdom (HTC 100)

Let all mortal flesh keep silence (HAMNS 256, HON 295, HTC 61)

Post communion prayer

Lord God,
the bright splendour whom the nations seek:
may we who with the wise men
have been drawn by your light
discern the glory of your presence in your Son,
the Word made flesh, Jesus Christ our Lord.

The Epiphany

The Baptism of Christ

The First Sunday of Epiphany

 ## Readings

Genesis 1.1-5

Light appears as one of the earliest elements of creation. Light and darkness are separated and light identified as good. The storyteller helps us to reflect that light is fundamental to existence, both physically and metaphorically.

Acts 19.1-7

This account of Paul's visit to Ephesus reminds us that baptism into faith in Jesus Christ is not simply an act of repentance but also confers the Holy Spirit, sustaining action.

Mark 1.4-11

John the Baptist appears in the desert, calling people to repentance. The place reinforces the challenge of his austere message, to turn away from sin and towards attention to God, and of his status as a prophet, one who points towards the Messiah. Many people go to see what is happening and are baptized. The baptism represents a drastic new beginning, in a wild place far from the traditional significant Jewish holy sites. A drastic change of direction is implied. Into this scene walks Jesus and undergoes baptism himself. The significance of this is marked by a sign of the Spirit, a dove and words from Isaiah 42.1, underlining the opening words of the Gospel, that it is about Jesus Christ, the Son of God.

Collect

Eternal Father,
who at the baptism of Jesus
revealed him to be your Son,
anointing him with the Holy Spirit:
grant to us, who are born again by water and the
    Spirit,
that we may be faithful to our calling
    as your adopted children;
through Jesus Christ your Son our Lord,
who is alive and reigns with you,
in the unity of the Holy Spirit,
one God, now and for ever.

 ## Talk/address/ sermon

The story in today's Gospel reading is the first mention of Jesus' adult life and for the next few weeks we shall be considering some of the really important incidents at the beginning of his adult ministry that made people realize that there was something really remarkable about this man. Something of the extraordinariness of Jesus, the man, is captured in those hymns and songs that we sing which tell of the wonderful things that he did (e.g. 'A man for all the people'). Look together at the words of one or two of these hymns and see what you can find out about Jesus that you can look out for in the readings you will hear in the coming weeks.

Congregational/ group activities

- Divide people into groups and give each group a large sheet of paper, a stick of glue and an envelope containing the words 'devil, rebellion, deceit, corruption and sins', together with coloured pens. Ask the groups to cut out the words and stick them on the large sheet of paper and add illustrations or other words to complement the words they have stuck on. All the words come from the Decision section of the Baptism service. Then ask the congregation to gather at the font to respond to the questions provided at the Decision in the baptism service. As each answer in the first section (about repentance) is made, one or two groups could screw up their sheets of words and illustrations and place them at the foot of the font. After each answer in the second section (about turning to Christ), light some candles and stand them around the font. After this is completed, the Gospel could be read, with people still standing around the font.

- Decorate the baptistry or font with things mentioned in the Gospel which relate to John the Baptist. Make origami doves out of white paper and invite people to place these on or in the font as the Gospel is read.

- If it is possible to organize a baptism during the service, this would be very appropriate. Children could make cards showing John the Baptist and the baptism of Jesus to give to the candidate. A list of things from the Gospel reading to show in the picture might be helpful. The whole congregation could be invited to join in the Commission which is provided in the Common Worship Initiation Services.

- Make a banner illustrating the Gospel reading to use at Baptism services, or a poster which can be photocopied and given to families who bring children for baptism.

Prayers/intercessions

Use the following prayers of intercession from the Baptism service:

> God of glory,
> whose radiance shines from the face of Christ,
> give your children such assurance of your mercy
> and such knowledge of your grace,
> that, believing all you promise,
> and receiving all you give,
> they may be transformed ever more closely
> by your Spirit into the image of Jesus, your Son.
> Father of life,
> **make known your glory.**
>
> God of light,
> whose life shines beyond all things,
> give us and all your Church
> the will to follow Christ
> and to bear his peace,
> that the light of Christ
> may bring confidence to the world,
> and faithfulness to all who look to you in hope.
> Father of life,
> **make known your glory.**
>
> God of power,
> whose word gives life to heaven and earth,
> pour your abundant gifts on all your creation,
> that the blind may see, the fallen may be raised,
> and your people find tongues to confess
> your promises of a broken world made new.
> Father of life,
> **make known your glory.**

Common Worship: Initiation Services (p. 75)

For the first prayer (God of glory), ask people to face each other in pairs and join hands. For the second prayer (God of light) ask everyone to face the door, where a group of people with candles should stand. You could open the door, but mind it doesn't blow the candles out! For the third prayer (God of power) ask people to pick up and hold Bibles (or if you haven't enough, service books) whilst the prayer is said.

Stories and other resources

'Baptism', in *Pick and Mix* (p. 15)

'Baptism' (p. 16) and 'Repentance and forgiveness' (p. 80), in *The Discovery Wheel*

Kathleen Crawford, *My Baptism Book*, NS/CHP, 1998

Jesus of Nazareth, Video 1, directed by Franco Zeffirelli

'Just like Jesus', in *Reign Dance*

Common Worship: Initiation Services, Church House Publishing, 1998

Drama

Sheila O'Connell Russell and Terri Vorndraw Nichols, 'The baptism of the Lord', in *Lectionary Based Gospel Dramas for Advent, Christmas and Epiphany*, St Mary's Press, Winona, Minnesota, 1997.

Music

Father, I place into your hands (JP 42, MP 133)

Father, lead me day by day (JP 43)

The journey of life (JP 468)

Jesus, I will come with You (JP 138)

You are beautiful (HON 569, MP 788)

I love you Lord Jesus (BBP 27)

A man for all the people (CP 27)

For God so loved the world (BBP 14)

How sweet the name of Jesus sounds (HAMNS 122, HON 220, HTC 211, MP 251, SHF 178)

On Jordan's bank the Baptist's cry (HAMNS 27, HON 401, HTC 601, MP 538)

Post communion prayer

> Lord of all time and eternity,
> you opened the heavens
>   and revealed yourself as Father
> in the baptism of Jesus your beloved Son:
> by the power of your Spirit
> complete the heavenly work of our rebirth
> through the waters of the new creation;
> through Jesus Christ our Lord.

The Second Sunday of Epiphany

 ## Readings

1 Samuel 3.1-10(11-20)

Although Samuel had been promised to God from the time of his birth by his mother Hannah, and has lived in the Temple from early childhood, he still has to accept God's call for himself. At first he does not recognize what is happening, but with Eli's encouragement he is ready to respond.

Revelation 5.1-10

The writer describes a vision of the lamb taking a scroll which is inscribed on both the back and front, and breaking its seven seals. At this, the four living creatures surrounding the lamb sing in its praise. The song is a carefully constructed acknowledgement of the work of Christ on earth, symbolized by the lamb.

John 1.43-51

Philip follows Jesus, building the community of disciples. His first action is to tell someone else, Nathaniel. The Gospel does not record that Nathaniel became one of the twelve, and indeed, he does not occur in any of the lists of the twelve (though some say he may be Bartholomew, whose name appears as one of the twelve though his call is not recorded). However, his initial doubt turns rapidly to recognition when he declares Jesus to be the 'Son of God, the King of Israel'. This incident, at the end of the first chapter of St John's Gospel, is the last in a series of personal testimonies to the identity of Jesus. The stage is set for the signs of his ministry, the first of which we encounter next week.

Collect

Almighty God,
in Christ you make all things new:
transform the poverty of our nature
　by the riches of your grace,
and in the renewal of our lives
make known your heavenly glory;
through Jesus Christ your Son our Lord,
who is alive and reigns with you,
in the unity of the Holy Spirit,
one God, now and for ever.

 ## Talk/address/ sermon

Ask each person to turn to their neighbour and tell them a piece of local news: it may be personal or about someone they know or something they saw in the local paper. (No scandal or gossip allowed!) In today's Gospel story we hear an account of the way a bit of local news spreads. Philip is doing the kind of thing we all do quite frequently: we go and tell our neighbours, friends or colleagues about something and a story gets round. It's not easy though. Nathaniel thinks Philip is rather stupid: 'Can anything good come from Nazareth?' But Philip is persistent and tells him to come and see. It's exactly the same situation we face in evangelism today. Evangelism works best from person to person: we can all invite our neighbours, friends, colleagues and so on. They are likely to be incredulous, even hostile, as Nathaniel was, but like Philip, we can say 'Come and see.'

 ## Congregational/ group activities

- The call of Samuel is the account of one person's awareness and response to God's call. Ask people to talk in groups and describe times when they have been aware in some way that God was asking something of them. Then address a second question. Samuel was asked by God to deliver an unpleasant and difficult message to Eli. Are we as a church community prepared to listen to the voices of children? What are they saying to us?

- When he meets Nathaniel, Jesus seems to know about and value him, making a startling promise to Nathaniel that he will witness God's action. Ask people to make a card to themselves showing and completing the sentences below.

Name ....

Jesus promises you that ....

In response to this promise, you are able to tell others of Jesus and promise them

....

- Make a big picture linking the calls of Samuel and Philip and God's call to each of us. Ask one group to make a quick picture showing the call of Samuel, another the call of Philip. A third group should write the words 'Jesus calls _____' and make little pictures of each person present, with their names underneath the drawings. Cut out all

the little pictures of individuals and stick them, along with the two biblical pictures, on a large sheet of card.

- The collect speaks of transformation. How might our lives be changed – as individuals and as a faith community? Make a list of changes we would like to see. How might they happen?

Prayers/intercessions

Offer prayers for our calling and response, and give thanks for the call of others. Pray for the people and missionary organizations that your church supports. Begin the time of intercession by interviewing one of the missionaries or reading out one of their recent letters.

How were they first called by God into their work?

What are the challenges, the joys and the problems they face each day?

What would they like the church to pray for them and for those they work with?

After praying through these issues, focus upon the ways we are called to follow Christ in our everyday lives. Use the prayer and response:

When we hear you call
Help us to follow you.

Stories and other resources

'Promises', in *Pick and Mix* (p. 139)

'Being valued', in *The Discovery Wheel* (p. 18)

'Jesus' early ministry', in *The Dorling Kindersley Illustrated Family Bible*, Dorling Kindersley, 1997 (p. 232)

'The call of Samuel', in *The Dorling Kindersley Illustrated Family Bible*, Dorling Kindersley, 1997 (p. 117)

Michael Perry, Patrick Goodland and Angela Griffiths, *Prayers for the People*, Marshall Pickering, 1992

Drama

Andrew Smith, 'Conversation pieces', in *Much Ado about Something Else: 20 More Sketches*, CPAS, 1996

Music

Hushed was the evening hymn (JP 85, MP 253)

The fields are white (JP 237)

I will make you fishers of men (JP 123)

Will you come and follow me (HON 560)

Just a tiny seed (BBP 67)

Wherever you go, I will follow, follow, follow (BBP 16)

Jesus called to Peter the fisherman (BBP 13)

All heaven declares (HON 14, MP 14)

Alleluia! Sing to Jesus (HAMNS 262, HON 26, HTC 170)

Just as I am, without one plea (HAMNS 246, HON 287, HTC 440, MP 396)

Post communion prayer

God of glory,
you nourish us with your Word
who is the bread of life:
fill us with your Holy Spirit
that through us the light of your glory
may shine in all the world.
We ask this in the name of Jesus Christ our Lord.

The Third Sunday of Epiphany

 ## Readings

Genesis 14.17-20

Abram returns from rescuing his nephew, Lot, who had been taken prisoner, and is greeted by the priest king Melchizedek, who brings bread and wine and blesses Abram. Abram gives him a tenth of everything.

Revelation 19.6-10

The writer draws upon powerful Jewish imagery in describing the marriage of the lamb, signifying Christ. The bride wears white clothes, symbolizing innocence, won by the good deeds of God's people. The wedding feast image draws upon the teaching of Jesus himself and alludes to the spiritual banquet in the kingdom of heaven, a powerful reassurance to readers at a time when the Church is suffering persecution.

John 2.1-11

Jesus attends a wedding with his disciples. His mother is also present. For some reason which we are not told, though we may care to speculate about it, the wine runs out and Jesus' mother comes to tell him about it. To alleviate the situation, Jesus turns the water in six large stone jars into wine. John tells us that this is the first of the signs which Jesus performed, encouraging his disciples' faith and revealing his glory. There may be significance in the fact that it is Jesus' mother who prompts the first sign: she is certainly a significant player in the story. Jesus acts at her prompting. The size of the water jars alludes to the abundance of the miracle and the fact that it is pointed out that the jars normally held water for Jewish rites of purification seems to suggest a transformation and new direction. In place of ritual acts, the writer is suggesting, Jesus offers transformation and abundant celebration.

Collect

Almighty God,
whose Son revealed in signs and miracles
the wonder of your saving presence:
renew your people with your heavenly grace,
and in all our weakness
sustain us by your mighty power;
through Jesus Christ your Son our Lord,
who is alive and reigns with you,
in the unity of the Holy Spirit,
one God, now and for ever.

 ## Talk/address/sermon

Gather ideas about what might be needed to celebrate a wedding. You could list these on a flip chart or overhead projector acetate. It may even be possible for you to have one or two real-life examples (e.g. a bride's veil, bottle of champagne, a bridesmaid's dress, ring, etc.). Contrast this with the list of items found in the Gospel story. If we act as detectives, we can find out quite a lot about the wedding that Jesus attended. Weddings were family affairs at this time and most of the guests would be members of the extended family. The fact that Jesus' mother interferes so readily when the crisis occurs and enlists his help would tend to suggest that they were also members of the family. Cana is not far from Jesus' family home in Nazareth. Weddings were important occasions for families, even more so than they are today, with feasting lasting up to a week. So when Jesus acted to solve the problem which arose, it may well have been within a family context. Yet the action is recorded in John's Gospel, described as the first 'sign' of Jesus, revealing his 'glory', his reflection of the wonderful presence of God in the world. Every action in the story is imbued with significance. The note on the reading (above) explains some of these. Lots of detective work is required in order to appreciate the significance of all the details in the story but its place, near the beginning of the Gospel, emphasizes to every reader that they are embarking on an extraordinary story.

 ## Congregational/group activities

- People often suggest that Christianity and Christians are dull. Yet in this story we see Jesus at the centre of a celebration. He acts as the life and soul of a party, transforming a special occasion into something extra special. Draw and cut out some big stone water jars, like the ones in the illustration. Have also some small pieces of white card (flash card size) stuck onto slightly larger silver or gold card. Use red pens to write on the flash cards ways in which being a Christian, knowing Jesus, adds a sparkle to life. This would work particularly well in mixed age groups with some discussion first. To complete the illustration, either stick the cards on the water jars, or turn the water jars nearly upside down, as though they are being used for pouring. Stick on the cards so that they look like ideas being poured out of the jars. Display your results so that everyone can see them.

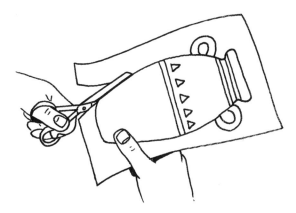

- Here is an idea which young children will especially enjoy. Ask children to bring along their Barbie (and other similar sized and male gender) dolls. Make sure you have two dolls to be the bride and groom and choose Jesus and his mother too. Sit around a simply constructed party table and tell the Gospel story in your own words or from a children's Bible or story book.

- Make little pots out of dough to take home, together with a little stand up card (like place cards at a party) with gold or silver lettering which says 'Jesus' first sign was at a wedding in Cana'.

- Ask one or two people to tell very briefly about something that happened at their own wedding celebration. You could sit them in a group on chairs at the front of the church and encourage them to pass round wedding photos as they are talking. Into this scene, an actor, John, appears and tells the Gospel story of the wedding as though he had been there (drawing comparisons between the modern wedding and the traditional Jewish wedding).

 ## Prayers/ intercessions

Use the intercession entitled 'World' which begins on p. 81 of *Patterns for Worship*, with the following introduction instead of the bracketed one given in the book:

> Faithful God, as we hear the story of your Son's first sign, we pray that we may always be open to your transforming presence in the world, saying faithful God:
> **glorify your name.**

 ## Stories and other resources

'The Marriage Feast of Cana' in *The Illustrated Children's Bible*, Dorling Kindersley, 1997 (p. 212)

Rachel Hall and Arthur Baker, *Jesus Goes to a Wedding*, Kevin Mayhew, 1993

Nick Butterworth and Mick Inkpen, *Jesus at the Wedding: The Cat's Tale*, HarperCollins, 1988

Joan Chapman, *Children Celebrate!*, Marshall Pickering, 1994 (pp. 1–3)

Edward Banyard, 'Strange miracle', in *Turn But a Stone*, NCEC, 1992 (p. 44)

 ## Drama

Dave and Lynn Hopwood, 'Water into wine', in *Telling more Tales,* CPAS, 1998

Robert Cuin, 'The wedding party', in Pam Macnaughton and Hamish Bruce (eds), *Together through the Bible*, NS/CHP, 1998

 ## Music

Come and praise the Lord our King (JP 34)

Come on and celebrate (JP 325, MP 99)

Hallelujah! for the Lord our God (JP 66, MP 205)

Lord of our life (HON 315, MP 441)

I will worship (SHP 66)

Jesus Christ is here (CP 26)

Father, Lord of all creation (HAMNS 356, HON 122)

God has spoken – by his prophets (HTC 248)

Jesus, Lord, we look to thee (HAMNS 380)

O for a thousand tongues to sing (HAMNS 125, HON 362, HTC 219, MP 496)

Post communion prayer

> Almighty Father,
> whose Son our Saviour Jesus Christ
>   is the light of the world:
> may your people,
> illumined by your word and sacraments,
> shine with the radiance of his glory,
> that he may be known, worshipped, and obeyed
>   to the ends of the earth;
> for he is alive and reigns, now and for ever.

The Fourth Sunday of Epiphany

 ## Readings

Deuteronomy 18.15-20

Moses tells the people of God to send a faithful prophet from among their own community. The people have said that they are afraid of the 'fiery presence' of God. It is recognized that it may be easier to hear someone from among their own community. The passage ends with a warning however: the prophet will speak with God's authority and to disregard him will carry consequences.

Revelation 12.1-5a

In the ancient world the movements of the stars were studied with great seriousness, as we learn from the story of the wise men, told in Matthew's Gospel. Each constellation was known and understood, marking important passages of time and the changing seasons. John builds upon this knowledge and uses it to create a style of Christian imagery. The sign in heaven, the woman robed with the sun, suggests the Virgo constellation and John superimposes upon this imagery from the prophets Daniel and Isaiah.

Mark 1.21-28

On the Sabbath Jesus visits the synagogue in Capernaum with his disciples and teaches there. Capernaum was a significant town with a large synagogue so his teaching would have been heard by a large number of people. They are amazed by what they hear, especially by the authority with which Jesus speaks. The only individual response recorded however, is from a man who is possessed, whom Jesus heals. Again the people are amazed and the news about Jesus spreads rapidly through the region of Galilee.

Collect

God our creator,
who in the beginning
commanded the light to shine out of darkness:
we pray that the light of the glorious gospel of
   Christ
may dispel the darkness of ignorance and unbelief,
shine into the hearts of all your people,
and reveal the knowledge of your glory
   in the face of Jesus Christ your Son our Lord,
who is alive and reigns with you,
in the unity of the Holy Spirit,
one God, now and for ever.

 ## Talk/address/ sermon

Ask people to discuss what they think Jesus might have been like. How do they imagine him? They could talk to those around them or you could invite a few people to share their ideas with everyone. It is tempting to construct a picture of Jesus as someone who was pretty way out, set apart from society, a leader of an exclusive group, perhaps, who acts and teaches for those who go out of their way to seek him out. But the opening of Mark's Gospel can be read in quite a different way. It begins simply, with brief accounts of his baptism and temptation and the call of four fishermen. The next we hear is of Jesus' arrival in the large fishing town of Capernaum where he visits the a synagogue to teach on the Sabbath. He is very much a part of the ordinary life of the community: very much the prophet from the local community described by Moses in the Old Testament reading. Yet people recognize at once that there is something about Jesus which is extraordinary, no more so than the sick man who enters the synagogue screaming. Jesus' response is low key, but assured and again extraordinary. The man is healed and news spreads. We receive the impression of a person who, while extra-ordinary, is very much at the heart of the local community. He is where the people are. That is where we, too, are called to be. We are not all great preachers or leaders but caring actions in the local community are immensely valued and, as in Galilee, news spreads fast.

 ## Congregational/ group activities

- Listen to the Gospel reading together. We are not told what Jesus said at the synagogue: we are just told what effect it had on the people who heard it. They were amazed. Think of other words which you might use instead of 'amazed'. What does each member of the group find amazing (surprising, etc.) about Jesus? Make a paper 'patchwork quilt' of amazing things about Jesus. Ask people to write the things they find amazing on hexagons and stick them together on a larger sheet of paper. Write, too, in big letters on hexagons, all the words you have found which you might use instead of 'amazing', and add these to the patchwork.

- Make a surprise 'fortune square'. Many children will know how to fold a square piece of paper to make a 'fortune square'. Fold a square piece of paper into four, then open it and fold across each diagonal. Open again. Fold each corner in so that the point touches the middle. Turn this over so that the folded in points are underneath. Fold the corners in to the centre again. Keeping it the same way up, fold it in half one way and open out, then in half the other way and open out. Then push it together and slide your forefingers and thumbs under the outside flaps. You are now ready to write on it. Under the inside flaps, write surprising things that Jesus said or did. On the inside flaps write 'SURPRISE' in eight different colours. On the outside flaps write the numbers. Then try out your 'fortune square' on each other before taking it home. For very small children, you may have to make the 'fortune square' for them, and they can just decorate it them- selves.

- Imagine that you are a group of people who were in the Capernaum synagogue when Jesus stood up and spoke, then commanded the evil spirit to come out of the man who shouted out. Talk about your feelings. Perhaps one person could imagine that they were the sick man and say how he felt. Then work together to write a letter to some imaginary friends who live elsewhere in Galilee.

Prayers/ intercessions

Lord, we bring you our love,
but we also bring you our perplexity.
We are not content with the church as it is;
we are not content that we make
so little impression on the world;
we know that we are not as we should be,
but what must be changed?

Are you calling us to withdraw
from a world that is weakening us?
Or beckoning us into an ever deeper involvement
in the life of those beyond the church?
What is the difference between building bridges
and compromising the Gospel?

As the old signposts are swept away,
help us Lord;
as we stand uncertain and hesitant,
help us Lord;
as we hear voices bidding us both forward and back,
help us Lord.

Searcher of minds and hearts,
teach us to distinguish between
the things to which we should hold fast at all costs
and the things we should gladly surrender
for your sake and the sake of the Gospel.
Help us to know you better
that we may love you better
and loving you better,
may we fear nothing
except the loss of your presence with us in the way.

Edmund Banyard, *Turn But a Stone* (p. 46)

Stories and other resources

Stuart Thomas, 'A new mind', in *Keep it in the Family*, Kevin Mayhew, 1993 (p. 62)

Lois Rock, 'Growing up' (p. 10) and 'Precious writings' (p. 14), in *The Time of Jesus*, Lion, 1998

Peter Graystone and Jacqui Thomas, *If I Had Lived in Jesus' Time*, Scripture Union, 1995

'Jesus heals and forgives', in *The Dorling Kindersley Illustrated Family Bible*, Dorling Kindersley, 1997 (p. 240)

'Information about Jewish worship and synagogues', in *The Dorling Kindersley Illustrated Family Bible*, Dorling Kindersley, 1997 (p. 206)

Edmund Banyard, *Turn but a Stone*, NCEC, 1992 (p. 46)

♫ ♫♪♫ ♫♫ Music

Father God, I wonder (JP 337, MP 128)

Hallelu, hallelu (JP 67)

God is so good (JP 53)

There is a Redeemer (HON 500, MP 673)

Jubilate Deo (BBP 2)

By your side (SHP 16)

Christ is our corner-stone (HAMNS 161, HON 77, HTC 564)

Firmly I believe and truly (HAMNS 118, HON 133, HTC 429)

Jesus Christ is waiting (HON 268)

Jesus, the name high over all (HTC 213, MP 385)

Post communion prayer

Generous Lord,
in word and eucharist we have proclaimed
the mystery of your love:
help us so to live out our days
that we may be signs of your wonders in the world;
through Jesus Christ our Saviour.

The Presentation of Christ in the Temple

Candlemas (2 February)

Candlemas is celebrated either on 2 February or on the Sunday falling between 28 January and 3 February

 ## Readings

Malachi 3.1-5

The prophet describes the day when the Lord will come to his Temple, using powerful imagery to describe the difference this will make. The imagery of the metal-worker's refining fire emphasizes the uncompromising nature of the power of God, but reflects the precious nature of the Temple.

Hebrews 2.14-18

The writer declares the importance of Jesus sharing in our human nature. For in knowing and understanding our humanity, he can stand beside us in our suffering and his death and, in confronting the power of evil, he sets free all who have been enslaved by the power of death.

Luke 2.22-40

Joseph and Mary take the baby Jesus to the Temple in Jerusalem. In the Temple two elderly and especially devout people, Simeon and Anna, witness to the unique significance of Jesus.

Collect

Almighty and ever-living God,
clothed in majesty,
whose beloved Son
   was this day presented in the Temple,
in substance of our flesh:
grant that we may be presented to you
with pure and clean hearts,
by your Son Jesus Christ our Lord,
who is alive and reigns with you,
in the unity of the Holy Spirit,
one God, now and for ever.

 ## Talk/address/ sermon

When we hear these three readings together, we are confronted by the power of the mystery of the baby Jesus. The prophet Malachi powerfully describes what will happen when the Lord comes to his Temple. No one will be able to stand before him until they have been cleansed in the most intense fashion, then they will be fit to make their offerings. In the Gospel story, we understand that the Lord really does come to his Temple. His appearance there is in marked contrast to that described by Malachi, and yet it is a startling occasion. Two elderly, holy people greet him there, a child in his parents' arms, and yet recognize him as the Messiah. And his importance is not simply to be in his power. The darker side of the story is no less important than the glory. It is perhaps significant that Luke chooses an elderly person, someone who has seen life and knows what has to be faced, to deliver this message. Finally the writer of the letter to the Hebrews reflects on this. Jesus' humanity is important for us, for we can be assured that he knows what we face. He has confronted suffering and death. Yet his place in the Temple reminds us that Jesus was more than man: his divine nature means that his suffering and death can be redemptive. In the Temple, the Jewish place of sacrifice, we catch a glimpse of the reason for this special child. And so, at the end of the Christmas season, we are strengthened to turn and face the coming season of Lent, with the assurance that the Christ-child, so close to us at Christmas, will remain beside us on the journey.

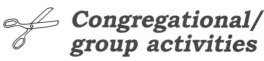 ## Congregational/ group activities

- Re-enact the story of Mary and Joseph's visit to the Temple. You could either write your own script or the *Dramatised Bible* might help you to use the biblical text effectively. Use elderly members of the congregation for Simeon and Anna and

younger people for Mary and Joseph. Can you get a real baby? Dress up. Learn to sing a simple version of Simeon's Song, the 'Nunc Dimittis'. They are beautiful words and well worth learning: singing them makes this much easier. When the story has been acted out, light individual candles and while they are alight, sing the song together.

- The festival of Presentation of Christ in the Temple is often known as Candlemas. In the middle ages, and in some places today, it is marked by a procession with the people carrying candles through the dark church, reminding us that Jesus is the Light of the World. If you have a large enough church, you could start the service with the lights out, in one part of the church (perhaps a side altar or the porch), and act out the story of the Presentation in the Temple there. After this, light the candles and sing the Nunc Dimittis (or some other appropriate song) while carrying the lighted candles through the darkness to where the main service will continue. Put the lights on when everyone has reached their places.

Prayers/ intercessions

It would be good if a number of children and young people could lead these prayers. Between the biddings, use a response that will be familiar to everyone.

Lord, as we grow older, help us to remember
That you are always there beside us,
Enfolding, supporting, uplifting us
With your love.

We pray for those whose old age
Is a time of freedom and opportunity,
Asking that they might use their days well,
Living lovingly, joyfully,
And in celebration of their true selves.

We pray for those whose old age
Is a time of limitation and frustration,
Asking that they might know the inner freedom
That your Spirit alone can bring,
Your Spirit of love and comfort, joy and peace.

We pray for those whose old age
Is richly peopled by family and friends,
Asking that they might be a source of strength
To those tossed by life's tempests,
Beacons of warm loving in dark times.

We pray for those whose old age
Is a time of loneliness and grief,
Asking that they might know God's loving presence,
Meeting him in the face of those caring for them,
Talking with him in their darkest hours.

Lord, as we grow older,
Life may become harder;
There are trials to face.
Help us to remember
That you are always there beside us,
Enfolding, supporting, uplifting us
With your love.

Christine Odell, from *The Word in the World* (p. 86)

Stories and other resources

'Candlemas', in *Pick and Mix* (p. 22)

Gordon and Ronni Lamont, 'Candlemas', in *Children Aloud!*, NS/CHP, 1997 (p. 40)

'Simeon and Anna bless Jesus', in the *Dorling Kindersley Illustrated Family Bible*

Joan Chapman, 'Candlemas', in *Children Celebrate!*, Marshall Pickering, 1994 (p. 53)

Stuart Thomas, 'The presentation of the Lord', in *Come to the Feast: Book 1*, Kevin Mayhew, 1997

Drama

Dave Hopwood, 'Light and dark', in *Playing Up*, NS/CHP, 1998

Derek Haylock, 'Light of the World', in *Plays on the Word*, NS/CHP, 1993

Music

For I'm building a people of power (JP 47, MP 151)

Jesus put this song into our hearts (JP 408, MP 376)

We really want to thank you, Lord (JP 268, MP 734)

Restore, O Lord, the honour of your name (HON 434, MP 579)

What a friend we have in Jesus (HON 541, HTC 373, KSHF 598, MP 746)

Post communion prayer

Lord, you fulfilled the hope of Simeon and Anna,
who lived to welcome the Messiah:
may we, who have received these gifts beyond
    words,
prepare to meet Christ Jesus when he comes
    to bring us to eternal life;
for he is alive and reigns, now and for ever.

Sunday between 3 and 9 February

(if earlier than the Second Sunday before Lent)

Proper 1

Readings

Isaiah 40.1-31

Isaiah poses a series of questions about the greatness of God. It is God who has created the world and he does not grow weary. He has no equal. He gives strength to those who turn and follow him.

1 Corinthians 9.16-23

Paul encourages the Corinthians in the best way to proclaim the gospel. For the Jews he became a Jew; to those outside the Law he became as one outside the Law; to those under the Law, he became as one under the Law; to the weak he became weak, so that he may win more of them for the sake of the gospel.

Mark 1.29-39

Jesus enters the house of Simon and Andrew where he cures Simon's mother-in-law who lies sick in her bed. Jesus goes on to cure many others who are sick or possessed. The next morning, Jesus goes off to pray alone. He is sought by Simon and his companions, who travel with Jesus into the nearby towns to proclaim God's word.

Talk/address/ sermon

God created us, and it is only in him that we can find meaning. As people that have been touched by the saving work of God, we have a duty to share with others his love in our lives. When others see we live lives given to God they seek answers to their own questions about him, and continue, if not begin, their own faith journey.

To help us deepen our faith we can ponder certain questions. Isaiah knew something of the grandeur of God. Where in your life do you see the greatness of God revealed? Paul encourages us to proclaim the gospel message. What is the good news of Christ that you proclaim? How is it made known in your life? In the Gospel reading, Jesus heals and then seeks to be alone in prayer. Do we make time and space to be alone with God for as long as it takes?

✂ Congregational/ group activities

*   Draw large pictures of parts of the body connected with the senses (e.g. hands for touch, ears for hearing). List all the ways in which we communicate with one another. Think of ways in our everyday lives that we can proclaim the gospel message by using our senses. List under the appropriate picture.

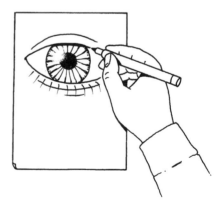

*   Use the following collective litany of praise on the greatness of God in our lives. Ask people to complete the sentence given to them on a piece of paper, beginning 'Praise God who . . .' (e.g. 'Praise God who . . . loves me', 'Praise God who . . . made the world'). Ask people to read them out in quick succession.

- The Isaiah reading speaks of the majesty of God over all creation. Bring a globe or a map of the world to church. Mark with flags (stuck onto the globe with Blu-tack) the places in the world in the news at the moment. Discuss how we can help to 'bring God's kingdom' to people in these countries. Talk about practical ways we can help and list topics for prayer.

- Give out a small piece of plasticine to each person. Whilst playing some quiet music, invite people to ask God, in silence, to mould and shape their lives whilst shaping their plasticine into something new. How would God wish to reform your life so that it may more fully reflect his greatness?

 ## Prayers/ intercessions

Use the following prayers of praise to link with the Isaiah reading and its focus on the greatness of God:

Praise to you, O faithful God!
You never fail those who trust in you,
but you allow them to share in your glory.
You fight for us against everything
that could attack or do us harm.
You are our shepherd,
and you free us from the snare.
You protect us who honour you, O God;
great is the sweetness that you give.

> Notker (c. 840–912)

Praise our God all you his servants,
honour him, you who fear God, both great and small.
Heaven and earth praise your glory, O Lord,
all creatures in heaven, on earth and under the earth;
let us praise and glorify him for ever.

> St Francis of Assisi (1182–1226)

Holy and loving God
open our eyes to see you,
open our minds to trust you;
open our hearts to love you
this day and for evermore.

> Christopher Herbert, *Pocket Prayers for Children*

 ## Stories and other resources

'Witness', in *Pick and Mix*

'Adverts', in Leslie Francis and Marian Carter, *Word for all God's Family,* Gracewing/Fowler Wright, 1996

'Jesus' friends', in *Building New Bridges*

Lesley and Neil Pinchbeck, *Theme Games*, Scripture Union, 1993

 ## Music

Father, I place into Your hands (JP 42, MP 133)

Be still and know (JP 22, MP 48)

Cleanse me from my sin (JP 27, MP 82)

Glory to our wonderful God (BBP 54)

Blessing and honour (BBP 9)

Let us sing and praise God for all that he has done (JU, p. 16)

Seek ye first the kingdom of God (MP 590)

Go forth and tell (HON 164, HTC 505, MP 178)

God is love: let heaven adore him (HAMNS 365, HON 170, MP 187)

O God, by whose almighty plan (HAMNS 406)

Collect and post communion prayer

Advent 1999 to Advent 2000	**The Fifth Sunday before Lent on p.128**
Advent 2002 to Advent 2003	**The Fourth Sunday before Lent on p.128**
Advent 2005 to Advent 2006	**The Fourth Sunday before Lent on p.128**

Sunday between 10 and 16 February

(if earlier than the Second Sunday before Lent)

Proper 2

 ### Readings

2 Kings 5.1-14

The King of Aram's commander, Naaman, has leprosy. The Israeli servant girl of Naaman's wife declares that the leprosy could be cured by God's prophet. The King of Aram sends a letter to the King of Israel to ask if he could cure Naaman. Displeased, the King of Israel tears his clothes. Elisha hears of this and asks that Naaman be brought to him. Elisha tells Naaman to wash in the Jordan seven times. Although annoyed at the prospect he goes out to bathe, and is made clean.

1 Corinthians 9.24-27

St Paul compares those who follow Christ with runners in a race. He exhorts the Christians in Corinth to be like athletes who train and run to win the race.

Mark 1.40-45

A man with a skin disease confronts Jesus and begs to be healed. Jesus cleanses him and tells him not to speak to anyone about it, but to visit the priest and make an offering of thanks. The man openly proclaims what Jesus has done for him, so that Jesus can no longer go into any town without crowds gathering to see him.

 ### Talk/address/ sermon

God accepts us as we are, whatever our condition or status. It is when we are ill or lonely or afraid or without hope that we need people most. Those people who had a skin disease were shunned by others in society for fear they too would become sick. The sick were shunned by those who were in fear. The same thing still happens today.

In the first reading annoyance was shown by the king who was asked to heal Naaman. He showed lack of faith. What are the times that we show our annoyance to God? Do you think we don't always have to be happy to know God's healing work in our lives? In the New Testament reading, St Paul exhorts the Christians at Corinth to train in their faith. What are the disciplines in our own faith journey which help us to take a closer step to God? Jesus heals the man from a skin disease. The man told those around him about his cure. Did he share his good news because he was thankful? In what ways are we excited about what God has done for us? What are the ways in which we show gratitude and thanks?

Congregational/ group activities

- Collect as many images of Christ as you can find: icons, postcards, crucifix, posters, etc. Ask the congregation to look at the pictures and think about the person of Jesus Christ who they know through faith. Ask the question 'if we are to follow Christ, what qualities do we need to grow closer to him, and what gift would we want to ask God for?' What things and what people help us in our lives to persevere in 'running the race' and keeping our eyes upon Jesus?

- Lay out a series of posters of images of Jesus on the floor (or on the walls of the church if you have space). Which ones do people like and why? What can we learn about Jesus through these images? What do these images tell us about the way that people have perceived Jesus through history?

- Use the following meditation to help people to reflect on their own walk with God. It is more appropriate for use with adults and older children. Ask people to close their eyes and imagine Jesus coming towards them as they rest by the water's edge. Think about the times in your life that you have become so tired and weary that you needed to rest and be refreshed. Can you remember any resting places in your life where you have been blessed by God? In your imagination what does Jesus say to you? If you are ready to take the next part of the faith journey with Jesus come out to the front and drink a tumbler of water. As you are doing so remember that God is there to cleanse and revive and restore us.

Prayers/intercessions

We pray for God's faithfulness to be known in our world, saying:

faithful God:

glorify your name.

In a world of change and hope,
of fear and adventure;
faithful God:
glorify your name.

In human rebellion and obedience,
in our seeking and our finding;
faithful God:
glorify your name.

In the common life of our society,
in prosperity and need;
faithful God:
glorify your name.

As your church proclaims your goodness
in words and action;
faithful God:
glorify your name.

Among our friends
and in our homes;
faithful God:
glorify your name.

In our times of joy,
in our days of sorrow;
faithful God:
glorify your name.

In our strengths and triumphs,
in our weakness and at our death;
faithful God:
glorify your name.

In your saints in glory
and on the day of Christ's coming;
faithful God:
glorify your name.

Patterns for Worship (p. 81)

Stories and other resources

'Keep it simple', in *The Word for All Age Worship*, Kevin Mayhew, 1995 (p. 54)

'Naaman is cured', in *In the Beginning* (p. 70)

'Healing', in *Pick and Mix* (p. 77)

Bob Hartman, *Cheer up Chicken*, Lion, 1998

Drama

'Christian Olympics', in *Plays on the Word*

Music

Jehovah Jireh (JP 404, MP 354)

Make me a channel of your peace (JP 161, HON 328, MP 456)

I cast all my cares upon You (JP 369)

Playing, running, skipping, jumping! (BBP 23)

If you climb to the top of the mountain (JU, p. 12)

We are climbing (CP 49)

A man there lived in Galilee (HAMNS 334, HON 3)

Jesu, lover of my soul (HAMNS 123, HON 261, HTC 438, MP 372, SHF 286)

Thine arm, O Lord, in days of old (HAMNS 285, HON 502)

Collect and post communion prayer

Advent 1999 to Advent 2000	The Fourth Sunday before Lent on p. 128
Advent 2002 to Advent 2003	The Third Sunday before Lent on p. 129
Advent 2005 to Advent 2006	The Third Sunday before Lent on p. 129

Sunday between 17 and 23 February

(if earlier than the Second Sunday before Lent)

Proper 3

Readings

Isaiah 43.18-25

God reveals that he is to do a new thing for Israel, even though the people have not called upon him to do so. It is God who wipes out the transgressions and sins of the people for his sake.

2 Corinthians 1.18-22

Paul tells the Corinthians that God is always faithful and ready to be there for his people. He always keeps his promises.

Mark 2.1-12

Jesus has returned to Capernaum, and whilst at a home a large crowd has gathered. A paralysed man can not be brought to Jesus through the door, so he is lowered through the roof. Seeing the man's faith, Jesus forgives his sin. Jesus confronts some scribes who are there who believe only God could forgive sins. Jesus then asks the man to take up his mat and walk. Those present all glorify God.

Talk/address/ sermon

God's love for us is very great, even though bad things happen; his love is greater than ours. When we look at the healing miracles of Jesus we see that faith is needed, though not necessarily on the part of the person being healed. Who had the faith in this story? Our healing involves wholeness – being healed not only in body mind or spirit, but in our relationships with others. In this context we can see that sin holds back recovery, holding us back from entering the place of transformation. We must also see that illness is not a punishment for sin (John 9.13), although our guilt can sometimes produce a physical illness. Jesus released those whom he healed, and brought new life to them.

Are there any doctors, nurses or others from the healing professions in your congregation? Invite them to talk about their work and what part their faith plays in it. What is the Church's role in healing? What can we thank God for today?

Congregational/ group activities

- Play a game of 'Consequences' with your group. Discuss ways in which promises made to you have been broken. What were the consequences of this?

- On Post-it notes draw or write of a time where you felt God had forgiven and released you. Ask everyone to stand and walk around, and to place the Post-it note on someone else's back. When this has been done, take the Post-it from one's back, sit down and give thanks 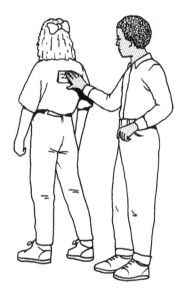 to God for what is written or drawn. Have the Post-it notes collected and placed upon the altar with thanksgiving.

- Give out small pebbles. Ask each person to focus on the pebble and to think about the things they would want to change in their life. Invite them to carry it with them during the week as a reminder that God has the power to heal and transform. Ask people to bring the pebble back the next Sunday, and place it in front of the altar.

Prayers/ intercessions

We pray for God's grace saying:

Lord, receive our praise:
and hear our prayer.

Lord God, through your grace we are your people;
through your Son you have redeemed us;
in your Spirit you have made us as your own.
Lord, receive our praise:
and hear our prayer.

We pray for . . . *(new Christians, the church)*
Make our hearts respond to your love.
Lord, receive our praise:
and hear our prayer.

We pray for . . . *(the world, society, the local community)*
Make our lives bear witness to your glory in the world.
Lord, receive our praise:
and hear our prayer.

We pray for . . . *(people in need, Christian service)*
Make our wills eager to obey, and our hands ready to heal.
Lord, receive our praise:
and hear our prayer.

We give thanks for . . .
Make our voices one with all your people in heaven and on earth.
Lord of the Church:
hear our prayer,
and make us one in heart and mind
to serve you with joy forever. Amen.

Michael Perry, from *Patterns for Worship* (p. 88)

Stories and other resources

'The man who came in through the roof', in *The Word for All Age Worship*, Kevin Mayhew, 1995 (p. 88)

'Forgiveness', in *Pick and Mix* (p. 64)

'Jigsaw Puzzle', in *The Word for all God's Family* (p. 110)

Leslie Francis and Nicola Slee, *Teddy Horsley: a Grumpy Day*, NCEC, 1994

Selina Hastings, 'Healing the sick', in *The Miracles of Jesus*, Dorling Kindersley, 1997

Music

Turn your eyes upon Jesus (JP 260)

Jesus' love is very wonderful (JP 139, JU, p. 14)

Amazing Grace (HON 27, MP 31)

God's love is deeper than the deepest ocean (JU, p. 90)

Loving Jesus, we will thank you (BBP 6)

All to Jesus I surrender (MP 25)

How great is our God (MP 245, SHF 173)

How good is the God we adore (HON 217, HTC 450, MP 244)

Through the night of doubt and sorrow (HAMNS 211, HON 517, HTC 466)

Collect and Post communion prayer

Advent 1999 to Advent 2000	The Third Sunday before Lent on p. 129
Advent 2002 to Advent 2003	The Proper 3 service material is not required for these years
Advent 2005 to Advent 2006	

The Second Sunday Before Lent

Readings

Proverbs 8.1,22-31

God's wisdom and understanding speaks for herself. She speaks her own praise and leads us to know her relationship with God. She had been in God from before the world was created and helped God create everything that exists.

Colossians 1.15-20

St Paul tells the Colossians that Christ is the image of the invisible God. In him and through him and for him all things were created. In him God dwells and through him God reconciles the world to himself.

John 1.1-14

John speaks of the Word being with God before anything was created. In fact the Word is God and all things are created through him. John the Baptist testifies to the dwelling of the Word in Jesus, who came to call people back into being true sons and daughters of God.

Collect

Almighty God,
you have created the heavens and the earth
and made us in your own image:
teach us to discern your hand in all your works
and your likeness in all your children;
through Jesus Christ your Son our Lord,
who with you and the Holy Spirit
    reigns supreme over all things,
now and for ever.

Talk/address/sermon

It is God who created the world. The Gospel points to the fact that there was a new creation when God and humanity became one in the person of Jesus Christ. God's Word speaks to us in many different ways. Every time we hear or speak or do or think about his Word, God is revealed anew.

How much time do you give in your life to hearing God's Word? How can we discern the Word of God without hearing it?

Re-read the Gospel slowly and give time to think about each sentence so that God may speak to us through them. New life in God comes through his Word.

Congregational/group activities

* Collect pictures from magazines, newspapers, postcards, etc. Ask people to take one picture and imagine that they have become a part of the scene. Ask people to meditate upon the question 'where is God in this picture and how does he bring this situation back to himself?'

* Draw around one person on a large sheet of paper. Ask for all the ways in which we can be Christ-like for one another. Write the responses in the outline and pin this where it can be seen by everybody.

- Ask for eight volunteers to look within the church for eight hidden envelopes, one per person. Within each one there is one word of this sentence: 'The Word became flesh and dwelt among us'. When all have been found and opened, the congregation are invited to put the words in the right order.

Prayers/ intercessions

Let our prayer rise before you like incense.
And our hands like an evening offering.
Lord God, remember the people you have made your own from the beginning:
May we see your image in others.
Creator God:
Come and renew us.

We pray for your Church:
May all who confess your name reflect your nature.
Creator God:
Come and renew us.

We pray for the places where we live:
Let them be places of life, healing and gift.
Creator God:
Come and renew us.

We pray for all we shall meet this week:
Grant them eternal life.
Creator God:
Come and renew us.

We pray for all who are ill and outcast:
Deliver them from their troubles.
Creator God:
Come and renew us.

We pray for those who have died:
Give them rest and peace
Creator God:
Come and renew us.

Stories and other resources

'Elijah's last journey', in Michael Forster, *The Word for All Age Worship*, Kevin Mayhew, 1995 (p. 48)

'Incarnation', in *Pick and Mix*

'Christ, the Light of the world', in Pam Macnaughton and Hamish Bruce (eds), *Together through the Bible*, NS/CHP, 1998

Drama

'Message received, but not understood', in *Plays for all Seasons*

 # Music

Hallelujah! for the Lord our God (JP 66, MP 205)

God whose love is everywhere (JP 353)

God loves you so much (JP 349)

Halle, halle, hallelujah! (JU, p. 80)

Glory to God, glory to God (JU, p. 78)

I am the bread of life (MP 261)

All creatures of our God and King (HAMNS 105, HON 9, HTC 13, MP 7)

Let us, with a gladsome mind (HAMNS 204, HON 302, HTC 23, MP 415)

Lord of the changing year (HTC 261)

Post communion prayer

God our creator,
by your gift
the tree of life was set at the heart of the earthly paradise,
and the bread of life at the heart of your Church:
may we who have been nourished at your table on earth
be transformed by the glory of the Saviour's cross
and enjoy the delights of eternity;
through Jesus Christ our Lord.

The Sunday Next Before Lent

 ## Readings

2 Kings 2.1-12

The prophets Elijah and Elisha are travelling from Gilgal, when Elisha swears he will never leave Elijah. As they reach the river Jordan, Elijah parts the water for them to cross to the other side. He knows he is about to leave Elisha, and so he asks Elisha to make a request to him. Elisha requests that a double portion of Elijah's spirit be given for him. This happens as horses and chariots of fire appear before him to take Elijah into heaven.

2 Corinthians 4.3-6

Paul tells the Corinthians that those who believe will see the light of the gospel of Christ. When we speak, the light of God shines within us so that we may proclaim Jesus Christ as Lord.

Mark 9.2-9

Jesus takes Peter, James and John to a mountain to be alone. Jesus is transfigured and there appear with him Elijah and Moses. Just as Peter, James and John want to make three dwellings for Jesus, Elijah and Moses, a cloud comes over them from which they hear the voice of God saying that Jesus is his beloved Son: listen to him.

Collect

> Almighty Father,
> whose Son was revealed in majesty
> before he suffered death upon the cross:
> give us grace to perceive his glory,
> that we may be strengthened to suffer with him
> and be changed into his likeness, from glory to
>   glory;
> who is alive and reigns with you,
> in the unity of the Holy Spirit,
> one God, now and for ever.

 ## Talk/address/ sermon

We were created by and for God. We have been chosen to work for his glory. It is God who loves, guides and supports us, and through us wants his love to shine. We have been touched by God's transforming love in action. What are the signs of God's glory in our world? List the ways in which we experience it (e.g. the sunrise, someone who makes us welcome, laughter).

How do we create places and spaces in which our relationships and attitudes can be transformed to reflect the love of God?

 ## Congregational/ group activities

• Place a large candle in front of the altar, this will represent the Light of Christ. Invite people to come and light a small candle from this large one and place in a candle stand or pot with sand in it in the four corners of the church where people can see them. Reflect on how we carry the Light of Christ within us and are called, collectively, to reflect God's Light in the world.

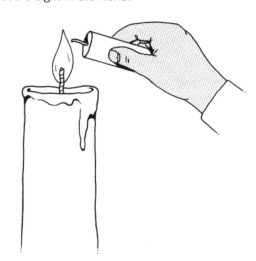

• Make a 'Glory Book': two pieces of large card with paper of a smaller size. Cover the card in silver foil and bind together with a shoe lace. Note in it all the ways in which we reflect God's glory through what we say.

- Brainstorm and list words which reflect the glory of God. Invite people to make up a personal prayer for the guidance of the Holy Spirit using some of these words. This can be carried with them and used throughout Lent as part of their Lenten discipline.

Prayers/ intercessions

Creator God, may we shine with your Light.
Strengthen us by your Spirit and fill us with your transforming love.
Silence:

Holy God, holy and strong;
May we reflect your glory.

Father, lead your Church to show your face to the world.
Help your children to walk in your ways of sacrificial love.
Silence:

Holy God, holy and strong:
May we reflect your glory.

Father, shed your transforming light where there is darkness of intolerance and injustice.
Strengthen the work of those who reconcile with your power to change and save.
Silence:

Holy God, holy and strong:
May we reflect your glory.

Father, be with us in the places where we live.
Bring to our living your likeness and peace
Silence:

Holy God, holy and strong:
May we reflect your glory.

Father, send your healing light upon all those who suffer.
Transform their anxiety and sorrow through your joy and hope.
Silence:

Holy God, holy and strong:
May we reflect your glory.

Father, we remember all those who have died.
May we, like them, share in your eternal glory.
Silence:

Holy God, holy and strong:
May we reflect your glory.

Stories and other resources

Selina Hastings, 'The transfiguration', in *The Miracles of Jesus*, Dorling Kindersley, 1997 (p. 22)

Susan Sayers, 'Christ in glory', in *Things to Do in Young People's Worship*, Kevin Mayhew, 1997

Transfiguration section, in *Festive Allsorts*

Music

May your loving Spirit (BBP 45)

Who made your eyes so you can see? (BBP 26)

Glory to our wonderful God (BBP 54)

Be still, for the presence of the Lord (HON 53, MP 50)

The peace prayer (Lead me from death to life) (CP 140)

When I look (SHP 147)

Over the mountains and the sea (SHP 106)

Christ is the world's true light (HAMNS 346, HON 78, HTC 323)

Lord Jesus, once you spoke to men (HAMNS 392, HTC 112)

Post communion prayer

Holy God,
we see your glory in the face of Jesus Christ:
may we who are partakers at his table
reflect his life in word and deed,
that all the world may know
his power to change and save.
This we ask through Jesus Christ our Lord.

The First Sunday of Lent

Readings

Genesis 9.8-17

Following the flood and the survival of Noah and his family in the ark, God establishes a covenant with Noah, his descendants, all humans and all living creatures. God promises never again to destroy the earth with a flood and sets a rainbow in the clouds as a sign of this covenant.

1 Peter 3.18-22

The writer reminds his readers that Christ suffered in order to bring them to God and is now alive in the Spirit. The saving power of baptism is likened to the ark which saved Noah and his family.

Mark 1.9-15

The story of the baptism of Jesus by John in the river Jordan. A dove, familiar as a symbol of peace and also of Israel, descends onto Jesus and a voice is heard from heaven. Jesus is then driven out into the desert for 40 days. After John is arrested Jesus returns and begins to preach the kingdom of God.

Collect

Almighty God,
whose Son Jesus Christ fasted forty days in the
wilderness,
and was tempted as we are, yet without sin:
give us grace to discipline ourselves
in obedience to your Spirit;
and, as you know our weakness,
so may we know your power to save;
through Jesus Christ your Son our Lord,
who is alive and reigns with you,
in the unity of the Holy Spirit,
one God, now and for ever.

Talk/address/ sermon

For a Christian, baptism is a link to Christ's suffering and death and to the covenant God has made with his people. Christians can take to the sea of life secure, as Noah was, in the knowledge of that covenant relationship. The story of Noah is well known, as it should be, but its point concerns the covenant and the revelation that such calamities are not God's will. After his baptism Jesus spent a long period of time developing a clear vision of his ministry before returning and beginning his preaching. What does your baptism mean to you?

Congregational/ group activities

*   Encourage people to remember and tell stories about their baptism. If notice is given beforehand photographs could be brought to church and shown. Notice any changes that have taken place in the practice of baptism and what remains the same. Light a candle for anyone whose baptism anniversary is this week/month. Let everyone who wants to celebrate their baptism do so by adding a photo, drawing, memory or statement of faith on a display in the form of an ark or a church.

*   Have a party for all those baptized during the past year. Arrange for the children to make the invitation cards. They can be hand-delivered by older members of the congregation.

*   Rainbows generate all sorts of creativity; offer an interesting set of art materials, shiny papers, cellophane, foil, as well as paint and crayons. Apart from collage pictures, what about making rainbow-coloured 'stained glass' windows, or rainbow mobiles?

*   The Bible reveals more of God's covenant. Make rainbow bookmarks to mark the relevant passages that are to be read this Lent.

*   Dramatize the Noah story, emphasizing God's covenant. You might dramatize part of a reading each Sunday in Lent and then present them all together to illustrate this Lenten theme.

- Make a Lenten tree by securing a branch in a weighted pot and decorating it with symbols made each week. This week's symbol might be stars, names, fonts or drops of water.

Prayers/intercessions

Write and decorate with rainbows a Lenten prayer to use in the group and at home during Lent. Decorate the following prayer:

Lord, you are love,
Lord, you are peace,
Lord, you are our gentle strength.
You are with us wherever we go
so we need not be afraid.
For your love, your peace and your strength
we thank you, now and always.

Christopher Herbert, *Pocket Prayers for Children*

Assemble a central table or cloth with dry sand, forming a small dune. Use 'The Desert of Prayer' in *Reign Dance*. During the meditation, small flowers could be placed in the sand, causing the desert to 'bloom'. Alternatively glass beads or other 'treasures' could be buried in the sand and 'unearthed' during worship. A time of prayer follows this meditation naturally.

Stories and other resources

Michael Foreman, *Dinosaurs and all that Rubbish*, Picture Puffin, 1972

Babette Cole and Ron Van Der Meer, *The Bible Beasties*, Marshall Pickering, 1993

Avril Rowlands, *Tales from the Ark*, Lion, 1993

Nicholas Allan, *Jesus' Day Off*, Hutchinson, 1998

'Noah and the flood', in *In the Beginning*

Marian Carter, *Rainbow People*, NCEC, 1992

David Adam, *The Edge of Glory*, SPCK, 1985

Drama

Edmund Banyard, 'The festival of weeks – a dialogue', in *All Year Round*, CCBI, 1998

'Mr Noah and the great flood', in *Telling Tales*

Music

Mighty is our God (JP 431)

My God is so big (JP 169)

Sing a new song to the Lord (JP 454, MP 599)

Be still and know (HON 52, MP 48)

Wait for the Lord (HON 528)

Give thanks to the Lord for he is good (JU, p. 30)

Forty days and forty nights (HAMNS 56, HON 145, HTC 103, MP 160)

Jesu, lover of my soul (HAMNS 123, HON 261, HTC 438, MP 372, SHF 286)

O love, how deep, how broad, how high (HAMNS 119, HON 383)

Post communion prayer

Lord God,
you have renewed us with the living bread from heaven;
by it you nourish our faith,
increase our hope,
and strengthen our love:
teach us always to hunger for him
who is the true and living bread,
and enable us to live by every word
that proceeds from out of your mouth;
through Jesus Christ our Lord.

The First Sunday of Lent

The Second Sunday of Lent

 ## Readings

Genesis 17.1-7,15-16

God confirms the covenant again with Abram, promising him an enormous number of descendants, to be emphasized by changing his name to Abraham, 'father of a multitude'. God promises to be the Lord of all these succeeding generations. The omitted verses describe how the descendants are to keep the covenant, namely by the practice of circumcision. Abraham's wife is also to change her name, from Sarai ('mockery') to Sarah ('princess'), for she is to have a son (Isaac), although she is 90.

Romans 4.13-25

Paul argues that faith in Christ will mean self-denial, obedience and suffering. Becoming a follower means questioning life and asking what it is really about.

Mark 8.31-8

Jesus tells the disciples that he will suffer rejection and death at the hands of the authorities, but will rise again. Peter is unhappy either with the idea of such a fate or at such open talk but receives a stinging rebuke from Jesus.

Collect

Almighty God,
you show to those who are in error the light of
    your truth,
that they may return to the way of righteousness:
grant to all those who are admitted
    into the fellowship of Christ's religion,
that they may reject those things
    that are contrary to their profession,
and follow all such things as are agreeable to the
    same;
through our Lord Jesus Christ,
who is alive and reigns with you,
in the unity of the Holy Spirit,
one God, now and for ever.

 ## Talk/address/ sermon

Being a faithful follower has its price, as the lives of people such as St Francis, Nelson Mandela and Dietrich Bonhoeffer demonstrate. The essence of discipleship lies perhaps in believing the promise which is offered and being willing to walk the walk of the teacher whatever may happen. Jesus makes it clear that he is asking for a life commitment, he is asking people to consider what their life is all about. Peter receives a rebuke for looking at his situation solely in human terms.

Call a few people to come and sit at the front or stand beside you before you begin speaking. After a few minutes ask them how they feel, their apprehension, embarrassment or discomfort at being in a different place and not knowing what might come next. This is a weak but telling illustration of what it is like to be a follower.

 ## Congregational/ group activities

* Abraham was promised as many descendants as there are stars in the sky or grains of sand on the sea shore. Give everyone a card shaped as or decorated with a star. Discuss how we are not only stars in our own unique way, but also stars because we are part of that promised inheritance. Ask everyone to put their name on the star and hang it on a display or put it in an offertory basket. At the end of the service, redistribute them so that everyone has someone else's to take home. They now have an individual to pray for in the future.

- Ask everyone to choose a new name, one that reflects the good things God has done or prepared for them.

- On sheets of A4 invite people to draw an outline figure of themselves and write on it some of their characteristics. In groups do the same for biblical disciples. Display them and do some guessing and comparing.

- Dramatize the story of Sarah, including her prayers in Genesis 16, for your covenant presentation.

- Make symbols for the Lenten tree: stars, signs (to help followers) or promises.

Prayers/ intercessions

The Iona community have a very simple liturgy that is appropriate to use for sad times or when people are facing difficult situations. The whole liturgy can be found on p. 55 of *The Pattern of our Days*. Alternatively, use the following prayer from this service during a time of confession:

Merciful God,
for the things we have done that we regret,
forgive us;
for the things we have failed to do that we regret,
forgive us;
for all the times we have acted without love,
forgive us;
for all the times we have reacted without thought,
forgive us;
for all the times we have withdrawn care,
forgive us;
for all the times we have failed to forgive,
forgive us.

For hurtful words said and helpful words unsaid,
for unfinished tasks
and unfulfilled hopes,
God of all time
forgive us
and help us
to lay down our burden of regret.

Kate McIlhagga, *The Pattern of our Days*

Stories and other resources

Michael Rosen and Helen Oxenbury, *We're Going on a Bear Hunt*, Walker Books, 1997

'The Call of Abraham', in *In the Beginning*

'Disciples' and 'Promises', in *Pick and Mix*

Michael Forster, 'God's incredible promise', in *The Word for All Age Worship*, Kevin Mayhew, 1995

Drama

John Bell and Graham Maule, 'The protector', in *Eh . . . Jesus . . . Yes Peter . . .?*, Wild Goose Publications, 1988

Mark Niel, 'If this is Lent, who borrowed?', in *Oh No, Not the Nativity!*. Scripture Union, 1998

Music

I do not know what lies ahead (JP 92)

I'm going to take a step of faith (JP 381)

One more step along the world I go (JP 188)

Father Abraham had many sons, many sons had Father Abraham (JU, p. 8)

I will sing for the Lord (BBP 78)

God has promised (CP 31)

Jesu, grant me this I pray (HAMNS 136, HON 260)

My God, how wonderful thou art (HAMNS 102, HON 343, HTC 369, KSHF 370, MP 468)

Take up thy cross (HAMNS 237, HON 465, HTC 114)

Post communion prayer

Almighty God,
you see that we have no power of ourselves to help ourselves:
keep us both outwardly in our bodies,
and inwardly in our souls;
that we may be defended from all adversities
which may happen to the body,
and from all evil thoughts
which may assault and hurt the soul;
through Jesus Christ our Lord.

The Third Sunday of Lent

 ## Readings

Exodus 20.1-17

The ten commandments or 'Words' give a summary of the law codes. The precepts are similar to those accepted in other cultures of the area but there are important differences. Israel has only one God; this God has chosen Israel as his people (and is able therefore to turn from them); the commandments are phrased directly in the second person, the person responsible for keeping God's laws is 'you'.

1 Corinthians 1.18-25

Paul is preaching the power and wisdom of God as revealed in Christ and the message of the cross. It sounds foolish to those such as the Greeks who value human 'wisdom' above all and it is a stumbling block to those like the Jews who would look for a 'sign'. Using words from Isaiah, Paul emphasizes that the way to know God is not through the wisdom of the wise but in the foolishness and weakness of birth as a human child and suffering as a man on a cross.

John 2.13-22

The other Gospels place the story about driving the traders from the Temple at the end of Jesus' ministry, but John has it at the beginning. The Jews ask Jesus for a sign to justify his action, but he only offers a conditional statement alluding to himself as the temple (the place where God may be known). He states that, if the 'temple' were destroyed, he would raise it again in three days.

Collect

Almighty God,
whose most dear Son went not up to joy
    but first he suffered pain,
and entered not into glory before he was crucified:
mercifully grant that we, walking in the way of the
    cross,
may find it none other than the way of life and
    peace;
through Jesus Christ your Son our Lord,
who is alive and reigns with you,
in the unity of the Holy Spirit,
one God, now and for ever.

 ## Talk/address/ sermon

The cross can be a meaningless decoration, in jewellery for instance, or perhaps it can never be really meaningless. Perhaps it always has some hint of the suffering of execution, the triumph of resurrection, the courage of the secret sign, the despair of loss, the hope of new life, the love of Jesus. Let everyone take a minute to count up mentally the number of crosses around in church and at home, then share thoughts on what they mean to you.

Divide the congregation into groups of four, each person adopting one of these roles: a trader, a priest, someone Jesus healed, and a child. Allow three periods of two or three minutes so that, in pairs, each person talks to the others in their group. Take comments back from the whole congregation focusing on one role at a time, starting with the children.

Congregational/ group activities

- Play a well-known game like snakes and ladders but announce changes in the rules during play (go down ladders, reverse direction, etc.). Afterwards share reflections on what rules are for and what makes good rules.

- Explore your church and discover how many crosses there are and why. Do some rubbings or sketches of some of them and make them into a collage. Discuss what the cross means to members of the group and invite them to make some suitable crosses of their own to add to it.

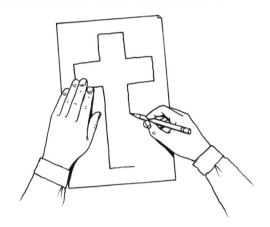

- Make tablets of stone or crosses for the Lenten tree.

- If you are building up a presentation about the Lenten theme of 'covenant' prepare a mime of Moses receiving the commandments or make some 'stone' tablets to display.

Prayers/ intercessions

Use the following prayers that focus upon our walk with God through difficult times:

Lord, you are our hope and strength,
staying with us in trouble,
walking with us in danger
and comforting us in our sadness.
Keep us always mindful of your love
that we may be strong and courageous
in all that we think and speak and do,
knowing that you are our closest and most loyal friend.

Christopher Herbert, *Pocket Prayers for Children* (p. 35)

Give us big hearts, dear God,
big enough to embrace everyone,
big enough to say sorry,
big enough to be humble,
big enough for you.

Christopher Herbert, *Pocket Prayers for Children* (p. 35)

Stories and other resources

Edmund Banyard, 'Freedom and law', in *Heaven and Charing Cross*, NCEC, 1996

'The Covenant Box', in *Instant Inspirations*

Gill Ambrose, *Plagues and Promises*, NCEC, 1998

'Cross', in *Pick and Mix* (p. 43)

 Drama

' The case of the golden calf', in *Playing Up*

 Music

God sent His Son (JP 58, MP 52)

I met You at the cross (JP 103)

A purple robe (JP 304)

All heaven declares (HON 14, MP 14)

As the deer pants for the water (HON 39, MP 37)

Overwhelmed by love (SHP 107)

Come let us sing of a wonderful love (MP 94)

All my hope on God is founded (HAMNS 336, HON 15, HTC 451, MP 16)

God be in my head (HAMNS 236, HON 166, HTC 543)

I know that my Redeemer lives, what joy (HON 232, HTC 169, MP 278)

Post communion prayer

Merciful Lord,
grant your people grace to withstand the temptations of the world, the flesh and the devil,
and with pure hearts and minds to follow you, the only God;
through Jesus Christ our Lord.

Mothering Sunday

The Fourth Sunday of Lent

 ## Readings

Exodus 2.1-10

The wonderful story of Moses' birth emphasizes his good Hebrew stock but places him slightly outside the slave community (with an Egyptian name) from where he can take a liberating role. The women play a large part in this cycle of stories and are presented as both caring and brave; this kind princess is going against the rules of her tyrant father.

or

1 Samuel 1.20-28

Hannah had been desperate for a son and prayed for one. When her prayer is answered she is very conscious of the child being a gift from God. When he has been weaned (at a much later age than now) Hannah takes him to Shiloh 20 miles north of Jerusalem to the house of the Lord where she offers him back to God.

2 Corinthians 1.3-7

Paul mentions consolation a great deal in this introductory passage, maybe following on from a rather severe telling off in a previous letter. We may suffer as Christ suffered but there is abundant consolation too.

or

Colossians 3.12-17

An encouraging reminder that as God's chosen people we must demonstrate godly qualities and clothe ourselves with love, which is what binds all together. Similarly we must be ready to teach, admonish and forgive each other.

Luke 2.33-35

Jesus is presented in the temple, reminding us of the story of Samuel. Simeon is inspired and sees clearly that the great role Jesus is to play will lead to liberation, but also to suffering which his mother will feel keenly.

or

John 19.25-27

The mother of Jesus stands near the cross where her son is being executed. Jesus sees her in her distress and places her in the care of the disciple he loved so dearly.

Collect

God of compassion,
whose Son Jesus Christ, the child of Mary,
shared the life of a home in Nazareth,
and on the cross drew the whole human family to
    himself:
strengthen us in our daily living
that in joy and in sorrow
we may know the power of your presence
    to bind together and to heal;
through Jesus Christ your Son our Lord,
who is alive and reigns with you,
in the unity of the Holy Spirit,
one God, now and for ever.

Talk/address/ sermon

God is described in the Bible as having fatherly and motherly qualities but Christians usually emphasize the fatherly ones. Today is an opportunity to think of our mothers; mother Church, the mother of Jesus and the motherhood of God. What happens if we dwell on some of the motherly qualities of God? Try saying the Lord's prayer beginning 'Our Mother . . .', what motherly qualities are brought to mind? Either beforehand or during the talk assemble a list of activities which are part of 'mothering'. Mothers do a lot of mothering, but so do others. Discuss in groups who are the people who do these activities for you.

Paddington Bear turned up with a label attached, saying 'Please take care of this bear'. Produce a suitable bear with label. One of the first things that happens to a baby born in hospital is that a label is attached. Produce a hospital wrist band. In a way it has a similar message, it has a family name on it, but what it means is 'Please take care of this child'. God doesn't need us to have a label, there is so much about each one of us that is reminiscent of God, but we could make ourselves one, to remind us that God is looking after us.

Congregational/ group activities

- Make cards for mothers and for all those who care for us. For younger children, paint the inside of egg cartons yellow. Cut out the individual cups and stick them onto A4 card to form the centre of a flower. Paint, draw or cut out paper leaves and petals to add to these flowers. For older children, make a decorated vase, painting patterns on clean, empty jars using glass paints.

- Make symbols of what mothers have done and do for us and hang them on the Lenten tree.

- Make a list of 'mothering' activities. Discuss in groups which are the ten most important and then put them in order of importance. Do a similar exercise for God's 'mothering' activity.

- Find out when and where each person was brought to church for the first time. What is it like for a mother and a baby coming to your church, especially if they have never been before? Share experiences and ideas for improvements.

- Dramatize the story of Hannah, her prayer and promise.

Prayers/ intercessions

Jesus, as a mother you gather your people to you: you are gentle with us like a mother with her children.
In your love and tenderness, remake us.

Often you weep over our sins and our pride: tenderly you draw us from hatred and judgement.
In your love and tenderness, remake us.

You comfort us in sorrow and bind up our wounds: in sickness you nurse us and with pure milk you feed us.
In your love and tenderness, remake us.

Jesus by your dying we are born to new life: by your anguish and labour we come forth in joy.
In your love and tenderness, remake us.

Despair turns to hope through your sweet goodness: through your gentleness we find comfort in fear.
In your love and tenderness, remake us.

Your warmth gives life to the dead: your touch makes sinners righteous.
In your love and tenderness, remake us.

In your compassion bring grace and forgiveness: for the beauty of heaven may your love prepare us.
In your love and tenderness, remake us.

St Anselm (1033–1109)

Stories and other resources

Sam McBratney, *Guess How Much I Love You*, Walker Books, 1994

Janet and Allan Ahlberg, *Bye Bye Baby*, Little Mammoth, 1989

Sue Doggett and Daniel Collins, *Hannah Keeps her Promise*, Bible Reading Fellowship, 1998

'Mothering Sunday' in *Seasons and Saints for the Christian Year* (p. 24), *Seasons, Saints and Sticky Tape* (p. 31), *Festive Allsorts* (p. 23) and *Together for Festivals* (p. 61)

Angela Ashwin, *The Book of a Thousand Prayers*, Harper Collins, 1996

Drama

Donald Dowling, 'Ta Ma or soft soap – a myth retold', in *Together for Festivals*

Brian Mountford, 'Some mothers do 'ave 'em', in *The Sower, Mrs Noah and a Dentist*, Tufton Books, 1998

Music

Bind us together, Lord (HON 60, JP 17, MP 54)

A naggy mum (JP 302)

He's got the whole wide world (HON 206, JP 78, MP 54)

We thank you God for mummies (BBP 53)

Welcome, welcome today, welcome to our family (BBP 59)

You can't stop rain (CP102, JP 297)

All things bright and beautiful (HAMNS 116, HON 21, HTC 283, MP 23)

Glorious things of thee are spoken (HAMNS 172, HON 158, HTC 494, KSHF 123, MP 173)

Now thank we all our God (HAMNS 205, HON 354, HTC 33, KSHF 386, MP 486)

Post communion prayer

Loving God,
as a mother feeds her children at the breast
you feed us in this sacrament
  with the food and drink of eternal life:
help us who have tasted your goodness
to grow in grace within the household of faith;
through Jesus Christ our Lord.

The Fifth Sunday of Lent

 ## Readings

Jeremiah 31.31-34

Jeremiah offers a message of hope and new life at a time of national despair. Israel has failed to keep its covenant with God, but God is prepared to enter into a new covenant relationship with the people. In future each and every person will know God from within; they will not need to be taught to have faith, the knowledge will be in their hearts.

Hebrews 5.5-10

This passage lies in the midst of a section where the author of the Epistle, a man who knows his Old Testament very well, describes the high-priestly role of Christ. In Psalm 2 God calls the Messiah 'son' and in Psalm 110 a priest. Jesus' priestly nature is seen in the way he represented humanity to God in prayer and learned through his human suffering what is involved in obedience to God.

John 12.20-33

After the triumphant entry into Jerusalem, some 'Greeks' appear wishing to see Jesus. The Gospel does not go on to reveal whether they saw him or not, but John uses them to represent the whole non-Jewish world. Their presence and the request that Andrew and Philip relay to Jesus draws out a heartfelt reply. For the rest of the world to see Jesus will require the death of the seed and the new life of the plant, the death of the self and eternal life as a follower. When Jesus asks the Father to glorify his name, some know God has spoken, but some hear only thunder.

Collect

Most merciful God,
who by the death and resurrection of your Son
   Jesus Christ
delivered and saved the world:
grant that by faith in him who suffered on the cross
we may triumph in the power of his victory;
through Jesus Christ your Son our Lord,
who is alive and reigns with you,
in the unity of the Holy Spirit,
one God, now and for ever.

 ## Talk/address/ sermon

A major strand in the readings for Lent has been the growing understanding of the covenant between God and his people. The passage from Jeremiah highlights the personal relationship with God which is part of the covenant; the passage from John indicates how the good news of God's love is to be revealed in the whole world.

'I will be their God, and they shall be my people.' This profound sense of belonging is our message to the world, which is crying out for security and freedom from fear and loneliness. As faith communities we need to see that ministry is ours to own, to share with each other and with the world, flowing from the eternal ministry of God. But not only do we have a ministry to offer, we also have one to receive, from all ages, and to encourage and enable that giving to happen.

 ## Congregational/ group activities

- Make a large map out of blotting paper of the area around your church (or of the country or even the whole world). Mount it on backing paper on a piece of board or wood. Invite everyone to commit themselves to God's work in that place by taking dead-looking cress seeds and planting them on the map. Afterwards, water the blotting paper and keep it in the dark until the seeds have germinated and bring it back next Sunday.

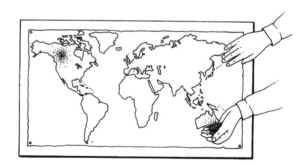

- Add symbols of seeds and new life to the Lenten tree.

- God's love is being revealed all over the world in many ways. Refer to newspaper cuttings from the previous few days to illustrate the point, or give out the newspapers and invite people to find the good news for themselves.

- Make big displays, such as Good News Boards and Bad News Boards. Use these as a focus for intercessionary, thanksgiving and meditative prayer.

- Prepare a mime or dance based on the reading from Jeremiah, or from John 12, to emphasize acceptance and not rejection.

- The life of Oscar Romero is celebrated at this time (24 March). His life was a wonderful example of how to find hope and stand up to injustice. Gather together foreign news from different newspapers. Where are some of the trouble spots in our world? What can we pray and do for these people? You might wish to select one country to pray for in the coming months. Your diocese will have links with churches in other countries and it might be useful to choose this as a starting point.

Prayers/ intercessions

Use the map, the Lenten tree, or the news boards as a focus for prayer.

Alternatively, use the following prayer to remember the suffering of Christ as Easter approaches:

Thanks be to God, who gives us the victory
through our Lord Jesus Christ.

We praise you, Lord Jesus Christ, Son of God,
for you submitted to the discipline of a son's
obedience, and perfectly revealed in your death
the loving nature of the Father.

We praise you, Lord Jesus Christ, Son of Man,
for as a champion of man and for his sake you
entered the battle against evil, and won the
complete victory over its power.

We praise you, Lord Jesus Christ, Servant of God,
for you accepted the suffering of those who
seek to be at one with those they serve, and by
your sacrifice made us one with God.

Thanks be to God who gives us the victory
through our Lord Jesus Christ.

Lent, Holy Week, Easter (p. 94)

Stories and other resources

Meryl Doney, *Ears and the Secret Song,* Hodder & Stoughton, 1989

Angela Elwell Hunt, *The Tale of Three Trees*, Lion, 1989

'One body with many parts', in *Instant Inspirations*

Inga Moore, *Six Dinner Sid*, MacDonald Young Books, 1998

Edmund Banyard, 'No easy road', in *Turn but a Stone*, NCEC, 1992

Angela Ashwin, *The Book of a Thousand Prayers*, HarperCollins, 1996

Drama

John Bell and Graham Maule, 'He was going on a journey', in *Wild Goose Prints 4*, Wild Goose Publications, 1990

Brian Mountford, 'The sin bin – an idea for a presentation', in *The Sower, Mrs Noah and a Dentist,* Tufton Books, 1998

 Music

God forgave my sin (HON 167, JP 54, MP 181)

In everything that I do (JP 391)

I am the way, the truth and the life (JP 89)

Two long pieces of wood (BBP 40)

I love you Lord Jesus (BBP 27)

Come and see, come and see (HON 88, MP 85)

My Lord, what love is this (HON 345, MP 476)

All in an Easter garden (CP 130)

Lift high the cross (HAMNS 72, HON 303, HTC 508,)

O Jesus, I have promised (HAMNS 235, HON 372, HTC 531, KSHF 400, MP 501)

Post communion prayer

Lord Jesus Christ,
you have taught us
that what we do for the least of our brothers and
sisters
we do also for you:
give us the will to be the servant of others
as you were the servant of all,
and gave up your life and died for us,
but are alive and reign, now and for ever.

Palm Sunday

Readings

Liturgy of the Palms

Mark 11.1-11

Jesus sends two disciples to fetch a colt from the village and then enters Jerusalem on it (fulfilling the prophecy of Zechariah) to adulation from bystanders, greeting him as the Messiah. Then in something of an anticlimax for the crowd he goes into the Temple.

or

John 12.12-16

Jesus has found a donkey for his entry into the city and the crowds cheer and greet him as their king. John makes it clear that the disciples didn't understand the significance of these events until much later.

Liturgy of the Passion

Isaiah 50.4-9a

The third Servant Song encourages Israel to stand firm whatever the present humiliations might be, to believe that God's salvation is at hand.

Philippians 2.5-11

Paul exhorts readers to have the mind of Christ, who emptied himself and became as a servant, who humbled himself and became obedient even to the point of death. As a consequence God raised him to a position of messianic lordship.

Mark 14.1-15.47 or Mark 15.1-39(40-47)

The long reading begins with the woman anointing Jesus with some very costly perfume. He dismisses objections about wasting money by praising her for what she has done as he sees there is little anyone can do for him now. Judas offers to help the chief priests arrest Jesus, but Mark offers no explanation. The Passion narrative then unfolds with its awesome power to engage hearers.

Collect

> Almighty and everlasting God,
> who in your tender love towards the human race
>   sent your Son our Saviour Jesus Christ
> to take upon him our flesh
> and to suffer death upon the cross:
> grant that we may follow the example
>   of his patience and humility,
> and also be made partakers of his resurrection;
> through Jesus Christ your Son our Lord,
> who is alive and reigns with you,
> in the unity of the Holy Spirit,
> one God, now and for ever.

Talk/sermon/ address

In the first reading Isaiah tells of the opposition and shameful treatment he faces and how every morning he hears the Lord and is helped to stand up to it all knowing all will be well. In the other two readings Jesus faces up to a horrific fate, strong in his relationship with God and in the knowledge that all will be well. Few of us have such trials in store but some of us have known God with us in difficult times and many of us have known that clear presence of God and share the sense of hope. With advance notice some may be ready to share such reflections.

Congregational/ group activities

*   Make palm branches, crosses or donkeys to hang on the Lenten tree. Order some palm branches along with the leaves or palm crosses and use them to lead a triumphal procession.

*   What would the people at the time have thought about Jesus and the events of Palm Sunday? In groups write newspaper headlines for the events of Palm Sunday and the rest of Holy Week. Think of appropriate headlines such as: 'Teenagers Tear Trees in Demonstration'; 'The Jesus who would be King'; 'Holy Hosannas to Cruel Crucifixion'.

- Make palm branches and write or draw on them something you want to shout about (or something you're just quietly pleased about). Shout hosannas! Find some other English 'shouting for joy' words (Hurray! Yippee! Cool!). Find something to shout about and shout!

- Arrange to have a live donkey from a local farm or city farm well in advance. Read one of the stories about the importance of the donkey in the events of Palm Sunday. Lead the congregation in a march or walk around the parish boundaries singing songs listed below.

Prayers/intercessions

We stand with Christ in his suffering.
For forgiveness for the many times we have denied Jesus, let us pray to the Lord.
Lord, have mercy.

For Christian people, that through the suffering of disunity there may grow a rich union in Christ, let us pray to the Lord.
Lord, have mercy.

For those who have the courage and honesty to work openly for justice and peace, let us pray to the Lord.
Lord, have mercy.

For those in the darkness and agony of isolation, that they may find support and encouragement, let us pray to the Lord.
Lord, have mercy.

That we, with those who have died in faith, may find mercy in the day of Christ, let us pray to the Lord.
Lord, have mercy.

Holy God,
holy and strong,
holy and immortal,
have mercy upon us.

Adapted from *Lent, Holy Week, Easter* (pp. 83–4)

Stories and other resources

Palm Sunday is retold in Walter Wangerin, *The Book of God*, Lion, 1996

'Palm Sunday', in *Festive Allsorts* (p. 24)

Jenny Hyson, *The Easter Garden*, Bible Reading Fellowship, 1998

Brian Ogden, *Too Busy to Listen*, Bible Reading Fellowship, 1998

Hall, Jarvis and Jefferson, *It's a Very Special Day*, NCEC, 1998

Drama

John Bell and Graham Maule, 'Stages on the way to the cross', in *Wild Goose Prints 4*, Wild Goose Publications, 1990

Andrew Brandon, 'An ass with attitude', in *Oh No, Not the Nativity!*, Scripture Union, 1998

Music

Make way, make way (JP 427, MP 457)

Hosanna, hosanna (JP 365, MP 242)

You are the King of glory (JP 296, MP 790)

Give me oil in my lamp (JP 50, MP 167)

I will enter his gates (HON 236, MP 307)

Trotting, trotting (CP 128)

Glory in the highest (HTC 582)

In the Cross of Christ I glory (HON 249, MP 338)

Stand up, stand up for Jesus (HAMNS 221, HON 457, HTC 535, KSHF 489, MP 617)

Post communion prayer

Lord Jesus Christ,
you humbled yourself in taking the form of a servant,
and in obedience died on the cross for our salvation:
give us the mind to follow you
and to proclaim you as Lord and King,
to the glory of God the Father.

Easter Day

 ## Readings

Isaiah 25.6-9

Celebration and thanksgiving for God's deliverance. The celebration comes in the form of a good feast with the best food and finest wine. It is also centred in the gift of the love of God, focusing on the immensity of his care and protection to bring the people out of the darkness of death and destruction to a new life.

Acts 10.34-43

Peter speaks to those gathered at the house of Cornelius, a centurion, with a summary of his teaching about Jesus. Peter tells them how he witnessed the death and resurrection of Jesus and was commissioned to preach and teach the good news and to testify that Jesus is the one appointed by God and spoken of by the prophets. Peter emphasizes his witness to a real relationship with Jesus and, through him, with God. It is through this realization and our personal development of a relationship that we receive forgiveness of sins and a new life in Christ.

1 Corinthians 15.1-11

Paul reinforces the teaching of the resurrection of Christ. He tells of Jesus' death, burial and resurrection and of the appearances he made to different people. Paul reveals his own personal experience. To him the appearance of Jesus was a most precious experience; definitely the turning point and dynamic moment of his life. This personal witness has a profound effect on all who hear him.

John 20.1-18

The account of the empty tomb and Jesus' appearance to Mary Magdalene. The personal response of Mary, Peter and John as they see what has happened is one of confusion and uncertainty as they try to understand the meaning of this miraculous event. When Mary encounters the risen Jesus, she mistakes him for the gardener, but recognizes him when he calls her by name. She goes back to the other disciples and witnesses to what has happened.

Mark 16.1-8

Mark's account of the resurrection centres on the experience of the women at the tomb. They arrive to anoint the body to find the stone rolled away. Inside the tomb they find a man in a white robe who tells them Jesus is risen and they will see him in Galilee. The women are afraid and confused and flee from the tomb, unable and unwilling to speak about their experiences.

Collect

> Lord of all life and power,
> who through the mighty resurrection of your Son
> overcame the old order of sin and death
> to make all things new in him:
> grant that we, being dead to sin
> and alive to you in Jesus Christ,
> may reign with him in glory;
> to whom with you and the Holy Spirit
> be praise and honour, glory and might,
> now and in all eternity.

 ## Talk/address/ sermon

Consider the theme of 'good news' and how we respond to receiving and giving good news.

We know now that the empty tomb is good news, but on the first Easter there must have been quite a combination of feelings amongst those who first saw the empty tomb and then the risen Lord. It is easy to understand the sense of confusion and fear felt by those first at the tomb. This could be developed into why the Resurrection is 'good news' still to us today. What are our own feelings about the cross and resurrection?

Consider the ways in which the church (the building) and the tone of the service have changed since Good Friday (e.g. flowers and perhaps other decorations, different kinds of music, use of colours in the vestments, altar frontal). Explain that these things, or the absence of them, reflect the very different moods of the two days and the contrast between them. This could then lead into teaching about the significance of Easter Day.

Use some sunflowers as a visual analogy to show that new life can come out of something that has died. The sunflower is something beautiful that grows, then at the peak of its beauty, the petals begin to fall and the flower soon dies. But the seeds from the old flower can be buried in the soil, and then they will grow into new sunflowers. Use as an introduction to the theme of Jesus bringing new life after death.

Take in a selection of Easter greeting cards. If possible, enlarge the illustrations onto overhead projector acetates. Talk about the pictures on the cards. Put on one side the ones which do not seem to have any Christian significance. Talk about the symbols which do have Christian significance. With carefully chosen cards, the events and some of the significance of the first Easter can be developed.

 ## Congregational/ group activities

- Make a series of paper plate faces to show the range of feelings experienced by the disciples from Good Friday through to Easter Sunday. Fasten them on to short garden sticks so that they can be held up at appropriate moments in the talk.

- Invite the congregation to add to a graffiti board with the heading 'Easter is . . .' or 'Easter means . . .'.

- If you have used a plain wooden cross as part of the Good Friday services, fasten oasis to the front of the cross and use to decorate with fresh flowers – you will need ones which have firm stems.

- Make an Easter banner which shows the empty cross, flowers around the base and the words 'Jesus is risen, Alleluia!' If the banner has been prepared beforehand and all the pieces have been pre-cut, this could be assembled quite quickly.

- Re-tell the events of Easter day using the figures in the Easter garden (see the story 'The boy who saw Easter' from *Children Aloud!* for ideas on a way to retell the story).

 ## Prayer/ intercessions

Prepare folded cards in the shape of the empty tomb, enough for one for everybody. Have available some pencils or felt pens. Invite the congregation to write or draw a 'good news' prayer on the inside of the 'tomb'. Allow a short time for each person to reflect on the prayer they have written (perhaps with some suitable music in the background), before the minister offers a collective prayer.

Place a large cross in a place which is visible to everyone. Have some pieces of Blu-tack ready near the cross. Give everyone a small piece of paper and have pencils/felt pens ready. Ask the congregation to spend a few moments thinking of someone or some situation who/which needs to find new life through Christ. Invite people to fasten their paper to the cross.

 ## Stories and other resources

Nicola Moon, *Billy's Sunflower*, Scholastic, 1997

Liz Curtis Higgs, *The Parable of the Lily*, Thomas Nelson, 1997

'The boy who saw Easter', in *Children Aloud!*

'Footprints', in *Together for Festivals*

Brian Ogden, *Too Busy to Listen*, Bible Reading Fellowship, 1998

Hall, Jarvis and Jefferson, *It's a Very Special Day*, NCEC, 1998

 ## Drama

'Easter group mime', in *Playing Up*

Andrew Brandon, 'The garden', in *Oh No, Not the Nativity!,* Scripture Union, 1998

♪ ♪♪♯♪ ♪♪♪ Music

Alleluia, alleluia (HON 24, JP 3, MP 30)

Children, join the celebration (JP 320)

He is Lord, He is Lord (JP 75, MP 220)

Jesus is Lord (JP 137, HON 270, MP 367)

Roll the stone (JP 449)

'Happy Easter' we will say (BBP 44)

Christ the Lord is risen again (HAMNS 79, HON 80, HTC 153)

Jesus Christ is risen today (HAMNS 77, HON 267, HTC 155, KSHF 269, MP 357)

Post communion prayer

God of Life,
who for our redemption gave your only-begotten
    Son to the death of the cross,
and by his glorious resurrection
have delivered us from the power of our enemy:
grant us so to die daily to sin,
that we may evermore live with him
    in the joy of his risen life;
through Jesus Christ our Lord.

The Second Sunday of Easter

 ## Readings

Exodus 14.10-31,15.20-21

Having been slaves in Egypt for many years, the Israelites escaped under the leadership of Moses. Following God's instructions, Moses led them between the parted waves of the Red Sea. The Egyptians tried to follow in pursuit but the water returned and they were all drowned. The Israelites were amazed: their faith in God, and Moses as his chosen servant, was restored, at least for a while!

Acts 4.32-35

This is a generalized summary of life in the early Christian community, which was characterized by unity, witness, and the renunciation of wealth and possessions. The proceeds from the sale of land and houses were shared out so that no one was left in need. The apostles were held in high regard because of the way in which they testified to the resurrection of Christ. This picture of the early Christian community is reinforced by the example of Joseph the Levite which follows, but needs to be considered alongside the later account of Ananias and Sapphira.

1 John 1.1-22

This Epistle is an exhortation to Johannine Christians, warning them against the views of dissidents. The prologue is a personal testimony to the presence of the pre-existent, life-giving Word of God revealed in Jesus, made out of a desire to see others sharing in the same faith. Light and dark are used as analogies with those who live according to God's commandments, and those who do not. Those who claim to live in the Light but do not live in accordance with their words, or deceive themselves into thinking they are without sin, are particularly criticized. But those who sincerely confess their sins can be assured of forgiveness through the death and resurrection of Jesus.

John 20.19-31

After Jesus has appeared to Mary Magdalene early in the morning, he appears to the disciples later in the same day whilst they are together in a locked room. There he shows them his wounds, passes on the Holy Spirit and confers on them the power to forgive sins. Thomas is absent from the group and can not believe what his fellow disciples tell him. He seeks the same visual evidence that they have been given. A week later Jesus appears to the disciples again, with Thomas present. Although Thomas has the chance to touch Jesus' wounds, he no longer needs that kind of evidence before he can believe. His profession of faith is the climax of this passage, and possibly of the whole Gospel: 'My Lord and my God!'

Collect

Almighty Father,
you have given your only Son to die for our sins
and to rise again for our justification:
grant us so to put away the leaven of malice and
   wickedness
that we may always serve you
in pureness of living and truth;
through the merits of your Son Jesus Christ our
   Lord,
who is alive and reigns with you,
in the unity of the Holy Spirit,
one God, now and for ever.

Talk/address/ sermon

There is perhaps part of our human make-up which makes us think that believing would be easier if we had proof, signs and evidence. Trust on its own can seem very difficult at times. The Israelites discovered this as they were standing on the shores of the Red Sea with water in front of them and the Egyptians in hot pursuit behind. Thomas also found this when he realized that he had not been present when Jesus first appeared to the rest of the disciples. Trust makes us vulnerable, but God does not let us down. God is with us always, in whatever situation.

Faith requires action. It should be changing the way we live. In the Gospel reading, Jesus commissioned his disciples: 'As the Father sent me, so I send you'. 'Send' implies an obligation to do, not just to be. Although the reading from Acts perhaps gives an idealistic picture of the early Christian community, it reinforces the message that faith is not only about believing, but also involves a way of living. Indeed, those who claim to follow Jesus, but whose pattern of living does not match their words and who do not confess their shortcomings, are singled out for particular criticism in the Epistle. The demands seem so daunting, but, for those who do recognize and confess their sins, they have the assurance of Christ's atoning action through death and resurrection.

 ## Congregational/ group activities

- Can we think of occasions when we have felt on the 'outside'? When we have not been a part of special experiences shared by others (in the playground, at home, in our workplaces, in a sports club)? What kind of situations make us feel 'on the outside'? Explore the feelings of Thomas at different stages in the Gospel reading. What is our response when we meet other people who feel 'on the outside'?

- Make paper plate faces on sticks to show the facial expressions of the disciples. Use two plates back-to-back to show how Thomas' feelings must have changed between the first and second incidents in the locked room.

- Prior to the service, make a simple two-dimensional picture to depict the world using blue for water and yellow for landforms. Cut it up into about six or eight large pieces to make a jigsaw. You will then need a backing board and some Blu-tack. Use as a visual aid to show the brokenness of our world. Our faith calls us to action. Invite helpers to piece the world together.

 ## Prayers/ intercessions

Arrange for all members of the congregation to have cards and pencils or felt pens. Refer to the reading from 1 John 1-2. Instruct the congregation to fold the cards into four. Invite them to write or draw something which symbolizes actions or situations for which they are sorry. In the first part this should be something for which they feel personally responsible. In the second, there should be something for which they feel responsible as a member of your church; in the third something for which they feel responsible as a citizen of this country; the fourth, something for which they

feel responsible as a member of the global community. Allow a few moments for quiet reflection, collect the cards in baskets and lay them on the altar or at the foot of a cross.

Use the 'broken world' visual aid. Start with the separate pieces. Pray for situations which mar the unity of God's world. Have ready a volunteer who will Blu-tack a piece of the world jigsaw onto the backing board. At the end of the prayers, the world will be complete.

 ## Stories and other resources

'Easter Rap', in *Children Aloud!*

Maggie Barfield (ed.), 'Let my people go', in *Let's Sing and Shout*, Scripture Union, 1998

'Amazing grace!', in *Reign Dance*

Anne Faulkner, *The Easter Alphabet*, Bible Reading Fellowship, 1999

 ## Drama

'Mr X', in *Playing Up*

 ## Music

God's not dead (JP 60)

Led like a lamb (JP 151, MP 402)

Saviour of the world (JP 216)

Jesus Christ (SHP 74)

Here is love (SHP 48)

Jesus in the garden (CP 129)

Because He lives (MP 52)

Jesus stand among us in thy risen power (HON 280, HTC 364, MP 380)

This joyful Eastertide (HON 509, HTC 165)

Post communion prayer

Lord God our Father,
through our Saviour Jesus Christ
you have assured your children of eternal life
and in baptism have made us one with him:
deliver us from the death of sin
and raise us to new life in your love,
in the fellowship of the Holy Spirit,
by the grace of our Lord Jesus Christ.

The Third Sunday of Easter

 ## Readings

Zephaniah 3.14-20

The Lord tells Zion to rejoice. He has overcome their enemies. He will gather his scattered people and restore esteem and property. The passage speaks of celebration and promise. God is the protector, the saviour, the all-powerful judge. It highlights the recognition and understanding of the effects of the special relationship with God, where there is promise of future joy and security in the knowledge of God's comfort, love and protection.

Acts 3.12-19

Peter's message to the Israelites is that through Jesus comes healing. The power of healing, and through this new life, comes from God through Jesus. This healing, spiritual and physical, is available for all people. The importance of repentance in order to receive forgiveness and a new life in Christ is strongly emphasized.

1 John 3.1-7

An exploration of what it means to be 'Children of God'. Becoming a child of God, accepting Jesus as saviour, results in dramatic change in who you are, your beliefs, priorities and principles, as well as how you behave. It is the confident knowledge of God's constant love and forgiveness, together with the security of his protection and guidance, which provides us with the courage to be different and the recognition and realization of the same. Those who do not know God find it difficult to appreciate and understand the changes in behaviour and attitude.

Luke 24.36-48

Jesus appears to the disciples. They have difficulty believing it is him or in understanding what is happening. The key features relate to recognition and realization being fundamental to understanding. Jesus refers them back to the teaching of the prophets and how all that has happened fulfils their prophecies. With his appearance to the disciples, Jesus is the living proof and they are witnesses of that. They are reminded of their responsibility to preach and explain the teaching about repentance and forgiveness, being key elements of life in Christ.

Collect

Almighty Father,
who in your great mercy gladdened the disciples
    with the sight of the risen Lord:
give us such knowledge of his presence with us,
that we may be strengthened and sustained
    by his risen life
and serve you continually in righteousness and
    truth;
through Jesus Christ your Son our Lord,
who is alive and reigns with you,
in the unity of the Holy Spirit,
one God, now and for ever.

Talk/address/ sermon

Explore ideas on recognition and realization leading to or reinforcing knowledge and understanding. Use examples from experience (such as when 'the penny suddenly dropped', when you realized you actually understood something). The need for proof, sometimes to be shown or to have active involvement, can help. This relates to the readings from Zephaniah and Luke.

How and where do we recognize God today? Through teaching, healing, example, action, people, events, etc.

Discuss the meaning of repentance and forgiveness. How do we feel and react? Relate this to our experiences and understanding of 'new life' and how we are changed and become different. This links in with the readings from Zephaniah, Acts and John's letter.

Explore key elements of what it means to be a Christian (perceived positives and negatives). This could be developed into an on-going visual activity over the weeks of Easter as different elements are revealed and explored. A display board headed 'A Christian is . . .' would provide an interesting focus developed over the weeks.

Share experience and fellowship. Use the reading from Luke to focus on the importance of the example of sharing a meal together and explore the symbolism of sharing in the Eucharist.

Congregational/ group activities

- Make cards or badges for 'A Christian is . . .' Explore different ideas with different age groups through discussion. Develop a display board for further use in the sermon slot.

- Explore the idea of sin = brokenness and healing = wholeness. Use a jigsaw puzzle cross (or several different cross designs) to symbolize the building up of wholeness through the cross.

- Look at books that show the change from one form of life to another (such as eggs to chicken, caterpillar to butterfly). Draw a timeline to show the animal at each stage of the transformation process.

- Discuss in appropriate age groups how we learn, how we know things and come to an understanding. Explore the effectiveness of experiences of such influences as teaching, reading, media, example, involvement, proof and faith.

- Organize an 'agape', a fellowship meal, interspersed with readings, songs and prayers.

 ## Prayers/ intercessions

Use prayers for the Church throughout the world, possibly using 'A Christian is . . .' cards.

Repentance and forgiveness: use cards with sad faces to create sorry prayers. Use an 'Action confession' using clenched fists to say sorry, with a simple response such as 'We are sorry' or 'Forgive us Lord'.

Finish the time of prayer with one of the following prayers:

> O Lord my God, take away from me all that blocks my way to you; give me all that speeds me towards you; rescue me from myself, and give me as your own to yourself.
>
> Nicholas von Flue (1417–87)

Lord Jesus Christ,
fill us, we pray, with your light
that we may reflect your wondrous glory.
So fill us with your love
that we may count nothing too small to do for you,
nothing too much to give,
and nothing too hard to bear.

St Ignatius Loyola (1491–1556)

 ## Stories and other resources

Eric Carle, *The Very Hungry Caterpillar*, H. Hamilton, 1994

'Repentance' and 'Forgiveness', in *The Discovery Wheel*

'Forgiveness', in *Pick and Mix*

Susan Sayers, Sections on 'Being made new' and 'Forgiveness', in *Come and See* (All Age Lenten Journey), Kevin Mayhew, 1990

Carol Watson , Section on 'Feelings and attitudes', in *365 Children's Prayers*, Lion, 1989

Lois Rock, 'New life', in *Glimpses of Heaven* (Poems and Prayers), Lion, 1997

Drama

Andrew Smith, 'The debtors . . . forgiveness', in *Much Ado About: 20 Sketches for Use with 11s–14s*, CPAS, 1994

Bob Irving, 'A woman who was a sinner', in *In a Nutshell*, NCEC, 1995

'Don't touch', in *A Fistful of Sketches*

Music

Rejoice in the Lord always (JP 208, MP 577)

Sing praise (JP 455)

Praise Him on the trumpet (JP 200)

Praise Him, Praise Him (JP 203)

Welcome the King (SHP 144)

We will lay our burden down (HON 538)

Alleluia, alleluia, give thanks to the risen Lord (HON 24, HTC S3, KSHF 5, MP 30)

I'm sorry (FG 23)

Creepy, crawly caterpillar (FG 32)

I know that my Redeemer lives, what joy (HON 232, HTC 169, MP 278)

The day of resurrection (HAMNS 75, HON 474, HTC 161)

Post communion prayer

Living God,
your Son made himself known to his disciples
in the breaking of bread:
open the eyes of our faith,
that we may see him in all his redeeming work;
who is alive and reigns, now and for ever.

The Fourth Sunday of Easter

Readings

Genesis 7.1-15,11-18;8.6-19;9.8-13

These interspersed readings trace the story of Noah, starting with God's instruction to Noah to enter the ark with his wife, sons and their wives, along with seven pairs each of the ritually clean animals, and one pair each of the unclean animals. The reading then gives details of the flood itself; the sending of a raven and a dove to see whether there is land fit for them to return; and the establishment of God's covenant with Noah and his descendants signified by the setting of a rainbow in the sky.

Acts 4.5-12

Peter and John are arrested and brought before the Sanhedrin because of the public reaction to the healing of the paralysed man at the Beautiful Gate. The question posed to Peter and John provides the introduction to the discourse which follows. 'Name' and 'power' are parallel concepts. Peter acknowledges that the empowerment to perform the cure comes through the invocation of Jesus' name. Peter's discourse challenges the Sanhedrin who had sought Jesus' death and the Sadducees who denied the possibility of resurrection. Peter proclaims the triumph of the risen Lord as the supreme authority.

1 John 3.16-24

Jesus' willing death for us should invoke in us the willingness to give our lives for others. One of the ways we can put this into practice is by sharing material goods with those in need. It is not enough to express our love for others just in words; it must also be expressed through actions, which are done in the right attitude.

John 10.11-18

This is part of a longer passage in which Jesus develops imagery of shepherds, sheep and the sheepfold. Jesus is the good shepherd. The term 'shepherd' is a well-known biblical symbol for ruler (e.g. Ezekiel 34). The good shepherd loves and knows his sheep as his own, but crucially is willing to lay down his life for his sheep. In contrast, the bad shepherd (i.e. the hired man) has no real concern for his sheep and abandons them when things get difficult. Jesus' willingness to lay down his life for his sheep arises out of his own voluntary self-offering made in love, as opposed to some unavoidable submission to another authority.

Collect

> Almighty God,
> whose Son Jesus Christ is the resurrection and the life:
> raise us, who trust in him,
> from the death of sin to the life of righteousness,
> that we may seek those things which are above,
> where he reigns with you
> in the unity of the Holy Spirit,
> one God, now and for ever.

Talk/address/ sermon

Following Christ will always involve taking personal risks. For Noah, taking action on hearing God's warnings and instructions must have been risky in terms of relationships with other people. One can imagine the reaction of bystanders as Noah and his family started to build the ark! Peter and John took risks in terms of their own personal freedom and safety in proclaiming the power of the risen Lord before the Sanhedrin. The reading from John's letter invokes us to be willing to share our material possessions with those in need. This, too, is risky in terms of personal comfort. Will there still be enough left for ourselves? The good shepherd, who was willing to lay down his life for his sheep, took the ultimate risk. Consider present-day experiences of risk-taking for Jesus.

Belief in God is not a 'self-protection' policy. It does not guarantee that we will be free from any kind of harm or misfortune. But we can be assured of power, greater than we could imagine, to do God's will, and an assurance that God is with us in whatever situation we find ourselves. Use the examples of Peter and John and the different ways in which their Christian discipleship developed.

Knowing that Jesus, the good shepherd loves and knows each one of us by name, and was willing, in an act of voluntary self-offering, to lay down his life for us, gives a sense of self-worth to each one of us which is beyond measure. This is in stark contrast to many of the values of our current society in which people are valued more in terms of material possessions, human worth and personal success. Moreover, as John's letter reminds us, God's kingdom allows for failures. Even when our own conscience suggests that we have fallen short, we can be confident of God's acceptance of us.

Congregational/ group activities

- Prepare a large picture of a sheep and a shepherd (ask a child to lie down on a length of wallpaper and draw round him/her and add a crook). Collect words and phrases which come to mind when we think of a sheep. Either write these words directly on to the sheep, or ask volunteers to write them on labels and stick them on to the sheep. Then do a similar exercise with the shepherds, asking for words and phrases which come to mind when we think of a good shepherd. Use as a lead-in to a talk about Jesus' relationship with us.

- Make a set of six or eight large warning signs (a triangle with a red border as in the road signs). Use words such as 'Warning: following Jesus always involves taking risks'. Invite suggestions of risks that people have been conscious of in their journey with Jesus. Write each suggestion on a separate triangle. Display them and use them as part of a talk on risk-taking.

- Give each person a picture of a sheep with a piece of double-sided sticky tape on the back. Ask each person to write their name on the sheep. Prepare some large sheets of paper on each of which are written a key verse or phrase from the Gospel reading (e.g. 'I am the good shepherd; the good shepherd lays down his life for his sheep'). If there are large numbers of people in your group, make duplicate sheets. At an appropriate time in the service, invite people to stick their sheep around the verse or phrase which means most to them at the moment.

Prayers/ intercessions

On either an overhead projector sheet or a large sheet of paper, draw three concentric circles. In the inside circle write 'This community', in the middle circle 'This country' and in the outside circle 'This world'. Before the intercessions, invite prayer requests for individuals and groups who feel they have no value in our society. Write them in the appropriate circles. Include these in the prayers of intercession.

A response prayer, reminding us of our dependence on God

> When we are anxious or afraid, Lord
> **help us to depend on you.**
> When we think we can do things in our own strength, Lord
> **help us to depend on you.**

When we have a difficult decision to make, Lord
help us to depend on you.
When there is no-one else to turn to, Lord
help us to depend on you.
When we forget our need of you, Lord
help us to depend on you.
Lord, we thank you that you are always there for us, even when we forget you. Help us to be constantly aware of your power and presence in our lives.
Amen

Stories and other resources

Pat Alexander (ed.), 'The soldier who took the blame', in *Song of the Morning*, Lion, 1997

V. Ironside, *The Huge Bag of Worries*, MacDonald Young Books, 1996

'Noah and the flood', in *Instant Inspirations*

The section on Noah, in Pam Macnaughton and Hamish Bruce (eds), *Together through the Bible*, NS/CHP, 1998

Drama

Brian Mountord, 'Mrs Noah's last stand', in *The Sower, Mrs Noah and a Dentist*, Tufton Books, 1998

Andrew Smith, 'One man and his voice', in *Much Ado About: 20 Sketches for Use with 11s–14s*, CPAS, 1996

Music

Mister Noah built an ark (JP 167)

Noah was the only good man (JP 432)

Old man Noah (JP 440)

Rise and shine (JP 210)

I love the pit-pit patter of the raindrops (BBP 79)

He came down that we may have love (JU, p. 36)

Jesus! the name high over all (HTC 213, KSHF 294, MP 385)

The God of love my shepherd is (HAMNS 110, HON 479)

Post communion prayer

Merciful Father,
you gave your Son Jesus Christ to be the good shepherd,
and in his love for us to lay down his life and rise again:
keep us always under his protection,
and give us grace to follow in his steps;
through Jesus Christ our Lord.

The Fifth Sunday of Easter

 ## Readings

Baruch 3.9-15,32-4.4

This is a homily on wisdom. The initial question asked is, 'Why is Israel still in exile?'

The answer is, because the Israelites have failed to recognize the real source of wisdom, they have, in fact, shown their ignorance in not recognizing God as the definite and powerful source of wisdom and life.

or

Genesis 22.1-18

The testing of the faith and obedience of Abraham. God orders Abraham to take his son, Isaac, to Moriah and to prepare to offer him in sacrifice, as was the custom. Abraham, with a heavy heart, sets off with Isaac to complete this order. As he is about to kill Isaac, God speaks to him through an angel and stops him killing his son. Abraham sees a ram caught in a bush which he kills and offers as sacrifice, and through this he recognizes that God is the great provider. God rewards Abraham's obedience with rich blessings and the promise of further blessings on future generations.

or

Acts 8.26-40

The account of Philip and the Ethiopian on the road from Jerusalem to Gaza. The Ethiopian is obviously interested and searching for information as he struggles to read from the book of Isaiah. Beginning with an explanation of this Scripture, Philip then goes on to teach the good news of Jesus to the Ethiopian, who becomes a believer and is baptized.

1 John 4.7-21

The essence of this reading is that God is love and from him all knowledge and practice of love comes. The immensity of God's love is not only in its constancy and its availability to all people, but also in the powerful element of sacrifice realized in his sending his son to earth as man. Through this passage we learn also about Jesus as the bringer of life, the builder of relationships between God and man, the saviour of the world and as the Son of God. The power of the Spirit working in us enables us to recognize and respond to God, his teaching and his presence, so that we can build our lives on him.

John 15.1-8

The image of Jesus as the vine and us as the branches is accessible and clear. The vine has to have its roots in good soil, well-prepared land – a firm foundation of belief/faith in God. The vine grows prolifically and therefore needs stringent pruning and particular care. The vine has two kinds of branches: fruit-bearing and non fruit-bearing. The analogy to types of practising and witnessing Christians is clear and links well with the gardener's realization of the need to feed and nurture as well as to cut back and discard.

Collect

Almighty God,
who through your only-begotten Son Jesus Christ
have overcome death and opened to us
    the gate of everlasting life:
grant that, as by your grace going before us
    you put into our minds good desires,
so by your continual help
we may bring them to good effect;
through Jesus Christ our risen Lord,
who is alive and reigns with you,
in the unity of the Holy Spirit,
one God, now and for ever.

 ## Talk/address/sermon

Use the 'gardening theme' with its analogy to us as practising, witnessing Christians. Visual aids and practical gardening gear can be used to demonstrate the need for pruning, for feeding and caring. What does the vine need to bear fruit for?

Love = sacrifice. Talk about the 'costs' of love (parents and children, some aspects of married life, the sacrifice made by God in love for us). Relate this to the readings from Genesis, John's letter and John's Gospel.

Sharing the 'good news' What does this mean, how can we share it, what might it cost and what opportunities are there? Build on the importance of good relationships, the learning and sharing by example, and the need for effective communication appropriate and relevant to different people and situations.

Congregational/ group activities

- Make a vine with branches, leaves and grapes using paper, felt and other scrap material. Use as a prayer vine with individuals' intercessions, or as a message board with 'instructions' about the Christian way of life.

- Create a 'Love is . . .' or 'Love means . . .' display board with some positive and some negative aspects.

- Make heart-shaped badges or cards with messages (e.g. God is love, God loves you) to distribute within the congregation.

- Lead a meditation based on the imagery of the vine and the branches, including the tending, feeding, pruning and nurturing.

- Organize a prayer walk, exploring God's creation and his gifts to us.

 ## Prayers/ intercessions

Create prayers in picture form, using the vine leaf and/or the grape shape. Make a display for church. Offer the individually created prayers within the service.

Use an adaptation of the meditation exercise suggested in the form of offering intercessions.

Lead intercessions with the regular headings (the Church, world, community, sick, deceased) within a theme of God as the provider and protector of all.

Use the following versicle and response:

Leader: for kingship belongs to the Lord,
All: **he rules over the nations**

 ## Stories and other resources

Margery Williams, *The Velveteen Rabbit*, Mammoth (Reed Books), 1992

Margaret Spivey, *I Can't Make a Flower*, Scripture Union, 1994

Nick Butterworth and Mick Inkpen, *Wonderful Earth*, Hunt and Thorpe, 1993

John Bell, 'Meditations', in *He Was in the World*, Wild Goose Publications, 1995

'Thanksgiving' and 'Worship and wonder' sections, in Jill Fuller, *Looking Beyond*, Kevin Mayhew, 1996

'Exploring' and 'Thanksgiving' sections, in Jill Fuller, *Gazing in Wonder*, Kevin Mayhew, 1996

'Creative visualisation' section, in Mary Stone, *Don't Just Do Something, Sit There*, RMEP, 1995

 ## Drama

'Phil and the Gent (Philip and the Ethiopian)', in *A Fistful of Sketches*

Music

Make me a servant, Lord (JP 162)

Father, lead me day by day (JP 43)

Jesus loves me (JP 140)

I am trusting You (JP 86)

This is my body (HON 506)

Ubi caritas (HON 525)

We have a gospel (HON 532, MP 728)

Bread of heaven, on thee we feed (HAMNS 271, HON 67, HTC 398)

Love divine, all loves excelling (HAMNS 131, HON 321, HTC 217, KSHF 353, MP 449)

Post communion prayer

Eternal God,
whose Son Jesus Christ is the way, the truth and
the life:
grant us to walk in his way,
to rejoice in his truth,
and to share his risen life;
who is alive and reigns, now and for ever.

The Fifth Sunday of Easter

The Sixth Sunday of Easter

 ## Readings

Isaiah 55.1-11

This reading opens with an invitation to a spiritual banquet. The only condition for participation is a thirst for God. God's promise is one of everlasting love. God, though transcendent, is close enough to be burdened by human sin. But forgiveness is also promised. There is a great gulf between God's ways and human ways, but God's purposes for humanity will prevail.

Acts 10.44-48

This reading is the climax of the action with Cornelius and Simon Peter, which is described throughout chapter 10, and is a pivotal point in the story of the Christian Church. For the first time, Gentiles (Cornelius and his household), who had not previously been converted to Judaism, received the gift of the Holy Spirit.

1 John 5.1-6

This reading connects the love of God with love of Jesus, and recognition of him as the Son. Faith in the incarnate Son as the Christ enables us to recognize others as God's children. Acknowledging Jesus' true character is an act of faith and is the means by which the forces in the world which are working against God are overcome. Although Jesus was proclaimed the Son of God after his baptism by water, it was by his shedding of blood on the cross that he was revealed.

John 15.9-17

This is a continuation of the 'true vine' discourse which Jesus gave to his disciples. Love – the essence of the life of God's people – is not something which just flows between the divine and the human. Indeed, the error of the old Israel had been to assume that the love of God was for them alone. This love must overflow into relationships between human beings. The limits of love are potentially endless. As Jesus was about to lay down his life for his friends, so Christian love is to be of this kind. The disciples were now friends of Jesus. They shared in a new intimacy because of all that Jesus had shared with them. The disciples were chosen by Jesus and commissioned in order to bear fruit for God.

Collect

God our redeemer,
you have delivered us from the power of darkness
and brought us into the kingdom of your Son:
grant, that as by his death he has recalled us to life,
so by his continual presence in us he may raise us to eternal joy;
through Jesus Christ your Son our Lord,
who is alive and reigns with you,
in the unity of the Holy Spirit,
one God, now and for ever.

 ## Talk/address/sermon

There can be a tendency for human beings to want to divide their fellows into simplistic categories: the good and the bad, the successes and the failures, the 'in' group and the 'out' group, the clean and the unclean. Sometimes people's view of God is mixed up with such classifications (consider examples from current world situations). The lesson that had to be grasped in the early Church was that the early Christians could not continue to classify people into Jews and non-Jews. The kingdom was available to all who believed in Christ and were committed to doing his will. In what ways do we continue to classify people, including ways within our churches? Are some people more accepted and included than others?

Congregational Group/activities

- Following the Gospel reading, tell a story about a person other than Jesus who has given up her/his own life for the sake of other people. We may never be in the position where we are called to lay down our lives for another person in the way that Jesus or others have done. However, we are called on a daily basis to consider the needs of others before ourselves. What is our instinctive response? In what ways do the values of our present society encourage or discourage us to put others before ourselves? What are the needs of our community? How might we find out and who should do this? What could/should we do about what we discover? What are our needs as a congregation? How might we be more effective with each other? What prevents us from relating more fully to each other?

- Give each person a sheet of A5 paper and a paper or pencil. Ask members of the congregation to fold their piece of paper in half vertically and then about one-third down horizontally. When the sheet is opened out, the fold should make a cross and it is possible to see four sections. Ask everyone to think of four people or situations whose needs they wish to put before their own. Write or draw words or symbols as signs for each situation. Encourage adults to help children as appropriate.

- Continue work on the banner or poster that you began last week on the theme of 'I am the vine, you are the branches'.

Prayers/ intercessions

Use the names written on the cross-shaped paper (produced during the congregational/group activities). Music can help to create a prayerful sense of quiet. Collect all the crosses up. Hold them up to God with the following words:

Lord Jesus Christ, we bring before you the needs of these people and situations. We have placed them around the cross in the knowledge that forgiveness and new life flow from your cross. Surround these people with your redeeming love, and show us what we can each do to help bring healing to each of these situations. We ask this in your name. **Amen**.

Use this prayer of confession, remembering the divisions that exist within our own churches:

Lord Jesus Christ, your disciple Peter said you have no favourites.
We confess that there have been occasions and situations when we have favoured some people more than others because of their age.
Forgive us. Help us to become a church which has no favourites.

We confess that there have been occasions and situations when we have favoured some people more than others because of their appearance.
Forgive us. Help us to become a church which has no favourites.

We confess that there have been occasions and situations when we have favoured some people more than others because of their opinions.
Forgive us. Help us to become a church which has no favourites.

We confess that there have been occasions and situations when we have favoured some people more than others because of their situation.

Forgive us. Help us to become a church which has no favourites.

We confess that there have been occasions and situations when we have favoured some people more than others because of limitations and abilities.
Forgive us. Help us to become a church which has no favourites.

We confess that there have been occasions and situations when we have favoured some people more than others because of their behaviour.
Forgive us. Help us to become a church which has no favourites.

 # Stories and other resources

Sam McBratney, *Guess how Much I Love You?*, Walker Books, 1996

Pat Alexander, 'The soldier who took the blame', in *Song of the Morning*, Lion, 1997

M. Waddell and B. Firt, *Can't you Sleep, Little Bear?*, Walker Books, 1990

'The Blitz and Coventry Cathedral', in *Instant Inspirations*

Robert Atwell, *Celebrating the Saints*, Canterbury Press, 1998

 # Drama

'Treat everyone the same', in *Telling more Tales*

 # Music

Shalom, my friend (JP 217)

The steadfast love (JP 250, MP 666)

Yesterday, today, for ever (JP 294, MP 787)

Come down, O Love Divine (HAMNS 156, HON 90, HTC 231, MP 89)

Holy Spirit, come, confirm us (HAMNS 471, HON 214)

Rock of ages (HAMNS 135, HON 437, HTC 593, KSHF 469, MP 582)

Post communion prayer

God our Father,
whose Son Jesus Christ gives the water of eternal life:
may we thirst for you,
the spring of life and source of goodness,
through him who is alive and reigns, now and for ever.

The Sixth Sunday of Easter

The Seventh Sunday of Easter

Sunday After Ascension Day

 ### Readings

Ezekiel 36.24-28

New life for Israel. God's promise is to cleanse, revive and inspire the Israelites to bring them back from darkness into new light. In return they will keep his laws and live in the land God gave to their ancestors.

or

Acts 1.15-17,21-26

Peter makes the announcement to the gathering of believers about the fulfilment of the prophecy of Judas' betrayal of Jesus and his subsequent death and now the need to replace him in the team of disciples. With God's guidance, Matthias is chosen by the drawing of lots, his gifts and experience being recognized.

1 John 5.9-13

Here John reinforces the message of God's testimony that through Jesus comes the gift of eternal life. This gift is given freely by God, but in order to receive it we have to be true believers in our minds, our lives and our witness.

John 17.6-19

As Jesus prepares himself to leave the earthly world, he prays for his disciples, commending them to God for their commitment to belief, obedience and witness. He prays for their safe keeping as they continue their commissioned ministry without his direct presence and guidance, and in a world where they will face hostility, disbelief and evil.

Collect

O God the king of glory,
you have exalted your only Son Jesus Christ
with great triumph to your kingdom in heaven:
we beseech you, leave us not comfortless,
but send your Holy Spirit to strengthen us
and exalt us to the place
    where our Saviour Christ is gone before,
who is alive and reigns with you,
in the unity of the Holy Spirit,
one God, now and for ever.

 ### Talk/address/sermon

Develop thoughts and ideas on what it means to be a Christian, relating to belief, service and witness. Reference could be made to the 'A Christian is . . .' display suggested in the previous weeks of Easter. Reflect further on this, possibly adding significant words or phrases.

Focus on the costs and rewards of being a true follower of Christ, referring to sacrifice, obedience, hostility and God's grace, the security of his love, guidance and protection.

Congregational/group activities

- Develop this idea with activities for different age groups, for example: 'Christian consequences' – a creative activity, where on a large piece of paper folded into three sections, individuals or small groups draw the head, the body and the legs and feet of the 'typical Christian'. It is more fun if the paper is passed on three times, so that the finished portrait is a collaborative production. After and during laughter, discuss the significant characteristics!

- In groups create a job description for a disciple, identifying necessary characteristics and a personal profile as well as the perceived requirements to fulfil the role.

- Develop a series of cartoons under the title of 'A Christian is . . .', 'A Disciple must . . .' or 'Christians/disciples are . . .'.

- Organize a Passover meal to focus on the Jewish tradition and its relationship to the Eucharist, and to highlight the significance of the use of blessings.

- The reading from John's Gospel concerns Jesus' prayer of blessing over his disciples. In today's terms this is a prayer of blessing for us, the Church in society and individuals in their Christian life, work and witness. There is opportunity to explore the significance of blessings in Christian pilgrimage, focusing on the sacraments and recognizing that blessings are given as a gift, a sign of love and protection. Explore the place and power of blessings at Baptism, Confirmation, Marriage, Confession, Vocation, and Holy Communion.

Prayers/ intercessions

Use the 'A Christian is . . .' cards suggested in previous weeks of Easter as a developing theme, focusing on identified qualities and the need of guidance, love, support and protection. Use prayers of thankfulness for all the gifts we have been given, developed and presented appropriately using words and/or pictures. Use prayer liturgies taken from *Take, Bless, Break, Share* (agapes, table blessings and liturgies).

Use the following versicle and response:

Leader: Creator God, we give you thanks

All: **Help us use your gifts for good.**

Stories and other resources

Joy Hutchinson, *Twelve Friends*, Scripture Union, 1991

'People Jesus met' and 'Jesus and his friends' from the series, Sue Kirby, *Bible Stories and Activities with the Under Fives*, CPAS, 1994

'Jesus' friends', in *Building New Bridges*

'Disciples', in *Pick and Mix*

'Disciples and discipleship', in Jonathan Mortimer, *See What I Mean,* CPAS, 1998

Simon Bryden-Brook, 'Blessings and liturgies', in *Take, Bless, Break, Share*, Canterbury Press, 1998

Drama

Richard Cole, 'A select group', in *Light Relief*, Bible Society, 1991

Bob Irving, 'Followers of Jesus', in *Crosstalk*, NCEC 1992.

John Bell and Graham Maule, 'The Call', in *Eh . . . Jesus . . . Yes, Peter . . .?*, Wild Goose Publications, 1987

Music

We're following Jesus (JP 487)

The journey of life (JP 468)

Abba Father (JP 2, MP 3)

Christ be my leader (JP 319)

Caring, sharing (BBP 8)

I, the Lord of sea and sky (HON 235)

I will make you fishers of men (JP 123)

I want to walk (JP 124)

We're following Jesus (JP 487)

Alleluia! sing to Jesus (HAMNS 262, HON 26, HTC 170)

Christ triumphant, ever reigning (HON 81, HTC 173, MP 77)

Crown him with many crowns (HAMNS 147, HON 103, HTC 174, MP 109)

Post communion prayer

Eternal God, giver of love and power,
your Son Jesus Christ has sent us into all the world
to preach the gospel of his kingdom:
confirm us in this mission,
and help us to live the good news we proclaim;
through Jesus Christ our Lord.

Day of Pentecost

Whit Sunday

 ## Readings

Ezekiel 37.1-14

Exiled in Babylon, the Jewish people are no longer free to live and worship as they want. In this time of desolation, the prophet Ezekiel has the tremendous vision of the Valley of the Dry Bones. Under the influence of the Holy Spirit, the dry bones become living people, illustrating God's power to restore his people to their own land. To describe the Holy Spirit, the prophet uses the word 'breath', a vivid reminder that the Spirit breathes God's life and power into our lives.

Acts 2.1-21

The Holy Spirit is given to the disciples of Jesus at Pentecost, as he promised. The gift also fulfils the prophecy of Joel in the Old Testament, that the Spirit would be given to people of every race and nation. As Jesus had promised, the Holy Spirit gives his disciples the right words to speak so that they can preach the gospel to all nations as he had commanded them.

Romans 8.22-27

Struggling along in the everyday world, we are not without hope and we don't need to be afraid about anything. The Holy Spirit is there with strength to overcome our weakness, and to lift us up to God in prayer, even when we do not have any words with which to pray.

John 15.26-27,16.4b-15

Jesus reassures his disciples that, when he is no longer with them on earth, the Holy Spirit will help them to remember him and know that he is still there. The Spirit 'shows up' the weaknesses of the world, and continually reveals more of the truth about God to the believers.

Collect

God, who as at this time
taught the hearts of your faithful people
by sending to them the light of your Holy Spirit:
grant us by the same Spirit
to have a right judgement in all things
and evermore to rejoice in his holy comfort;
through the merits of Christ Jesus our Saviour,
who is alive and reigns with you,
in the unity of the Holy Spirit,
one God, now and for ever.

Talk/address/ sermon

The Holy Spirit is God's power working within us. Talk about different powerful people (rulers, dictators, those who are wealthy, etc.) and about powerful objects (such as spaceships, aeroplanes, cars, etc.). Where does the power come from? Is it put to good use or bad use? Stress how, without this power, the people and objects mentioned cannot work properly. A good example from everyday life is the torch. Have a torch or torches with batteries and some without to show that only the ones with batteries inside can give light. With the Spirit inside us, we can show the light of Christ to the world.

Congregational/ group activities

- Prepare pre-written greetings cards in different languages. Everyone receives a card with their service sheet. After the Acts 2.1-21 reading, ask people to turn to their neighbour and give the greeting in the language on their card. Although we may not understand the language we can understand the meaning.

- Prepare for each person one pre-cut torso, four long-shaped balloons, one round balloon, and masking tape. Inflate the balloons and attach to the torso with strips of mask-

ing tape. Joined together these make a body shape, which can be used to illustrate the reading from Ezekiel about God breathing life into dry bones.

- Some people may like to have a lasting memory of Pentecost. By making prayer wheels we can pray continuously for the world and its peoples. Cut out a small and a large circle from card. Photocopy an image of a globe or world map. Decide on the countries or places you specifically want to remember in your prayers. Using a ruler and pencil, divide the large circle into those areas. Write or illustrate your prayers in your own way in the sections. Stick the world map onto the small card and attach through the middle with paper clip.

- Use coloured paper strips and make long paper chains and wrap them around some volunteers. Then use to illustrate how restrictive a chain of captivity can be, and our need to break free. However, there is also another side to this image. If the chains wrapped around us are of prayer, then they can be all embracing and enfolding, wherever we may be.

Prayers/ intercessions

In between each 'section' a short chorus such as 'Spirit of the Living God' may be used. The first section could be entitled 'The Spirit gives new life' (vision of the dry bones), in which we remember how the Spirit, the breath of God, brings new life, even when all seems dead. Our prayer is also that the Spirit will give new hope, even to people who feel that all is hopeless.

Holy Spirit, Lord and Giver of Life, strengthen us by your power and love

'The Spirit comes to the Church' (the day of Pentecost). Here we praise God for the gift of confidence to Peter and the disciples, so that they could stand up without fear and declare their faith. Give thanks for the gifts of understanding and fellowship between people of all different kinds, for the unity which laid the foundations of the Church. Pray that this unity will continue in the Church, and for that same gift of power to carry on the work of the apostles.

Holy Spirit, Lord and Giver of Life, unite us in your power and love

'The Spirit removes evil and brings God's truth to us' (our Lord's promise). Pray that God will help us teach his truth to all people by our words and deeds. Remembering that the fruits of the Spirit are love, joy and peace, we ask God that the gift of his Spirit will keep us from harm and help us to walk away from evil. Pray that our minds will always be open to the Spirit's guiding hand

Holy Spirit, Lord and Giver of Life, lead us by your power and love

Stories and other resources

'Pentecost', in *Seasons and Saints for the Christian Year*

Leslie Francis and Nicola Slee, *The Windy Day: Teddy Horsley Learns about the Holy Spirit*, NCEC, 1987

Jan Godfrey, 'Pentecost for 5's and under', in *Praise, Play and Paint!*, NS/CHP, 1995

Donald Dowling, 'Blow, blow, wind of God', in *Together for Festivals*

Melissa Musick Nussbaum, 'The Valley of the Dry Bones', in *Stories for the Forty Days*, LTP Publications, 1997

Drama

' Pentecost Day', in *Telling Tales*

Music

Spirit of the living God (JP 222, MP 613)

When God breathes (JP 497)

Give me oil in my lamp (JP 50, MP 167)

This is the day (JP 255, MP 691)

I believe (SHP 57)

May your loving spirit (BBP 45)

The King is among us (HON 483, MP 650)

O breath of life, come sweeping (HON 356, HTC 237, MP 488, SHF 388)

Come, Holy Ghost, our souls inspire (HAMNS 93, HON 92, HTC 589, MP 90)

Breathe on me, Breath of God (HAMNS 157, HON 69, HTC 226, MP 67)

Post communion prayer

Faithful God,
who fulfilled the promises of Easter
by sending us your Holy Spirit
and opening to every race and nation
the way of life eternal:
open our lips by your Spirit,
that every tongue may tell of your glory;
through Jesus Christ our Lord.

Day of Pentecost

Trinity Sunday

 ## Readings

Isaiah 6.1-8

The prophet's great vision of God convinces him of his own weaknesses, but when he knows that he is cleansed and forgiven by God, he is able to answer his call. As a result Isaiah becomes a great prophet, speaking about God to people who have forgotten him, and bringing them a message of peace and hope.

Romans 8.12-17

God the Father, Son and Holy Spirit are completely united as one God, and St Paul shows us that we also become united with God. Through the Holy Spirit we become children of God, able to call him 'Father'. If we are children of God then we are with Christ because we share fully with him in his kingdom.

John 3.1-17

Like many people, Nicodemus cannot easily understand Jesus when he is talking about God and about something which is spiritual, rather than physical or 'seen' with our human eyes. Jesus points to himself as the source of knowledge about God. If we want salvation or true fulfilment in the realm of Father, Son and Holy Spirit, then we must believe: put our trust in God as he is shown to us in Jesus.

Collect

Almighty and everlasting God,
you have given us your servants grace,
by the confession of a true faith,
to acknowledge the glory of the eternal Trinity
and in the power of the divine majesty to worship
the Unity:
keep us steadfast in this faith,
that we may evermore be defended from all adversities;
through Jesus Christ your Son our Lord,
who is alive and reigns with you,
in the unity of the Holy Spirit,
one God, now and for ever.

 ## Talk/address/ sermon

Our everyday experiences and observation tell us that, although it may not be logical, 'three' can be also 'one' just like the Trinity. The triangle has three sides, but is only one figure. The tricycle has three wheels, but is only one machine. A triangle cannot have only two sides: it would be incomplete. Also, the tricycle is no good if one or two wheels are missing! In the same way, Father, Son and Holy Spirit work as a team. Each member shows a different 'side' of God but they are completely joined together for the purpose of loving and caring for us and his world.

 ## Congregational/ group activities

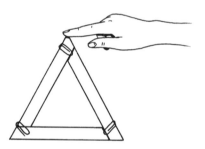

- Three together is one unit! On Trinity Sunday have as many visual images to illustrate the theme as possible. Have as many examples as you can borrow needing three to make one, such as a tripod for a camera, an artist's easel, a trike or a triangle. In each case three parts are needed to make a whole object and to get the balance right. Demonstrate the strength of the triangular shape by using three cardboard strips and brass paper clips. Compare the strength of the triangular shape with that of a square or other shape made with four strips of cardboard.

- Use the idea of a yacht. With a large cardboard box make a boat shape to represent God the Father, a mast with upright and cross piece to represent God the Son, then a sail to represent ourselves. We need the wind of the Holy Spirit to make the whole work. The three parts of the yacht together form one unit.

- Throughout the history of our faith, we have tried to personalize and visualize the Trinity: the Father,

Son and Holy Spirit. We can never fully know, but through sharing ideas and through biblical and theological reflection we can enrich what knowledge and understanding we have. Play the 'If' game. If God were a bird, what kind of bird would he be and why? Try this game with other kinds of animals or objects.

Prayers/ intercessions

Looking at God as Trinity, we see the Father who makes life, the Son who saves life, and the Spirit who strengthens life. We thank God for the wonder and beauty of the world he has made and for the gift of our daily bread. We pray for grace to use his gifts in the proper way.

God the Father, maker of all things.
Help us to believe and trust in you

We thank Jesus for his care for the sick and troubled, for showing us the love of God by dying on the cross and rising from the dead, opening the door for us into God's glorious kingdom. Pray that we will love and follow Jesus as he leads us to Heaven.

God the Son, who saves us from evil and death.
Help us to believe and trust in you

Give thanks to God the Holy Spirit for the gift of new life as he brings his power into our world. We pray that we will always be ready to receive the Holy Spirit into our lives and use his power to bring light to all people.

God the Holy Spirit, Lord and Giver of Life.
Help us to believe and trust in you

Stories and other resources

'Trinity Sunday', in *Festive Allsorts*

Joan Chapman, 'Trinity', in *Children Celebrate!*, Marshall Pickering, 1994

'St Mark' and 'St Patrick', in *Seasons, Saints and Sticky Tape*

Martin Wallace, 'Pilgrimage with God', in *The Celtic Resource Book*, NS/CHP, 1998

Drama

Andrew Smith, 'United . . . (the peace of God)', in *Much Ado About something else: 20 More Sketches for Use with 11–14s*, CPAS, 1996

Music

Thank you, God, for sending Jesus (JP 233)

We really want to thank You, Lord (JP 268, MP 734)

Praise God, from whom all blessings flow (JP 199, MP 557)

Father, we adore you (JP 44, MP 139)

Hallelujah, my Father (HON 194, MP 206)

Bless the Lord, my soul (HON 61)

Holy Hokey (JU, p. 22)

Father of heaven, whose love profound (HAMNS 97, HON 124, HTC 359)

Holy, holy, holy, Lord God almighty (HAMNS 95, HON 212, MP 237)

May the grace of Christ our Saviour (HAMNS 181, HON 333, HTC 370)

Three in One and One in Three (HON 515, HTC 12)

Post communion prayer

Almighty and eternal God,
you have revealed yourself as Father, Son and
   Holy Spirit,
and live and reign in the perfect unity of love:
hold us firm in this faith,
that we may know you in all your ways
and evermore rejoice in your eternal glory,
who are three Persons yet one God,
now and for ever.

Sunday between 29 May and 4 June

(if after Trinity Sunday)

Proper 4

 ### Readings

Continuous

I Samuel 3.1-10

Samuel hears God's call and answers, and when he repeats God's message to Eli, the old priest recognizes that God has spoken to the boy. This reading shows how God calls people of all ages and types to his service.

or Related

Deuteronomy 5.12-15

As part of the ten commandments, the people of God are told to observe the Sabbath day and to keep it holy. It is a day to be set apart from the rest of the week as a Sabbath to God.

2 Corinthians 4.5-12

Being human and limited, we are, as Paul says, like 'clay jars' but the Light of God shines through us. No matter what happens, however many difficulties we face, God is within us.

Jesus dies and rises again in our lives, and so we can bring new life and hope to others.

Mark 2.23-3.6

The strict rules about keeping the Sabbath day as a day of rest were unfair, because people needed to eat. It also wouldn't be right to use this rule as an excuse not to help someone in need. Jesus allows his disciples to eat and heals a sick man, because, as he says, the Sabbath day is given for us to choose to do good if we know it is right to do so.

 ### Talk/address/ sermon

Consider all the tasks we are asked to do in our daily lives. Some of them may appear to be beyond our abilities, but we are free to say 'yes' or 'no' just as Jesus showed that he and his friends were free to do what they wanted on the Sabbath. And yet, we often find that saying 'yes' can result in a great sense of achievement and satisfaction. We think of people like Samuel who have said 'yes' to God and as a result have done some wonderful things: people such as The Virgin Mary, St Paul, Francis of Assisi, and many others. What God wants us to do will not be easy, but when we open the door to him, his light and power come to us, giving us the strength we need to do his work.

 ### Congregational/ group activities

- Make a list with both adults and children of accidents or any emergency which has to be dealt with straight away. What do we do in circumstances like this? Who is there to help us? What do we do when God calls us to do things? How do we recognize the call? What do we do? Encourage all ages to share experiences and to act out the situations. Alternatively, make a collage picture to record what you have shared.

- The power of story-telling can be used through the use of silhouette puppets. Set up an overhead projector sheet or screen, and make shadow-puppets on sticks to use behind the screen, to dramatize the emergencies identified in the first activity, or in Samuel's story.

- Make jars with night lights, to illustrate God shining through us. You will need jam jars, coloured paper, a person-shaped template, glue sticks and night lights. Draw round the shape and cut out, then discard. Stick the coloured paper round the jar and place the night light inside. When lit, the light shines through the person.

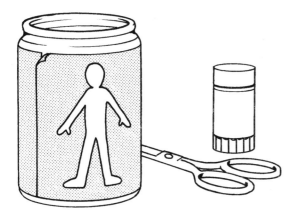

 ## Prayers/ intercessions

Think of people who have said 'yes' to God, and those who help us in emergencies. Thank God for people such as saints, priests, church members, and all who have answered God's call. Pray that, like them we will be ready to do whatever God wants us to do in his world.

God said 'who will go for me?'

Here I am, send me

Pray for all who are called to be leaders in our world, that they will let the light of God work through them to bring peace and hope to people of all nations.

God said 'who will go for me?'

Here I am, send me.

Give thanks for the doctors, nurses, paramedics, and all carers who will go out at any time to care for suffering people, and we thank God that Jesus continues his work of healing through them. We pray that God will help us to use any opportunities we have of caring for others.

God said 'who will go for me?'

Here I am, send me

 ## Stories and other resources

'The call of Samuel', in *In the Beginning*

'Moses and ten timely tips', in *Livewires Live*

'The covenant box', in *Instant Inspirations*

Gill Ambrose, *Plagues and Promises*, NCEC, 1998

 ## Drama

'The great adventurers: episode 2', in *Plays for all Seasons*

'Light and dark', in *Playing Up*

 ## Music

Colours of day (JP 28)

I am a lighthouse (JP 87)

I'm going to shine, shine, shine (JP 392)

God has put a circle round us (BBP 46)

Let today be the day as I go along my way (BBP 5)

Jesus called to Peter the fisherman (BBP 13)

Come, let us with our Lord arise (HAMNS 449, HTC 375)

Lord, be thy word my rule (HAMNS 232, HTC 250)

Christ, whose glory fills the skies (HAMNS 4, HON 82, HTC 266, MP 79)

Collect and Post communion prayer

Advent 1999 to Advent 2000	
Advent 2002 to Advent 2003	**The Proper 4 service material is not required for these years**
Advent 2005 to Advent 2006	

Sunday between 5 and 11 June

(if after Trinity Sunday)

Proper 5

 ### Readings

Continuous

1 Samuel 8.4-11

Samuel has become a well-known and respected preacher of God's word, but he is angry when the people ask him to find a king for Israel. A human king will make them into his slaves, their true king should be God who loves and cares for them.

or *Related*

Genesis 3.8-15

Adam and Eve hide from God in shame because of their nakedness. The Lord passes sentence on the serpent for tricking Adam and Eve into eating the fruit of the forbidden tree.

2 Corinthians 4.13-5.1

People often think that the only things that matter are what you can hear and see around you. St Paul wants us to look beyond the ordinary things of life to the eternal gifts of God. Whatever is eternal may not be seen straight away, but it lasts for ever. If we look for God's eternal kingdom, then it will not matter what happens to our human bodies. Our souls are with God.

Mark 3.20-35

When Jesus lived on earth, people used to say that misfits or those who suffered inexplicable illnesses were 'possessed by the devil'. Jesus is casting out the devil from those who need his help and, as he points out, 'how can the devil get rid of the devil?'

 ### Talk/address/ sermon

Make a list of all the objects and possessions that we want to buy. How long have we wanted them for? How often have we changed our minds about what we really want? If and when we get our 'wants' how long do we keep them? We can see that all these wonderful things we have do not last for ever.

By contrast, make a list of our needs, such as food, love, friendship and needing to belong. These needs never change, and are a part of all of our lives. The people of Israel had a particular 'want'; they wanted a king, but what they really needed was to trust in God and love him. He will never change his mind about us, and, unlike the things around us here today and gone tomorrow, he will never desert us.

 ### Congregational/ group activities

- Humanity with unlimited power becomes greedy, yet God can provide for his people and their emotional and material needs. Have a flip-chart and paper, with large pens. Fold the paper into three sections. Section 1 is the 'Ruler's list'. Section 2 is the 'People's list'. Divide the group into two teams, rulers and people's sides. The ruler's side picks out all the things a ruler would choose, i.e. jewels, fine clothes and money. The people's needs are things such as housing, justice, education and choice. Bring the groups together and write on Section 3, 'God's list', with everyone helping.

- A Christian community will only survive if there is sharing with others. To illustrate this, ask everyone to write their immediate family's names on the sticky-strip side of Post-it notes. Stick on to a piece of transparent plastic cut out in the shape of

a church. Turn the shape round and you have the whole Christian family. It isn't any good being hidden away in your own world. You need to come out and share with others. A Christian community only thrives if everyone shares together

- Play 'Pass the Parcel' to illustrate St Paul's letter to the Corinthians. As well as sweets, have 'gifts from God' hidden in the parcel (i.e. 'God cares for us', 'God send his love to us', either written or in pictures). Afterwards talk about these gifts using the pictures and messages.

- What qualities do we look for in a ruler? Make a list of these. Who do we know who has been a good ruler? Who has not? Who do I have power over in my own life (e.g. younger brothers or sisters, or pets)? Am I a good 'ruler', or not?

Prayers/ intercessions

Make a prayer basket and put in it pieces of paper on which the people's needs are written. The various things are mentioned and then the basket can be placed on the altar.

As each item is named, someone may lead a suitable response, for example:

Whatever we ask the Father in the name of Jesus.
He will give it to us.

Seek first God's kingdom and his goodness.
And everything else will come to you.

Lord, you open wide your hand.
And fill all living creatures with your goodness.

Stories and other resources

Martin Wallace, 'St Ninian', in *The Celtic Resource Book*, NS/CHP, 1998

C.S.Lewis, *The Last Battle*, Puffin, 1956

'St Hugh', in *Festive Allsorts*

'Family tree prayers', in *Children Aloud!*

Drama

Margaret Cooling, 'The Temptations of Jesus', in *Ten Minute Miracle Plays*, Bible Society, 1995

Gordon and Ronnie Lamont, 'Family rap and family drama', in *Children Aloud!*

 ## Music

Brothers and sisters (JP 21)

Have you seen the pussycat (JP 72)

In our work and in our play (JP 108)

Bind us together, Lord (JP 17, MP 54)

Oh, the Lord is good (SHP 103)

Lord of the Dance (CP 22)

In Christ there is no east or west (HAMNS 376, HON 244, HTC 322, MP 329)

Join all the glorious names (HTC 214, KSHF 301, MP 392,)

Love is his word (HON 322, HTC 481)

Collect and post communion prayer

Advent 1999 to Advent 2000	The Proper 5
Advent 2002 to Advent 2003	service material is not required
Advent 2005 to Advent 2006	for these years

Sunday between 12 and 18 June

(if after Trinity Sunday)

Proper 6

 ### Readings

Continuous

1 Samuel 15.34-16.13

As Samuel had predicted, things are going wrong with the 'king' of Israel. He is not happy with Saul, and God tells him to look for another king. He is guided to Bethlehem, where he looks for a king among the sons of Jesse. They are an impressive group, but in the end God calls the youngest, David the shepherd boy, to be king after Saul. Later events show that he was the right choice.

or Related

Ezekiel 17.22-24

This short passage depicts a beautiful image of God planting a sprig tree on a high and lofty mountain, under which every kind of bird finds shelter.

2 Corinthians 5.6-10[11-13],14-17

We have to go on our journey trusting in God even though we can't see him face to face. When we have faith in Jesus we become 'new people'. The old fears, the old selfishness, the old weaknesses no longer control us. We are forgiven, strengthened, and we see everything through new eyes.

Mark 4.26-34

Jesus is teaching the people by parables, stories with an illustration taken from everyday life which help us to learn more about God. Here he talks about God's kingdom being like a seed growing secretly in the ground, and a mustard-seed, the smallest there is, becoming a huge tree! God's kingdom is growing all the time, even though we may not notice it, and from the smallest beginnings it grows into the largest kingdom there can be.

 ### Talk/address/ sermon

Life is full of changes: new things happen every day, new gifts come to us, and we are always having to make choices, just as Samuel had to choose a new king. As we go through all these changes, we are growing in different ways: hopefully getting taller, but also learning more about God and his world. Jesus tells us that growth is a central part of God's kingdom – the tiny seed becomes a vast tree. We feel that there must be an end to all this changing and growing, it all must stop somewhere. But in God's kingdom, he never stops giving and loving, and all the while he is making room for everyone in heaven.

 ### Congregational/ group activities

- The theme of altering our vision and seeing things with new eyes can be reinforced here in all-age discussion groups, by collecting a display of anything which magnifies or makes things look different (e.g. a microscope, magnifying glasses, mirrors, binoculars, a kaleidoscope). How do they change the way we see things? Provide cardboard tubes, cellophane and sticky coloured paper for groups to cut out and make their own kaleidoscopes.

- Collect newspaper articles and stories on environmental issues, especially articles that show how we are gradually destroying the planet. This is to illustrate how our unthinking actions have only helped us in the short term. They may help us in the short term, but they have devastating long-term effects. But God also has a long-term plan. His kingdom is growing all the time and we need to think of the future of mankind and listen to him.

Stories and other resources

Stephen Cottrell, *Praying through Life*, NS/CHP, 1998

Anne Evans, *Room for God*, NS/CHP, 1998

'St Francis', in *Festive Allsorts*

Joan Chapman, 'God loves us and all creation', in *Children Celebrate!*, Marshall Pickering, 1994

'Creation', in *Livewires Live*

Carine Mackenzie, *The Caring Creator*, Christian Focus, 1992

Drama

Matt Sands, 'The bungee jump', in *'Get a Life' and Other Sketches for your Youth Group*, Scripture Union, 1998

 ## Music

How lovely on the mountains are the feet (JP 84, MP 249)

Majesty (JP 160, MP 454)

The journey of life (JP 468)

Just a tiny seed (BBP 67)

I am a new creation (HON 221, MP 254)

Praise the Lord in everything! (CP 33)

Blest are the pure in heart (HAMNS 238, HON 63, HTC 110, MP 58)

For the fruits of his creation (HAMNS 457, HON 138, HTC 286, MP 153)

Hail to the Lord's anointed (HAMNS 142, HON 193, HTC 190, KSHF 146, MP 204)

- We can see God's long-term plan in all that grows around us. Collect various types of seed, from quick growing grass and cress seeds, to acorns, conkers and other tree seeds. Plant the different varieties. Sometimes they almost grow before your eyes, other times they will take a very long time. Sometimes in churchyards there is a conservation area. How about starting a small tree nursery? Then care for them in a safe area until they can be planted in the church garden or church yard.

 ## Prayers/ intercessions

The prayers this week might revolve around the themes of 'going' and 'growing' (including 'changing') and journeying with God. Pray for guidance and protection, that we will end up where God wants us to be, and not be taken off the road by evil or turned aside from his love. Pray for the Spirit to help us make the right choices. Give thanks for a wonderful changing world, and for the great vision of heaven as the place for all God's people.

Use the responses:

Lord of our journey
Walk with us

Lord of the changing world
Stay with us

Lord of heaven
Take us into your kingdom

Collect and post communion prayer

Advent 1999 to Advent 2000	The Proper 6 service material is not required for these years
Advent 2002 to Advent 2003	
Advent 2005 to Advent 2000	Use the collect and post communion prayer for the First Sunday after Trinity on p. 130

Sunday between 19 and 25 June

(if after Trinity Sunday)

Proper 7

 ### Readings

Continuous

1 Samuel 17.32-49

This is the famous passage about David and Goliath. The impressive height and armour of Goliath are described at great length. In comparison, the young shepherd boy has to rely on a sling, some stones and his faith in the Lord God.

or Related

Job 38.1-11

Job is trying to answer the question as to why he and other good people suffer. After all, his sufferings are undeserved. What has he done against God to warrant this treatment? He and his friends try to argue with God, to question him, in an attempt to 'pin him down' to give a good reason for this problem. God is telling Job that he has no business to question him. He is the creator and giver of life: no human being can impose any limits on him.

2 Corinthians 6.1-13

Paul's sufferings and endurance for Christ's sake are proof of his sincerity, and of the Grace of God at work in his life. They also confirm the fact that the values and virtues of the kingdom of God reverse the values of this world. His apparent weakness is, in fact, strength, dying means living. He wants the Corinthians to be as frank and sincere in their talk with him as he is with them, because they are all 'fellow-workers' with Christ.

Mark 4.35-41

The Sea of Galilee was, as now, subject to storms which were often short but very violent. Jesus uses his divine power to calm the elements, not to establish his authority over the natural world, but to build up his disciples' faith. Understandably they are afraid, and he is able to reassure them that they really are in the presence of the Son of God. This is a foretaste of the reassurance he is able to give them at his resurrection, and through his promise of the Holy Spirit

 ### Talk/address/ sermon

We may not know exactly why suffering goes on in the world, but what we do know is that God does not leave us to suffer without any help. He calls people to come to the rescue and care for his suffering people. Examples of those who do this are seen in Mother Teresa, Sheila Cassidy, Florence Nightingale, and others. They worked in very difficult situations but were able to do a lot for those in need. They also show how God's love overcomes suffering and removes fear, bringing a new calm in the storms of life. Suffering doesn't go away, but God gives us power to cope with it.

The David and Goliath story shows that where God is, the unpredictable can happen. God can change our lives, turning them upside down, but as the Mark reading demonstrates, Jesus is always with us when we feel unsure or frightened.

 ### Congregational/ group activities

- There are many written and visual examples of people who have been sustained by their faith in God: those who have worked with the poor and destitute or have been punished and imprisoned for their beliefs. Choose stories, pictures or videos to show the group of people such as Nelson Mandela, Mother Teresa or Sheila Cassidy. Discuss how they overcame the most adverse conditions because of their faith in God.

- Make prayer scroll boxes. Have a 'brainstorm' to choose the themes for the prayers (e.g. night-time, when we are afraid, when we feel alone, unloved, and the good times as well). Write or illustrate the prayers on small sheets of paper. Roll up round a pencil and place in a box you have made specially for the purpose. Use them daily for prayer.

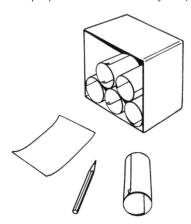

- Life is full of inequality, just as David found when confronted with Goliath. A good way to help understand this is to have a 'tug of war'. You will need a long piece of rope for this. First have a contest between the Little and Large teams (adults vs children). In an unequal world this is the way we would do it. But we need to do it God's way; so this time mix up the teams to get the balance.

Prayers/ intercessions

Pray for Christians who are suffering because of their faith, and for people who are victims of conflict. Give thanks for carers, and for God's gift of inner peace. Within reason, it is always good to name particular people who are suffering, and also if possible to mention some local doctors, nurses and others who look after sick and needy people. Either individual members of the congregation can be encouraged to read out a name or names, or alternatively have them written on pieces of paper for the prayer leader.

Use the following versicle and response:

Leader: Though we walk through the valley of the shadow

All: **You are always with us.**

Stories and other resources

'St Paul', in *Seasons, Saints and Sticky Tape*

Nick Butterworth and Mick Inkpen, *Jesus and the Storm: The Mouse's Tale*, HarperCollins, 1996

The section on David and Goliath, in *Instant Inspirations*

Jim Dainty, *Mudge, Gill and Steve,* NS/CHP, 1997

Drama

Dave Hopwood, 'David and the Giant', in *Acting Up*, NS/CHP, 1995

Dave and Lynn Hopwood, 'David the giant-killer and David and Goliath', in *Telling Tales*, CPAS, 1997

Music

Put your hand in the hand (JP 206)

May the mind of Christ my Saviour (HON 334, JP 165, MP 463)

Jesus, I will come with You (JP 138)

Give thanks with a grateful heart (HON 154, MP 170)

All I once held dear (SHP 2)

One day when we were fishing (BBP 18)

God is love (CP 36)

I cannot tell why (HON 226, HTC 194, KSHF 185, MP 266)

Holy Spirit, truth divine (HTC 235)

Eternal Father, strong to save (HAMNS 292, HON 114, HTC 285, MP 122)

Collect and post communion prayer

Advent 1999 to Advent 2000	The First Sunday after Trinity on p. 130
Advent 2002 to Advent 2003	The Second Sunday after Trinity on p. 130
Advent 2005 to Advent 2006	

Sunday between 26 June and 2 July

Proper 8

 Readings

Continuous

2 Samuel 1.1,17-27

David's lament over the death of Saul and Jonathan on the battlefield. The phrase which stands out is 'How the mighty have fallen' – a kind of chorus that has become a modern idiom. Part of this lament responds in typical form to the bravery of the warrior king, but coupled with it are the tender reflections of a respected king and his beloved son and friend.

or *Related*

Wisdom of Solomon 1.13-15,2.23-24

God is a creator who takes no delight in death and destruction. He created us in his own image and for an eternal purpose.

2 Corinthians 8.7-15

A reading about giving to enable others to have a new start. The wealthy part of the Body needs to be generous to the poor parts. The pivotal verse is v.9, and should form the base of all giving. At the heart is Jesus' grace in making himself 'poor' so that we might become 'rich'. His example of humbling himself is set, and provides the model for us.

Mark 5.21-43

Two lovely stories of new beginnings – one for a middle-aged woman, one for a little girl. Both experience the power of Jesus. The woman decides to touch Jesus' cloak – and that action of faith brings healing. Jesus senses the power leaving him (v.30). Her admission and his word confirm the healing. The little girl (probably thought to be of little consequence in Jewish society) is of great value to her father Jairus. So he asks Jesus to come and heal her. Jesus' arrival is delayed by the incident with the woman, and a message comes to say that the girl is dead. Jesus simply continues and on reaching the house raises her with a touch of the hand and a word of command.

Jesus' love and power is such that it reaches to those who would not be regarded as worth it! This reflects on the nature of God's love, and the dismissiveness of mankind – and his love provides new beginnings where we would often give up.

Talk/address/sermon

The Gospel points us towards the God whose love is unfailing, and who provides a hope for the future. The Gospel tells us too that there is not only life after death . . . there is also life after bereavement.

The Epistle and Gospel readings give a lovely way into asking 'Who do we think is important, and why?' The Gospel points out that Jesus gives a real value to people who may not have been seen as very valuable in those days. The Epistle puts all this in financial terms . . . very like Western culture! What does Jesus' example tell us to do for those who are poor or who have little 'value' in society's eyes? The response can be as practical as you like!

Jesus' immediate response to Jairus' plea gives an idea of Jesus' compassion – so often a part of his healing. The story is about a loved little girl and a father with faith in what Jesus could do. The woman who touches Jesus' cloak is full of faith in what Jesus could do too. The release of power and the touch of his hand both bring complete restoration. Use this to offer prayers for healing.

The readings are about new beginnings for a sick lady and a dying child and a suffering poor church and a wealthy neighbour – and about the effect of Jesus' grace. Jesus encourages fairness and generosity. He brings healing and new life. He offers forgiveness and a new hope and future. All these elements tell us of the value God sets on each one of us, drawing people to meet this Jesus for themselves.

Man's frailty even in heroism can be contrasted with the unfailing nature of God's love. This can be used well using stories from the *Guinness Book of Records*, set against the stories of some 'fallen' heroes (e.g. Mike Tyson, Ben Johnson, etc.).

Congregational/ group activities

- Act out the Gospel in a dramatic reading. This is a great one for the children's group to do as it involves a number of characters. The visual impact can be very good and helps people to remember the practical, down-to-earth nature of Jesus. The actions and characters can be mimed to the words.

- Make some simple paper flowers. Prayers can be written on the petals. The flowers can be made into a collage picture, or put on garden canes and displayed in a vase. Use the Psalm to focus on the hope and love of God .

- Ask for three volunteers and divide a bag of sweets among them – unfairly! Give one person one sweet, give the second ten, and the third the rest of the bag. Ask if that's fair? And if you haven't already had any cries of 'That's not fair!', ask the person with one sweet whether they think that's OK. The answer will always be 'No!' This simply illustrates that we have a keen sense of justice when it comes to sweets, but not so much when it comes to real money. Gather all the sweets back in, and give each one sweet . . . and use the rest to give lots of other children one sweet too. This shows how far sweets can go round the church . . . so why not be fairer with other resources?

Prayers/ intercessions

Use the following prayer during a time of confession:

Lord God – we have tried to rule the earth with our power and force, and have found that we are always in conflict with one another.
How the mighty have fallen!

Lord God – we have tried to subdue the earth with our cleverness and technology, and have found that our greed is destroying the world.
How the mighty have fallen!

Lord God – we have tried to reach you with our good deeds and charity, and found that we cannot wipe away our sinfulness.
How the mighty have fallen!

Lord God – we have become proud and headstrong, and found that we do not really trust you.
How the mighty have fallen!

Lord forgive us for standing in our own strength.
As we bow before you, help us to stand in your mighty power,
and learn to live by trusting your love
through Jesus Christ our Lord, **Amen.**

Stories and other resources

Paul Vallely, *Daniel and the Mischief Boy*, Christian Aid/HarperCollins, 1993

'William and Catherine Booth', in *Seasons and Saints for the Christian Year*

Martin Wallace, 'St Columba of Iona', in *The Celtic Resource Book*, NS/CHP, 1998

'Christian Aid Week', in *Seasons, Saints and Sticky Tape*

Drama

'Love is like this . . .', in *Playing Up*

'Jesus and the little girl', in *Telling Tales*

 ## Music

I cast all my cares upon You (JP 369)

Yesterday, today for ever (JP 294, MP 787)

I will offer up my life (SHP 65)

Lord, I come to you (SHP 84)

Praise Him (CP 40)

Before the heaven and earth (HTC 612)

Heal me, hands of Jesus (HTC 319)

My Lord, you wore no royal crown (HTC 118)

Collect and post communion prayer

Advent 1999 to Advent 2000	The Second Sunday after Trinity on p. 130
Advent 2002 to Advent 2003	
Advent 2005 to Advent 2006	The Third Sunday after Trinity on p. 131

Sunday between 3 and 9 July

Proper 9

Readings

Continuous

2 Samuel 5.1-5,9-10

David is made king – a new task for him, yet drawing on his previous experience. The people not only knew of David's exploits on the battlefield, but also God's promise to him. This promise reflects back to David's experience as a shepherd.

or Related

Ezekiel 2.1-5

The voice of the Lord speaks to Ezekiel. The prophet is commissioned to go to the rebellious people of Israel and speak God's word to them.

2 Corinthians 12.2-10

Paul's weakness is God's strength. In this passage, Paul concentrates on the 'thorn' that caused him such distress – the nature of this 'thorn' is never explained. This thorn made him humanly 'weak' in his work as an evangelist, but made him trust God all the more as a result. Therefore, he boasts in his weakness, so that Christ's power can enable him to complete his task.

Mark 6.1-13

The reading begins in Nazareth, where Jesus is unable to work because of their lack of faith. Having amazed the crowds wherever he went, this time he is amazed at the people's response to him. This leads him to send out the twelve disciples in pairs, taking the message of the kingdom to a wider audience. The disciples obediently go, and find that people are healed and delivered as they preach the message of repentance.

Talk/address/sermon

Several of the readings today look at how God commissions people. David is made king, in accordance with God's promise – and God is with him.

Paul is called by God to be an evangelist to the Gentiles, and has to trust in God for his strength because of his 'thorn'. The disciples are sent out with Jesus' authority to carry the kingdom more widely.

The Epistle gives an important contrast between our own experience (which it is easy to boast about, or rely on) and on our weakness. Paul is writing to a Church that was eager to boast of its spiritual life. Instead he points them to Christ. Boasting only focuses on ourselves, and consequently our eyes are taken off Jesus. Recognizing our weakness leads us to rely on God's power rather than our own resources or past. We need to rely on Christ's mighty power, not our own.

Congregational/group activities

* Use volunteers from the congregation (adults would probably be better for this than children). Play a 'Who's the strongest?' competition. Organize one or two 'events' like who can hold a two 2-litre bottle of water at arm's length for the longest – so bring a stop watch too! Have the world record times at your fingertips (from a look in the *Guinness Book of Records*) – this shows that our strongest is still weak compared to others. When compared to God's strength, ours seems insignificant. So we need to rely on his strength. A good way of finishing this off would be to ask a child to hold these same bottles, but with an adult helping by holding up the child's arms from below, and you will probably find that they can hold them up for longer than the strongest adult. This illustrates the promise that 'God was with him' (2 Sam 5.10), and with God's help we can be strong, even though weak on our own.

* If you live in a rural community, you may have a shepherd in your congregation. If not, invite one along. Set up an interview with them on what they do. The questions can include: what time do you get up? What things do you need to be a shepherd? How many sheep do you look after? What are the problems with looking after sheep? What happens if a sheep falls ill, or goes missing?

What's the funniest thing that ever happened to you or your sheep? Do you think a shepherd would make a good king? (If you can't interview a shepherd, why not write a sketch as if you are interviewing a shepherd for the job of king.) You will hopefully have provided yourself with enough ammunition to explore why God used shepherds as leaders for Israel. What can we learn from this today about leadership in the Church?

• Divide the congregation into groups, and provide each group with a large cardboard thorn and a pen. Ask each group to write on the thorn the things that make them weak. After five minutes, collect them and staple the corners together to make a ring of thorns, like a crown. Offer these to Christ in prayer, even hanging the crown over the cross on the communion table. Use the verse in 2 Corinthians 12.9-10 to remind us of his promise of grace and strength.

Prayers/ intercessions

This is a prayer offering (for use with the crown of thorns activity):

Jesus said 'My grace is all you need, for my power is made perfect in weakness'.
Lord, you know my weaknesses; I offer them to you so that you may show your perfect strength in me.

Jesus said 'My grace is all you need, for my power is made perfect in weakness'.
Lord you know my strengths; I place them into your hands that you may use me for your glory.

Jesus said 'My grace is all you need, for my power is made perfect in weakness'.
Lord you know me; help me to trust you.

So may the Grace of our Lord Jesus Christ, and the love of God, and the fellowship of the Holy Spirit, be with us all, evermore, **Amen.**

This is a shout of praise, based on Psalm 48:

Great is the Lord, and most worthy of praise!
. . . for your strength and protection as our fortress.
Great is the Lord, and most worthy of praise!
. . . for your unfailing love.

Great is the Lord, and most worthy of praise!
. . . for your name, worshipped in all corners of the world
Great is the Lord, and most worthy of praise!
. . . for your heart of justice, and hand of integrity
Great is the Lord, and most worthy of praise!
. . . for your gentle leading as the good shepherd
Great is the Lord, and most worthy of praise!
. . . for being our God for ever and ever!
Great is the Lord, and most worthy of praise!

Stories and other resources

Roger Hargreaves, *Mr Small,* Thurman Publishing, 1972

David Watson, chapter 13, 'Strength out of weakness', in *Fear no Evil*, Hodder & Stoughton, 1984

Martin Wallace, 'St Aidan of Lindisfarne', in *The Celtic Resource Book*, NS/CHP, 1998

Sue Doggett, *Jonah and the Little Black Cloud*, Bible Reading Fellowship, 1998

'Jonah and the whale', in *Instant Inspirations*

Drama

Michael Catchpool and Pat Lunt, 'Mission to Pontefract', in *The Log in my Eye*, Kevin Mayhew, 1998

 ## Music

Give thanks to the Lord (JP 345)

Hallelujah! for the Lord our God (JP 66, MP 205)

Sing a new song to the Lord (JP 454, MP 599)

Are we the people (SHP 8)

Inspired by love and anger (HON 252)

Wherever I am I'll praise him (MP 762)

Father, hear the prayer we offer (HAMNS 113, HON 120, HTC 360, MP 132)

Lord of all hopefulness (HAMNS 394, HON 313, HTC 101)

O Christ, the master carpenter (HTC 135)

Collect and post communion prayer

Advent 1999 to Advent 2000	The Third Sunday after Trinity on p. 131
Advent 2002 to Advent 2003	
Advent 2005 to Advent 2006	The Fourth Sunday after Trinity on p. 131

Sunday between 10 and 16 July

Proper 10

 ### Readings

Continuous

2 Samuel 6.1-5,12b-19

The arrival of the Ark of the Covenant into Jerusalem represents the welcoming and blessing of God resting among the people. David has tried to do everything in style, with a huge army of men in procession, a new cart to transport the Ark, and with great celebration. David himself leads the second stage of the Ark's journey, assuming his priestly role as king of Israel. The Ark is received into Jerusalem with penitent sacrifices, and at the end a meal that everyone shares in. There are interesting links with God's presence, repentance, communion, and sacrifice here which can be explored further.

or Related

Amos 7.7-15

The prophet is shown a vision of the Lord standing beside a wall with a plumb line in his hand. The Lord will set a plumb line in the midst of the Israelites and will bring devastation to their sanctuaries and high places.

Ephesians 1.3-14

Here we see Paul's perspective of God's choice for us – that we should be holy and blameless, his adopted children, recipients of his glorious grace in Christ, gain redemption and forgiveness through his blood, unity under Christ and the gift of the Spirit. No wonder Paul overflows with thanks to God!

Mark 6.14-29

This is an odd passage to link with – the beheading of John the Baptist. His execution comes as the result of a rash promise as a favour to a sensual dancer. There is such a marked contrast here between the other three readings of the greatness of God and our place in worship, and the jealousies and degradation when men's hearts are not seeking him.

 ### Talk/address/ sermon

We cannot force our way into God's presence on our terms, only on his. The Old Testament passages show David's attempts and reflections on doing this, with the Ark as the focus. Paul writes in the light of the cross. Through the cross, we see God making forgiveness and a new life of worship not only a possibility, but part of his eternal plan for us. This is a good opportunity to focus on the place of confession within worship.

John's preaching against Herodias presented a moral holiness that Herod did not like – it was embarrassing to be confronted with one's sins! Herod recognized John's holiness (v.20), but in the end was tricked into killing him. John's holiness came from knowing and serving an uncompromising holy God – the God we see in the two Old Testament readings. If we catch sight of this fierce holiness, how does this affect our worship and our behaviour?

Paul ends his words of spiritual blessings with the one who brings those blessings into our experience – the Holy Spirit:

His presence brings cleansing and a new start

His presence brings new life and purpose

His presence brings a new unity and family

His presence brings new worship/praise

His presence guarantees that there is more to come.

What a wonderful reflection of what it means to be a Christian!

 ### Congregational/ group activities

- One of the set psalms for today is Psalm 24. This is a psalm reflecting on God's great creative majesty, and therefore how any person can come into his presence. It fits very well with the 2 Samuel reading. Here we see God in command over all creation, and man's desire to come into his presence, but how? There is the need for penitence and cleansing and then God's blessing comes in person. The second half of the psalm could reflect the shouts that welcomed the Ark into Jerusalem. These verses can be used as a shout of praise to begin the time of worship.

- Discuss what it means to have 'clean hands and a pure heart' (Ps 24). 'Clean hands': the things we do should be right in God's eyes. A great illustration of this is Lady Macbeth's desire to wash the stain of blood out of her hands, and her inability to do it. We need to be cleansed by God through the cross (Eph 1.7). Our actions must have an honesty and integrity about them. 'Pure heart': our actions reflect what's in the heart. A purity of heart leads to good actions. Therefore God deals with our hearts – giving us new hearts that can know and follow his purposes. Our response is to come into God's presence to worship and receive his blessings through the Spirit within (Eph 1.13) that enables us to continue to live and praise him.

Prayers/ intercessions

This 'shout of worship' is based on Psalm 24. In this rendering, the children represent the 'gates', the adults are the 'ancient doors'!

Adults:	Lift up your heads, O you gates (*children stand*)
Children:	Be lifted up, you ancient doors (*adults stand*)
All:	**that the king of glory may come in.**
Children:	Who is this king of glory?
Adults:	The Lord strong and mighty, the Lord mighty in battle.
	Lift up your heads, O you gates (*children raise arms*)
Children:	Lift them up, you ancient doors (*adults raise arms*)
All:	**that the king of glory may come in**
Adults:	Who is he, this king of glory?
Children:	The Lord almighty! He is the king of glory!

This prayer focuses on the way that God blesses us:

God has blessed us with spiritual blessings in Christ
By choosing us to belong to him
He has blessed us, thank you Lord

By making us one in Christ with each other
He has blessed us, thank you Lord

By forgiving us through the cross
He has blessed us, thank you Lord

By giving us a new purpose
He has blessed us, thank you Lord

By giving us a new song of worship and praise
He has blessed us, thank you Lord

By pouring his Spirit into our hearts
He has blessed us, thank you Lord

By making us his children, and giving us
a future with him
He has blessed us, thank you Lord. Amen

Stories and other resources

'How to make an Ark of the Covenant', in *In the Beginning* (p. 41)

Steve Pearce and Diana Murrie, 'Pilgrim's story', in *All Aboard!*, NCEC, 1996

Martin Wallace, 'Holy times and holy places', in *The Celtic Resource Book*, NS/CHP, 1998

Drama

Andrew Smith, 'The sheep stuffer's sentence', in *Much Ado about Something Else: 20 More Sketches*, CPAS, 1996

'Families', in *Playing Up*

Music

Cleanse me from my sin (JP 27, MP 82)

God of all mercy (JP 350)

Make way, make way (HON 329, MP 457)

Purify my heart (SHP 112)

It's hard to say 'I'm sorry', 'I'm sorry' (BBP 75)

Collect and post communion prayer

Advent 1997 to Advent 1998	**The Fourth Sunday after Trinity on p. 131**
Advent 2002 to Advent 2003	
Advent 2005 to Advent 2006	**The Fifth Sunday after Trinity on p. 131**

Sunday between 17 and 23 July

Proper 11

 ### Readings

Continuous

2 Samuel 7.1-14a

David's conscience is pricked as he realizes that he has a palace, and God's Ark is housed in a tent. Nathan the prophet is commanded to deliver God's message: that he is happy to be in the Tabernacle because it represents the constant travelling presence of God with Israel. But a time will come when David's son will build a Temple, once the people have become settled and established.

or Related

Jeremiah 23.1-6

The Lord is angered by the shepherds (or leaders of his people) who have scattered his sheep and driven them away from him. The Lord will attend to their evil-doing and become the shepherd himself of the remnant of his flock.

Ephesians 2.11-22

Paul reminds the Ephesian church that they are one in Christ – brought into the people of God by Jesus. He is our peace with God and with each other – whatever our race. Christians are therefore true citizens of the New Jerusalem ('the City of Peace'), new creations in Christ and the dwelling place of his Spirit. Here is God's promise to David coming true!

Mark 6.30-34,53-56

These are two short passages about Jesus being recognized and in demand. Jesus teaches the vast crowds out of his compassion for them – a people who are like sheep without a shepherd. This picks up the theme from Proper 9 about the significance of shepherding in the Bible. On the other side of the lake people still recognize him, and run to collect all the people they can find who needed healing. Here is a great hunger that was met by Jesus – all who touched him were healed (v.56). He was passive in this healing, rather than active.

 ### Talk/address/ sermon

The Gospel reading reflects on the hunger there was for Jesus. It arose out of reports of what he was doing elsewhere, of recognizing him, and of faith in what he could do there and then. Where is the hunger in our day? Is it for things or for happiness?

The Gospel suggests that people would be hungry for Jesus if they heard reports of what he was doing elsewhere, and knew about who he was so they could recognize him. This would encourage trust that Jesus is still the same today, and could meet their need.

How can we respond to this? Part of it might be in obedience to Jesus' commands to go out and share the gospel with others. But another part is having the compassion that Jesus had, a compassion that his Spirit brings today.

This passage look at the theme of God's promise – the kingdom:

- God's promise to David (Old Testament/psalm) – a faithfulness and love forever, and a continuing line.

- God's promise through Christ – the eternal line is established through the King of Kings.

- God's promise to us – a part in his kingdom through the cross and the Spirit.

Using this framework, we can see our part in God's promise to David through Christ. This can also be shown using this second framework:

- God's promise to David – an established 'dwelling place' among his people, including a faithful love.

- God's promise through Christ – people recognize Jesus and discover the presence of God's kingdom in healing, teaching and compassion.

- God's promise to us – the Spirit living in his people today, experiencing that eternal love of Christ, promised of old. How is the kingdom seen and experienced through the Church today and ourselves?

- Paul tells the Ephesians of the unity they have in Christ – a unity and peace with God and a unity with one another (Jew or Gentile). This is established through the cross, and brought into our present reality by the Spirit within us.

- This is a good text to help us to explore Christian unity in Churches and across nations – and to pray for the peace of Christ.

 ## Congregational/ group activities

- Why not explore fasting during the following week, using hunger to draw us closer to God, or sharpen our focus on him? This could be done in church groups, and then sharing the experiences the following Sunday. Covenant to miss one meal each day, and use the time to read and pray. For the younger ones, try not having any pudding, but looking at the Bible and praying instead. There is a prayer in the next section that may be helpful. Did the experience make me hungry for God, or simply hungry? Did I find it harder or easier to pray? Was it helpful to have a regular time each day to give to God? Did I find God saying things to me?

- Write down the different kinds of promises that we make in our daily lives – things such as marriage vows, that on a £5 note, Brownie/Cub promises, etc. Explore what they mean – and so determine the nature of 'promise'. They will all involve some element of doing or being something of value for someone else. They can be promising to do something now, or something in the future.

- What happens when people don't keep their promises? How do we feel? It would be interesting for each person to commit themselves to one promise, and then see how they get on with it the following week! God's promises about his kingdom are about now and the future. They are promises we can hold onto today, and look forward to as well. God's promises are trustworthy, because he keeps his word.

 ## Prayers/ intercessions

Perhaps people could be encouraged to fast during the week, reflecting on the Bible passages for this week, and the following prayer:

Lord Jesus,

As I offer my prayers to you,
may I hear your words to me.
Fill my emptiness with your presence;
change my weakness into your strength;
transform my desires;
and draw me close to your heart. **Amen**

Meditate on the promises of God. A good exercise in prayer is to read a Gospel, making note of the promises Jesus gives. If you have time, this can be prepared, and a list given to the congregation. Encourage everyone to take one promise a week, and use it in prayer – allowing God to show how that promise can be realized in our experience in different ways. This is a great way of building faith, and learning verses in the Bible, and is for young and old alike.

 ## Stories and other resources

Brian Ogden, 'The lost sheep', in *Sometimes the Donkey is Right*, Bible Reading Fellowship, 1998

'The City of Peace', in Robin Sharples, *Livewires Live*, BRF, 1998

'Promises', in *Pick and Mix*

 ## Drama

Michael Catchpool and Pat Lunt, 'The cake appreciation society', in *The Log in my Eye*, Kevin Mayhew, 1998

♪ ♪♪♯♪ ♩♪♫ Music

Jesus' hands were kind hands (JP 134)

Lord, You are the Light (JP 424)

Gather around, for the table is spread (HON 152)

Domine Deus (JU, p. 84)

I worship you, almighty God (SHP 67)

From darkness came light (CP 29)

Christ is the world's light (HAMNS 440, HTC 321)

Faithful Shepherd, feed me (HON 117, HTC 29)

Peace, perfect peace, in this dark world of sin (HON 413, HTC 467, MP 555)

Collect and post communion prayer

Advent 1999 to Advent 2000	The Fifth Sunday after Trinity on p. 131
Advent 2002 to Advent 2003	
Advent 2005 to Advent 2006	The Sixth Sunday after Trinity on p. 131

Sunday between 24 and 30 July

Proper 12

Readings

Continuous

2 Samuel 11.1-15

This is a sordid tale of lust, adultery and murder, about David's abuse of his new power as king. David, instead of leading his men in battle, stays at home and sees Bathsheba bathing. He arranges for her to be brought to him, and they sleep together. This deed results in her pregnancy, and so their affair will soon become public knowledge. So David arranges for her husband to come home with the idea of getting him to sleep with his wife, hoping to pass off the child as Uriah's. When Uriah refuses, remaining loyal to his comrades at war, David arranges for Uriah to be killed. What a contrast between the honourable Hittite, and the frightened, scheming king!

or Related

2 Kings 4.42-44

This story is directly related to the Gospel account of the feeding of the 5,000. Here Elisha provides 20 loaves of barley and some grain – plenty to feed 100 people, with food left over.

Ephesians 3.14-21

This is Paul's prayer for the Ephesian church. It is a prayer of intimacy as Paul 'kneels' to pray, when his tradition would have been to stand in prayer. Perhaps this shows how his relationship with God has changed. He prays for inner strength, Christ's indwelling Spirit, a root of Christ's love, and power to participate in that love.

John 6.1-21

Jesus feeds 5,000 with a child's packed lunch. This is such a lovely demonstration of the power of the kingdom, where a small offering was transformed to meet the needs of a vast crowd with plenty to spare.

Talk/address/ sermon

This talk looks at the three 'Ls' of David's sin:

David's *laziness* – staying at home instead of leading his army meant he was in a place that he shouldn't have been, and bored!

David's *lust* – the seeing, the investigation, the taking another man's wife as his own, and the consequences meant he was going to be found out.

David's *last resort* – David decides to try and cover up his sin, but Uriah is not co-operative. So his murder is arranged, to make it look like an accident of war. This shows how easy it can be for sin to spread, and get worse and worse.

Use Paul's prayer for the Ephesian church to preach about the cross as the demonstration of God's great love for us and how wide, long, high and deep is his love. What do we do with this love? Grasp it and understand what Jesus did for us on the cross. Be rooted and established in it through Christ's indwelling. Know it – to share in it and participate in it in an active response.

The Gospel story focuses on a small, insignificant gift being put into Jesus' hands – and Jesus transforming it. We can put ourselves in his hands, however small or insignificant we feel, and see Jesus take that gift, thank God for that gift, and use it to his glory. This is a lovely story to use with children, and very powerful for adults too.

The 'old power' of evil scheming is seen in the Old Testament reading – a power that is used for its own ends. Jesus displays the 'new power' of the kingdom of God – transforming a gift given for the benefit of others. His death on the cross is the ultimate example of that power, and the place that this power is released for us to share in. The Spirit who lives within us is the Spirit of power, love and self-discipline.

Congregational/ group activities

- Why not organize a shared meal after the service with all the food in cross shapes. This is easy to make by cutting cross-shaped chips (and slightly more taxing when thinking about meat and vegetables!). However, well-presented plates can be very effective. Let the children prepare as much of it as they can, and certainly do use any of their ideas, then you can be sure they will eat it! Shared meals can be wonderful as a practical expression of love – as well as great fun.

- Power games. This is a game in which a leader shouts out instructions, and the people obey. Some can be active things (clap hands, bend down and touch toes, etc.), but make sure you have some which involve strength (pick up the person sitting next to you). Those who are slow, or can't do the action, have to sit down. Work down to the 'strongest' person – this can often be a child as they are likely to be sitting next to another child and so find the tests of strength relatively easy. Play the same game, only this time ask the winner of the first game to call out instructions. Add in wrong instructions (such as 'give me all the money in your pockets and purses'). Remind the people that he or she is the strongest – and wait for the reaction. You can get cross with the people if they refuse to comply. This pair of games illustrates the abuse of power and how some people gain a position of strength and then misuse it for their own ends.

 ## Prayers/ intercessions

This is a prayer that focuses upon the cross:

Lord, thank you for your cross of love.
When I am struggling in the depths, your love restores me
When I am wandering far away, your love can reach me
When I am soaring high with joy, your love holds me
Thank you for your cross of love
Amen

Use the following prayer during a time of confession:

When I have looked at others with the wrong attitude
Forgive me Lord

When I have lied to cover up my own deeds
Forgive me Lord

When I have misused the power you have given me to hurt others
Forgive me Lord

When I have lost sight of you
Forgive me Lord

Open my eyes to see your love,
Open my heart to receive your love,
Open my hands to live in love, now and always,
Amen.

 ## Stories and other resources

Lesley and Neil Pinchbeck, 'The Whizz Quiz', in *Theme Games*, Scripture Union, 1993 (p. 107)

J. Mortimer, 'The feeding of the 5,000', in *See What I Mean*, CPAS, 1998

Brian Ogden, 'Feeding the 5,000', in *Sometimes the Donkey is Right,* Bible Reading Fellowship, 1998

Drama

'Feeding 5,000 people', in *Telling more Tales*

 ## Music

Who took fish and bread (JP 286)

I will offer up my life (SHP 65)

God is good to me (JU, p. 10)

Everyone in the whole wide world (JU, p. 2)

Join with us (CP 30)

In the presence of your people (MP 341)

Creator of the earth and skies (HAMNS 351, HTC 320)

Just as I am, without one plea (HAMNS 246, HON 287, HTC 440, KSHF 304, MP 396)

O Love divine, how sweet thou art (HAMNS 124)

Collect and post communion prayer

Advent 1999 to Advent 2000	The Sixth Sunday after Trinity on p. 132
Advent 2002 to Advent 2003	
Advent 2005 to Advent 2006	Use the collect and post communion prayer for the Seventh Sunday after Trinity on p. 132

Sunday between 24 and 30 July

Sunday between 31 July and 6 August

Proper 13

 ### Readings

Continuous

2 Samuel 11.26-12.13a

Nathan rebukes David – Nathan the prophet is sent to David with a parable of an abuse of power, a rich man over a poor man. David's anger is roused, and having pronounced his judgement, Nathan brings God's accusation, and word of judgement. Notice that when David sins, God speaks to him through someone else. Sin separates us from God – and David is brought to recognize his sin by Nathan.

or Related

Exodus 16.2-4,9-15

The Israelites are not content in their journey through the wilderness and complain that the Lord has brought them out of slavery only to die of starvation. The Lord sends quail in the evening and manna in the morning to feed his people.

Ephesians 4.1-16

Paul urges these Christians to work together in unity and so not divide the Church against itself. Within the Body there is room for all kinds of jobs, roles, ministries – that way the Body functions properly. The purpose is to build up the Body to maturity in both faith and action. Christ is the Head of the Body – an interesting reflection on the arguments on the nature of 'headship' in the Church.

John 6.24-35

The crowd pursues Jesus and calls for more miraculous signs to prove his validity. Jesus reveals his identity and authority to the people, but they miss it – again! He tells them of the Father's seal of approval on him; of how they must believe in the one God sent; how his Father gives bread from heaven that leads to eternal life. As you read these verses, you can feel Jesus' frustration growing as the crowd seem to miss the point each time, until the point when Jesus declares that he is the bread of life.

 ### Talk/address/ sermon

What is the Body? It is a unity of different parts, all working together. This is one of the Biblical pictures of the Church. It is not a uniformity (where everyone does the same thing) but a unity (where different people hold together).

What is my place in the Body? Paul tells us that we have different parts to play, so this is an important question for many Christians, young and old.

Whose Body is it? It is the Body of Christ (the head). He directs the Body, so let's ask him where we fit in. He wants the Body to be united and strong (mature).

'Lord, from now on, give us this bread' (John 6.34)

Here the people are asking a request of Jesus – to give them bread from heaven to feed the world. But Jesus is talking about himself – not a wonder loaf!

He comes from heaven, a gift from the Father.

He lasts forever, leads to eternal life.

He requires our trust.

This request could be our response to saying 'yes' to Jesus – a sign of commitment to Christ.

 ### Congregational/ group activities

- Use one of the set psalms for today as a basis for a time of confession. Psalm 51 resulted from Nathan's visit – a cry for mercy. Here are heartfelt words of confession, and the desire for cleansing so that their relationship can once again be restored. David is broken before God, trusting himself and his kingdom into God's mercy. Notice how the state of David's relationship with God is reflected at a national level – the king represents his people, a priestly role. Read through the psalm slowly, pausing after each few verses to reflect on our own need for confession.

- Lay a large piece of lining paper on the floor, and ask for a volunteer to lie on it, and be drawn round. Then cut out the figure, and then cut it into pieces and give a piece to everyone in the church (keeping the head to one side). Ask everyone to put the pieces together to remake the figure. This is much harder than it sounds and will probably take ages! This simply shows that, although we each have a part, we are not very good at putting it together again. This is why we need Jesus to be the head. If your congregation manage to put all the pieces together easily, then talk about the fact that the head needs to be in place – Jesus.

 ## Prayers/ intercessions

Use the following prayer, as we remember that we are all part of the one Body – the Church.

Thank you for the Church in this country. We pray for all Christians in our city/town/village. Help us to work together in your kingdom.
Lord strengthen us, for we are one Body.

We pray for those working abroad – for our missionary links (by name), and for our link Diocese of (name). May your love continue to spread into the hearts of people everywhere.
Lord inspire us, for we are one Body.

We pray for those who struggle with divisions in the Church. Thank you for your Spirit who brings peace into unity. We pray for that peace in your Church today
Lord unite us, for we are one Body.

We pray for all members of your body as we discover the roles you have for us. Help us to encourage one another, and build each other up.
Lord equip us, for we are one Body.

We pray for our mission together, to pray for your kingdom to come here on earth, as it is in heaven. We look to you, our head, for your will and your wisdom.
Lord lead us, for we are one Body.

May we grow together in peace, united by the Spirit in our love for you, and so grow up into you, our Lord and Saviour, Jesus Christ, **Amen.**

 ## Stories and other resources

Steve Pearce and Diana Murrie, 'Fellow travellers', in *All Aboard!*, NCEC, 1996

Robin Sharples, 'Belonging', in *Livewires Live,* BRF, 1998

'One Body with Many Parts', in *Instant Inspirations*

'Composer God', in *Reign Dance*

Lesley and Neil Pinchbeck, *Theme Games*, Scripture Union, 1993

 ## Music

I am the Church (JP 367)

All over the world (JP 5, MP 18)

Bread is blessed and broken (HON 66)

Help us to help each other, Lord (HON 208)

My Lord, what love is this (HON 345, MP 476)

As we are gathered (MP 38)

Bread of the world in mercy broken (HAMNS 270, HON 68, HTC 396)

Come, risen Lord, and deign to be our guest (HAMNS 349, HON 96)

Lord Jesus Christ, you have come to us (HAMNS 391, HON 311, HTC 417, KSHF 342, MP 435)

Collect and post communion prayer

Advent 1999 to Advent 2000	**The Seventh Sunday after Trinity on p. 132**
Advent 2002 to Advent 2003	
Advent 2005 to Advent 2006	**The Eight Sunday after Trinity on p. 132**

Sunday between 7 and 13 August

Proper 14

Readings

Continuous

2 Samuel 18. 5-9,15,31-33

Absalom has turned against his father, King David. A battle is inevitable and David knows that he will defeat his son. He does not, however, want harm to come to Absalom and orders his army commanders to deal gently with him. Absalom's troops are soundly defeated. As the battle draws to a close he has the misfortune to become helplessly caught in a tree, in the vicinity of Joab. Joab has little sympathy for a son of David who would turn against the king and orders his men to kill Absalom. The news of his son's death is broken to David by a Cushite who regards this killing as no less than a sign of God's vindication of David against his enemies.

or Related

1 Kings 19.4-8

Elijah's life has been threatened by Jezebel. He has fled into the desert and would happily lie down and die. He has had enough, and feels that he is of no more use to God than his forbears. He falls asleep and is awoken by an angel who offers him water and a fresh cake to strengthen him for his journey. The food and drink sustain him for 40 days until he reaches Mount Horeb.

Ephesians 4.25-5.2

The Ephesians are exhorted to speak truthfully to one another, to deal appropriately with their anger, to be honest, to speak constructively, to be kind and forgiving. In this way they will live in the love of Christ.

John 6.35,41-51

Those who have known Jesus all his life refuse to take his claims to be the bread of life very seriously. Despite their mutterings, Jesus insists that God will help them to recognize him. Just as their forefathers were brought manna in the wilderness to sustain them, so God has sent him to bring bread which will mean eternal life for them. He is the means to this eternal life and he will give his life so that people might understand what God is offering to those he created and loves.

Talk/address/sermon

The reading from 2 Samuel is a moving account of the effects of love, betrayal, loyalty and passion. David is distraught, and Joab is angry. In his love for his son David becomes vulnerable; Joab wants only revenge and punishment for Absalom. Both might say they want justice.

In the 1 Kings reading Elijah feels exhausted and a failure. How can we be sustained when we feel we have had enough, done enough and none of it has been good enough? Elijah does not just *feel* like running away, he *does* run away. Then he gets the distinct message that he must keep going and he is sustained in doing so. How do we discern the difference between 'giving up' and 'letting go'? What does it really mean to speak the truth? How can speaking the truth be reconciled to kindness and tenderheartedness? Is there a link here with assertiveness?

Listening to the Gospel reading, should we be so surprised that some of those who have known Jesus and his family all his life are resistant to his astonishing claims? If this was someone we knew, what would he/she have to do in order to convince us of the truth of his/her identity?

John tells us that Jesus described himself as the 'bread of life'. If that is the case he must be basic, sustaining, tasty, nourishing and a good accompaniment to other 'foods'! What does Jesus show us about what is fundamental to the enjoyment of a full and rich life?

Congregational/ group activities

- The Old Testament readings contain stories of anger, weariness, malice, death and sadness. Give small groups a character to address (such as David, Joab, the Cushite or Elijah). The groups then prepare a minute-long statement designed to convince their character of Jesus being the bread of life who will bring them true hope.

- Discuss the difference between 'giving up' and 'letting go' of, for example, a gym/football club, an A-level course, church, home, their own country, someone they love.

- Use the Ephesians reading to produce an illustrated 'Charter for Living in the Love of Christ'. Ask one or two people to prepare for this by spending an hour/a morning/a day trying to 'speak the truth'! Share with the congregation just how realistic/amusing/difficult it was.

- Produce a variety of breads. Have everyone touch, smell, taste them. Encourage conversation about baking bread, what people like on bread, what foods it enhances, etc. Can anyone remember the bread strike? What would we miss about it if we could not have it? What might we replace it with? Then ask why people think Jesus would call himself the bread of life.

- Make a giant picture or poster showing what things people believe are 'basic' to leading a sustained, nourishing and tasty life

Prayers/ intercessions

Link prayers for current concerns with the words:

Leader: God where there is (*anger/sadness/malice/conflict/joy/ fun/tenderheartedness etc.*)

Let us see your truth

All: **And so live in your love.**

Use the poster prepared above as a focus for silent prayer.

Use loaves/slices/rolls of bread as symbols of praise, thanks, confession and supplication. As the symbols are placed in an appropriate place and the prayer has been said, use the relevant words below, saying

Leader: God, when we taste (*anxiety/joy/ concern/sorrow/injustice etc.*)

All   **Help us to remember that you are the bread of life.**

Stories and other resources

Hiawyn Oram, *Angry Arthur*, Red Fox, 1993

Pat Hutchins, *The Doorbell Rang*, Mulberry Books, 1989

Steve Pearce and Diana Murrie, 'Bread of life', in *Children and Holy Communion*, NS/CHP, 1997

'Elijah hears a still small voice', in *In the Beginning*

'Jesus shares a meal', in *Instant Inspirations*

Drama

'Good news and bad news', in *Plays on the Word*

Music

God is good, we sing and shout it (HON 168, MP 185)

I am the bread of life (HON 222)

Let us praise the Lord our God (BBP 3)

God forgave my sin (HON 167, JP 54, MP 181)

The joy of the Lord is my strength (JP 240)

When I'm feeling down and sad (BBP 74)

Author of life divine (HAMNS 258, HON 48, HTC 395)

May the mind of Christ my Saviour (HON 334, HTC 550, MP 463)

O Jesus, King most wonderful (HTC 484)

Collect and post communion prayer

Advent 1999 to Advent 2000	The Eight Sunday after Trinity on p. 132
Advent 2002 to Advent 2003	
Advent 2005 to Advent 2006	Use the collect and post communion prayer for the Ninth Sunday after Trinity on p. 133

Sunday between 14 and 20 August

Proper 15

Readings

Continuous

1 Kings 2.10-12,3.3-14

King David dies after reigning for 40 years, leaving his throne to Solomon his son. Solomon wants only to be a good king, governing the people properly. God is pleased with Solomon's intentions and promises to honour them, bestowing upon the new king wisdom and discernment. Since Solomon shows no desire for personal wealth and glory, God promises to reward him with both and, if Solomon keeps God's commandments, he is promised a long life.

or Related

Proverbs 9.1-6

In this poem wisdom is a woman who prepares a feast and invites the simple, the senseless and the immature to share in it. By doing this they will gain insight and walk in the way of wisdom.

Ephesians 5.15-20

The Ephesians are told to be careful and live wisely, understanding God's will and praising him for what he has done through Jesus.

John 6.51-58

Jesus speaks of being the living bread, the source of eternal life and of giving his life for the life of the world. His listeners interpret his words literally and are puzzled about the prospect of eating his flesh. Jesus does not respond to that particular point, continuing to emphasize that he is the food and drink of life now, and of eternal life. We are dependent upon him just as he is dependent upon God.

Talk/address/sermon

There is simplicity about Solomon's desires and ambitions in the extract from 1 Kings. In his humility he knows that he is entirely dependent on God. He recognizes that he has an enormous task, but seems to have an understanding of what is important if he is to do his job well. Part of his reward is a wise and discerning mind: what are the features of these qualities?

Simplicity, senselessness and immaturity are not desirable qualities according to the writer of Proverbs. What are the meanings behind these words? How do we lay them aside and what insight will we gain by doing so? The same action might be described by some as wise and others as foolish. What does this mean for Christians as they attempt to discern the will of God?

What does Paul mean by being careful when he, like others, has taken the risk of following Jesus?

What does Jesus really mean by eating his flesh and drinking his blood? If he is speaking in metaphor, why does he not spell out what he means?

The reading from John is a reminder of our inextricable link with Jesus and God. If we take care in discerning his will, and take the risk of sharing in his body and blood, what insight will we gain into the richness of life which is promised us?

Simplicity and foolishness are often regarded as Christian virtues – how does that equate with the Proverbs reading?

Congregational/ group activities

- Describe through word, picture or mime the ideal king. Does it fit with the 1 Kings reading?

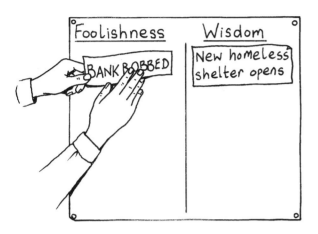

- Make two headings on a large sheet, 'Foolishness' and 'Wisdom', then list beneath each one appropriate types of action and behaviour. Do you find any that are included in both lists? Why might that be the case? Alternatively, tear articles and pictures out of newspapers and decide whether they should be stuck under the 'Wisdom' poster or the 'Foolishness' poster. Should any be included under both?

- Have a mini debate, which argues the motion 'Being careful is being boring?'

- Give each group two large paper plates, preferably of different colours, and some pieces of paper. Ask everyone to draw or write one or more aspects of Jesus' life that they would like to 'eat and drink'. Place them on the first plate. Which are the aspects that you would prefer not to partake in? Write or draw these and place them on the second plate.

Prayers/ intercessions

Pass around the pieces of paper from the first plate (as designed in the congregational/group activities),

ensuring that everyone knows that this is the plate of things about Jesus' life that people *want* to partake in. Play music and allow time for the pieces of paper to be looked at or read. Do the same with the second plate, being sure that everyone knows that these aspects of life in Jesus are not so attractive. No comments need to be made.

Stories and other resources

William Mayne, *The Mouse and the Egg*, Picture Lions, 1982

Nancy Sweetland, *God's Quiet Things*, Lion, 1994

'The Last Supper', in *Building New Bridges*

'Jesus shares a meal', in *Instant Inspirations*

'Solomon's Temple', in *In the Beginning*

Drama

John Bell and Eric Maule, 'The protector', in *Eh . . . Jesus . . . Yes, Peter . . .? No. 2*, Wild Goose Publications, 1988

♪ ♫♯♫ ♪♫ Music

The wise man built his house upon the rock (JP 252)

Spirit of the living God (JP 222, MP 613)

This is my body broken for you (HON 506)

Love will never come to an end (CP 99)

God of the morning (CP 105)

Jesus' love is very wonderful (JU, p. 14)

Awake, awake, fling off the night (HAMNS 342, HON 49)

Lord of all power, I give you my will (HAMNS 395, HTC 547)

When morning gilds the skies (HAMNS 146, HON 551, HTC 223, KSHF 603, MP 756)

Collect and post communion prayer

Advent 1999 to Advent 2000	
	The Ninth Sunday after Trinity on p. 133
Advent 2002 to Advent 2003	
Advent 2005 to Advent 2006	The Tenth Sunday after Trinity on p. 133

Sunday between 21 and 27 August

Proper 16

 ### Readings

Continuous

1 Kings 8.[1,6,10-11],22-30,41-43

Elders and leaders are summoned by Solomon to witness the placing of the Ark of the Covenant into the inner sanctuary of the newly built temple. A cloud then fills the temple, preventing the priests from ministering and filling them with the glory of God. Solomon stands before the altar, praising God, thanking him for fulfilling his promise and praying that those who sit on the throne of Israel will always be of David's lineage. He begs God to take heed of the prayers of all those who honour him in his temple, including foreigners, so that everyone in the world will come to worship him.

or Related

Joshua 24.1-2a,14-18

Joshua gathers the elders and leaders of the people of Israel, exhorting them to make up their minds as to whether they will serve God or those gods that were worshipped in Egypt. They need to make up their minds now. Joshua, however, makes it absolutely clear that he and his household will worship God alone.

Ephesians 6.10-20

The Ephesians are to arm themselves with the armour of God: righteousness, peace, faith, salvation and the word of God. They are to pray in the Spirit at all times and they must pray for Paul who, whilst imprisoned, continues to be an ambassador for the gospel.

John 6.56-69

Speaking in the synagogue in Capernaum, Jesus says that whoever eats of him eats the bread of life and will have eternal life. Some of his followers find this very difficult and are no clearer when he explains that life is not restricted to the human body: it is what he teaches that gives spirit and life. He knows that not everyone can accept what he says and seems unsurprised when a number of followers leave. Jesus asks the twelve disciples if they too want to go, but Peter, on behalf of everyone, professes belief in his claims. Jesus responds by saying that one of their number will betray him.

 ### Talk/address/ sermon

The account from 1 Kings is of a deeply spiritual event in which priests are overwhelmed by the glory of God, and Solomon can do nothing other than praise God. Is it the case that complete obedience allows God's glory to be revealed? How can complete obedience be achieved?

With the Joshua reading in mind, is there a tendency for us to apologize for our faith? What is our bottom line? Which things will we not compromise on? Where is the evidence?

Each of the words righteousness, peace, faith, salvation and word conjure up all sorts of pictures. What is our understanding of any of them?

If you were one of Jesus' followers in the Gospel reading, would you go or stay?

What is it that motivates us and gives us energy and zest for life? How are we sustained?

How can we get a taste of Jesus? Is there a link between this and the 1 Kings reading, where Solomon and the priests seemed to be enjoying a 'feast' of God's glory? If we did get a taste, would we want to follow him?

Congregational/ group activities

- During the service, either with a group of volunteers or with the whole congregation, play a game of word association, starting with the word 'obedience'. Do any of the words relate to the idea that comes across in the 1 Kings reading, i.e. that obeying God reveals his glory?

- Offer volunteers the choice between particular sweets, drinks, biscuits, etc. When they have chosen, ask them how they made their decisions. What was easy? What was hard? What might have happened if they had not made up their minds? Relate this to the situation of the elders and leaders in the story from Joshua who were urged to make up their minds quickly.

- Have some pre-prepared cardboard armour. Label each with one of the words from Ephesians (such as righteousness, peace, faith, salvation and word). In the appropriate number of groups, give everyone a time limit to illustrate their piece of armour with relevant drawings and words. You may need more than one set of armour. When the time is up dress a volunteer in the armour so that person displays the apparel of one who is trying to live a Christian life.

- Act out a situation where a character has the opportunity to forgive or not to forgive; to be charitable or not to be charitable; to think positively rather than negatively, etc. Freeze when the choice has to be made and then ask which is the course of action that gives spirit and life, perhaps speculating why.

- Have an upside-down picture of the world. Bearing in mind both the Ephesians reading and the reading from John's Gospel, what is it about Jesus' teaching that is the other way round to what we often want to do, but that is life-giving?

Prayers/ intercessions

Break some bread. As each piece is broken give thanks for particular life-giving situations, repent for destructive ones and pray for those which still may be one or the other. Finally give thanks for the fact that Jesus' teaching, death and resurrection show that even the most desperate situation can be transformed into a life-giving one.

Pray for the world, the Church, the local community, the sick and those who have died, using the versicle and response:

Leader: Jesus, who gives spirit and life.

All: **We want to go your way.**

Stories and other resources

Liz Rosenberg and Jim Lamarche, *The Carousel*, Orchard Books,1995

Robert Munsch , *Love You Forever*, Firefly Books, 1986

Gill Ambrose, *Plagues and Promises*, NCEC, 1998

'Solomon's temple', in *In the Beginning*

Drama

Anita Haigh, 'Follow me', in *Rap, Rhyme and Reason*, Scripture Union, 1996

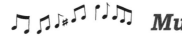 ## Music

Glory to God in the highest (JP 51)

Glory to You, my God (JP 52)

Glory to God (JU, p. 78)

The love of God be with you (JU, p. 86)

Christ is made the sure foundation (HON 76, HTC 559, KSHF 54, MP 73)

Lord Jesus, once you spoke to men (HAMNS 392, HTC 112)

Thine for ever (HAMNS 234, HON 504, HTC 556)

Collect and post communion prayer

Advent 1999 to Advent 2000	The Tenth Sunday after Trinity on p. 132
Advent 2002 to Advent 2003	
Advent 2005 to Advent 2006	Use the collect and post communion prayer for the Eleventh Sunday after Trinity on p. 133

Sunday between 28 August and 3 September

Proper 17

Readings

Continuous

Song of Solomon 2.8-13

The writer's lover is approaching the object of his love. He is strong and agile, seeing only the beauty of his beloved. He beckons his love out to where the winter is past and the new life of spring is bursting forth and full of promise.

or Related

Deuteronomy 4.1-2,6-9

Moses tells his people that they must observe the laws given to them by God if they wish to take possession of the land promised to them. Strict observance of these laws will demonstrate their wisdom and unique relationship with a righteous God. Not only must they themselves follow the laws strictly, they must pass them on to future generations.

James 1.17-27

Readers are reminded that everything good comes from an unchanging God. Each person is born in God's truth to become a first-fruit. They must be quick to listen, slow to speak and slow to anger. Human anger does not lead to the kind of righteousness required by God. God's people must trust the truth into which they are born, ridding themselves of immorality. Do what God says, implores the writer, and know its freedom and blessings. Hold your tongue, look after the orphans and widows, and do not be tainted by the world.

Mark 7.1-8,14-15,21-23

The Pharisees take issue with Jesus because the disciples fail to honour the ritualistic washing of hands in preparation for eating. Jesus accuses the Pharisees of putting man-made laws before those of God. He tells those around him that being 'unclean' is nothing to do with the state of what is taken into the body: it is a person's words and actions that indicate his/her state of uncleanliness. It is what comes from a person that is significant, because it is from within that evil thoughts, greed or malice come.

Talk/address/ sermon

With the Song of Solomon in mind, what signs of new life around us and in the wider world is God beckoning us to come and see? God promises more than we can imagine.

What are the commands of the Lord God, referred to in the Deuteronomy reading and which the Israelites are urged to keep?

Reflect upon how the way we live speaks of our beliefs and values. What are the signs of our faith community? How do people know we are Christians?

With the reading from James in mind, what are the first-fruits of those who own the truth into which they were born?

Explore the issue of appropriating anger, in the light of the James reading.

How do ritual and tradition help to uphold God's law and how can their effectiveness be tested?

How can the uncleanliness spelt out in the Gospel reading be transformed?

Congregational/ group activities

- Create a collage or picture of the scene to which the loved one is beckoned in the Song of Solomon. Alternatively, design a picture with your own ideas of what constitutes new life and promise.

- Without reference to the Bible, make a list of the ten commandments. Check its accuracy against the biblical accounts and perhaps give a prize for the winning team?

- Give everyone a 'T'-shaped badge (double-sided sticky tape on the back might be easier than safety pins). The 'T' is for the truth we are born into. Decorate the badge with words, pictures, colours which illustrate that truth.

- Play a game of 'Opposites', finding opposites to the words in the final paragraph of the Gospel reading such as 'greed' and 'generosity'.

- In groups make lists of things that make people angry. How many of these are common to the group? Which of these things should change? Are there situations where the change actually needs to take place in us? Identify them. How might we instigate effective change?

 ## Prayers/ intercessions

In preparation, invite a church group to identify situations locally and in the wider world where situations of greed, malice, deceit, slander, etc. have been transformed, or might be transformed. These are signs of truth. Ask the group to pray about these very concisely, using the following versicle and response to link the prayers:

Leader: Through the word of truth
All: **Transform your world O Lord**

Focus on the poster and play appropriate music.

Play some music and encourage everyone to bring their badges and stick them to a cross. The badges could be reclaimed later and taken home as a reminder that Christ is our truth.

 ## Stories and other resources

Dyan Sheldon, 'The Whale's Song', in *The Hutchinson Treasury of Children's Literature*, Hutchinson, 1995

Peter Thamm, *The Raucous, Underhand, Smooth-Backed, Yellow, Spotted Bean Beetle*, Lutheran Publishing House, 1988.

Leslie Baker, *Morning Beach*, Little, Brown and Company, 1990

'The Chain of Life', in *Reign Dance*

 ## Drama

Anita Haigh, 'Actions speak louder than words', in *Rap, Rhyme and Reason*, Scripture Union, 1996

Paul Powell, 'The alternative 10 commandments', in *Scenes and Wonders*, NS/CHP, 1994

Music

Jehovah Jireh (JP 404, MP 354)

Christ's is the world (HON 83)

Big blue planet, swinging through the universe (BBP 62)

Get up out of bed (JU, p. 4)

For health and strength and daily food (JU, p. 100)

Almighty Father, who for us thy Son didst give (HAMNS 338)

For the beauty of the earth (HAMNS 104, HON 137, HTC 298, MP 152)

Teach me, my God and King (HAMNS 240, HON 466)

Collect and post communion prayer

Advent 1999 to Advent 2000	The Eleventh Sunday after Trinity on p. 133
Advent 2002 to Advent 2003	
Advent 2005 to Advent 2006	The Twelfth Sunday after Trinity on p. 134

Sunday between 4 and 10 September

Proper 18

 ### Readings

Continuous

Proverbs 22.1-2,8-9,22-23

To have a good name is preferable by far to having wealth. God is the maker of everyone, rich and poor. Wicked people will be destroyed; generous people will be blessed. The poor must not be exploited. If they are, God will deal out the same treatment to those who abuse them.

or Related

Isaiah 35.4-7a

Isaiah encourages those who live in fear by assuring them of God's divine retribution. He anticipates a time when the blind will see, the deaf will hear, the lame will walk and those without speech will shout with joy. Wilderness, desert, burning sand and any thirsty ground will gush with water.

James 2.1-10,[11-13],14-17

In this letter readers are urged not to show preference to the rich at the expense of the poor. God has chosen the poor to be rich in faith, but discrimination humiliates and insults them. Those who show favouritism might only seem to be breaking one point of law. Mercy must be shown to others if there is a wish to be dealt with mercifully by God, and any words of faith must be accompanied by action.

Mark 7.24-37

Jesus is near Tyre. He does not want to attract attention but cannot avoid it. A Greek woman, born in Syrian Phoenicia, implores Jesus to drive an evil spirit from her small daughter. Jesus says he must let the children have all they need to eat before tossing their leftovers to the dogs. The woman replies by saying that even the dogs can have the crumbs discarded by the children. Jesus, impressed by her reply, heals her daughter. From the area of Tyre he travels on to Decapolis. Here a man who is deaf and has a speech impediment is brought to him. Jesus heals the man and commands the assembled company not to tell anyone. They ignore him and his fame travels fast.

 ### Talk/address/ sermon

How do we disentangle measurement of self-esteem from degrees of material success when our society tends to show esteem by financial reward? Also with Proverbs in mind, what evidence do we have of the generous being blessed?

The Old Testament readings emphasize vengeance. What does this say about the circumstances of the writers and what does it say about the nature of God? Jesus told stories such as the parable of the prodigal son which give a very different picture.

No matter how hard we try it is difficult for many not to be impressed by rich and famous people. Why is this? What does it teach us about ourselves – and them?

The reading from James encourages us to live with total integrity, so that everything we do demonstrates what we believe. How can we be helped to identify the obvious contradictions between our beliefs and lifestyle without being disabled by guilt?

The Gospel reading gives the impression that Jesus wants some peace and quiet, but it seems that he cannot help responding to the needs of the poor and sick. His behaviour, indeed his whole life, demonstrates the person he is.

 ### Congregational/ group activities

- Provide groups with scenarios (through the written word, newspaper reports or pictures) where people have been unjustly treated. In relation to the Old Testament reading how should their persecutors be treated? In terms of Jesus' teaching and life style (particularly his words on the cross) how should they be treated?

- The Isaiah reading paints one picture of how things will be when God comes. Can the congregation paint another picture (literally or with words), using contemporary images, of what they regard to be features of a redeemed creation?

- What would you think/feel/do if a famous footballer or pop star were coming? Why do you think we all behave in these ways when faced with famous people? How do you think they feel?

- It seems as though Jesus wanted a break from being famous, but not from showing God's love to people. If you were asked to organize a day off for him, what would you plan?

Prayers/ intercessions

Have scenarios from the first activity read out. Then use these versicles and responses:

Leader: To those upon whom pain and injustice are inflicted

All: Let your love and mercy be known, O Lord.

Leader: To those who inflict pain and injustice on others

All: Let your love and mercy be known, O Lord.

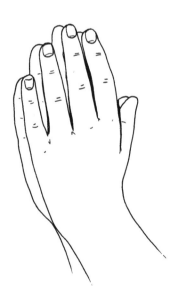

Stories and other resources

Nicholas Allan, *Jesus' Day Off*, Hutchinson, 1998

Pamela Allen, *Herbert and Harry*, Puffin Books, 1990

'The wisdom of the mouse deer', in *The Lion Book of World Stories*, Lion 1998

Jill Murphy, *Five Minutes' Peace*, Macmillan, 1980

'Two little boys', in *Reign Dance*

Drama

Anita Haigh, 'Forgiving or forgetting', in *Rap, Rhyme and Reason*, Scripture Union, 1996

Anita Haigh, 'Love in the twenty first century', in *Rap, Rhyme and Reason*, Scripture Union, 1996

Music

Fill your hearts with joy (JP 339)

How great is our God (JP 82, MP 245)

Jubilate, everybody (JP 145, MP 394)

Keep a light in your eyes for the children of the world (BBP 24)

Do not be afraid (HON 111, MP 115)

You shall go out with joy (HON 571, MP 796)

O Lord, hear my prayer (HON 379)

God is love: let heaven adore him (HAMNS 365, HON 170, MP 187)

O for a thousand tongues to sing (HAMNS 125, HON 362, HTC 219, KSHF 394, MP 496)

The Kingdom of God is justice and joy (HTC 333)

Collect and post communion prayer

Advent 1999 to Advent 2000	
Advent 1999 to Advent 2000	**The Twelfth Sunday after Trinity on p. 134**
Advent 2002 to Advent 2003	
Advent 2005 to Advent 2006	**The Thirteenth Sunday after Trinity on p. 134**

Sunday between 4 and 10 September

Sunday between
11 and 17 September

Proper 19

 ## Readings

Continuous

Proverbs 1.20-33

Wisdom calls to the people telling them that, because they have ignored her rebuke, she will laugh at their misfortune. She will abandon those who have not listened. Those who do listen, however, will live in safety.

or Related

Isaiah 50.4-9a

Isaiah has been instructed by God to know the word which sustains the weak. Isaiah has been obedient to God. More than that, he has been persecuted for his obedience. He knows he is not disgraced because what he does is in obedience. Isaiah will face anything because he knows that God will help him.

James 3.1-12

This is a strong reminder of the responsibility we have whenever we speak. The tongue is a small part of the body but its power is colossal. God should not be praised by the same tongue that pours curse on others.

Mark 8.27-38

Jesus asks the disciples who other people say he is and who they themselves believe he is. Peter answers that Jesus is the Christ; Jesus' immediate response is to warn them not to tell anyone. He then goes on to warn them of his forthcoming suffering and death. Peter's protests at this makes Jesus very angry. He tells all his followers that his way is indeed the way of suffering and death. Only by giving life will life be gained.

 ## Talk/address/ sermon

What is wisdom? What is foolishness? What is behind sayings like 'One man's wisdom is another man's folly'?

Why is God so often characterized as vengeful in the Old Testament when his son teaches forgiveness and love of enemies in the New Testament?

What sorts of things sustain us in an apparently superficial way (e.g. watching a favourite programme on television, meeting a friend, having a late-night whisky, walking the dog, going away for a day, shopping, playing or watching football)? Are these really so superficial? Is God there in them? If so, how? If we recognize God in those situations, are we more likely to recognize his presence when our need of him is great?

What we say can build people up or undermine them. Misunderstandings can damage relationships. To what extent do we appreciate the power and reponsibility we have when we speak?

 ## Congregational/ group activities

- What do you most like doing to relax and refresh yourself? Write and/or illustrate a prayer of thanks to God for these things.

- Make up new lyrics to complete verses of the song 'The wise man built his house upon the rock.' It could be changed to 'The wise one . . .'. Illustrate your song.

- Give groups a piece of flip chart paper and ask them to describe through words, pictures or symbols who Jesus is and why he is still so important to people today.

- Invite people of different ages to make up a discussion panel. Prepare them by telling a short story (or showing a video) of someone who has suffered for their faith, and inviting them to reflect honestly upon whether or not they think it was worth it – and why. Tell the congregation the same story and then let them hear the reflections of the panel.

- Make an instant, massive poster with lots of colour to represent the glory of God. Display the poster and ask everyone to stand where they can see it. Read the passage from the Gospel, then in silence have a large cross laid against the poster.

 Prayers/ intercessions

Use the prayers produced in the group activity.

In silence, think of some one you know who annoys you. Picture that person. What do you feel like saying to them? Now think of what you could say that would build them up.

Offer all this to God in silence.

With or without the massive poster suggested in the last activity, pray for different situations locally and more widely, using the following versicle and response:

Leader: Jesus, the Christ, in seeing who you are
All: **Let us take up our cross and follow you.**

Stories and other resources

Anthony Browne, 'Willy and Hugh', in *The Hutchinson Treasury of Children's Literature*, Hutchinson, 1995

Angela Elwell Hunt, *The Tale of Three Trees*, Lion, 1989

'St Benedict', in *Seasons and Saints for the Christian Year*

'Obedience', in *Pick and Mix*

Drama

'Love is like this', in *Playing Up*

 Music

Jesus, I will come with You (JP 138)

King of kings and Lord of lords (JP 148)

All heaven declares (HON 14, MP 14)

As the deer pants for the water (HON 39, MP 37)

I love you, Lord (HON 233, MP 287)

The family of Man (CP 69)

O Jesus, I have promised (HAMNS 235, HON 372, HTC 531, KSHF 400, MP 501)

Take my life, and let it be (HAMNS 249, HON 464, HTC 554, KSHF 496, MP 624)

O worship the King all glorious above (HAMNS 101, HON 393, HTC 24, KSHF 428, MP 528)

Collect and post communion prayer

Advent 1999 to Advent 2000	The Thirteenth Sunday after Trinity on p. 134
Advent 2002 to Advent 2003	
Advent 2005 to Advent 2006	Use the collect and post communion prayer for the Fourteenth Sunday after Trinity on p. 134

Sunday between 18 and 24 September

Proper 20

 ## Readings

Continuous

Proverbs 31.10-31

This is the famous epilogue to the book of Proverbs, praising the wife of noble character. It is an acrostic poem that describes the desirability of the woman that, like wisdom itself, is worth more than precious rubies.

or Related

Wisdom of Solomon 1.16-2.1,12-22

The ungodly lie in wait for the righteous, because his very way of life condemns their sins. The very sight of him is a reproach to the ungodly and for this reason they will test him with insults, torture and death itself to see if God really will come to his aid.

Jeremiah 11.18-20

The Lord reveals to Jeremiah a plot against his life. Jeremiah had been like a 'lamb led to the slaughter', unaware that his enemies were plotting against him.

Mark 9.30-37

Jesus' ministry in Galilee is now complete. From this point onwards he is travelling on his way to Jerusalem to suffer and die. His disciples argue about who is the greatest of them all. Jesus tells them that whoever wants to be first must also be the servant of all. He takes a child in his arms and tells his disciples that whoever welcomes such a child as this welcomes Jesus.

 ## Talk/address/ sermon

Gather together pictures of as many heroes of modern culture as you can find (pop stars, film stars, politicians, etc.). What makes them so popular? Why does our society consider them the 'greatest' of all? Who does our society consider the least? Show pictures of some of the people marginalized by our society such as the homeless, children or the elderly. Talk about how each person is of infinite worth to God. Can we identify the differing gifts of each age group? What do the elderly give us, and children? How can our church ensure that it welcomes all?

Invite a guest speaker from a charity such as Crisis or Christian Aid to talk about their work amongst many of the undervalued people in our society.

 ## Congregational/ group activities

- Write out as many modern proverbs as your group can remember (such as 'a stitch in time saves nine', 'absence makes the heart grow fonder', 'too many cooks spoil the broth'). How true are such generalized words of wisdom? What are the limitations of proverbs?

- The passage in Proverbs is an acrostic poem. Ask the group to think of different aspects of wisdom and to create an acrostic using the letters of 'Wisdom' or 'Proverbs'.

- St Matthew is commemorated on 21 September. Draw symbols for the four Gospel writers (the lion, ox, eagle and human face). How does the Gospel of Matthew differ from the other Gospels? In what way does he display Jesus as the 'Lion King'?

- Ask each person in the group to identify their hero. What makes them so special? What makes them so heroic? Compare them with Jesus' own explanation of 'the greatest'. Who would we say has shown this kind of greatness in their own lives? Who am I a hero to, or how might I become one?

- Begin a 'Journeys of Jesus' poster or banner, that you will add to over the next few weeks. Draw a map of the holy land and indicate the areas that Jesus visited on his way from Galilee to Jerusalem. Ask each person in the group to take off their shoes and socks and draw around their feet. Cut out these shapes, colour them in and stick them around the edge of the banner or poster.

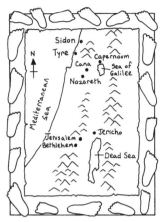

I know, O God,
that wherever I travel,
you will be with me.
There is nowhere I can go,
nothing I can face
which is beyond your love and strength.
And so I place myself
into your care and keeping,
knowing that at all times
and in all places,
I am in your hands.

Christopher Herbert

Prayers/intercessions

Use the wisdom prayers written during the congregational/group activities as a focus for your prayers.

Continue with the theme of journeying in faith. Use the following prayers on the theme of journeying:

Alone with none but thee, my God,
I journey on my way.
What need I fear when thou art near
O king of night and day?
More safe am I within thy hand
than if a host did round me stand.

St Columba (AD 521–97)

May the road rise to meet you
May the wind always be at your back
May the sun shine warm upon your face
The rain fall soft upon your fields
And until we meet again
May God hold you
In the hollow of his hand.

Traditional Celtic blessing

Stories and other resources

Steve Pearce and Diana Murrie, chapter 3, 'First class', *in All Aboard!,* Bible Reading Fellowship,1996

'St Augustine', in *Instant Inspirations*

'Follow Me', in *Livewires Live*

Drama

'Careless talk', in *A Fistful of Sketches*

 ## Music

One more step along the world I go (JP 188)

If you want to be great (JP 389)

Make me a servant, Lord (JP 162)

Praise the Lord of all creation (BBP 12)

The earth is yours, O God (CP 6)

Think of a world without any flowers (CP 17)

A man there lived in Galilee (HAMNS 334, HON 3)

God of grace and God of glory (HAMNS 367, HON 174, HTC 324, MP 192)

Praise to the Holiest in the height (HAMNS 117, HON 426, HTC 140, MP 563)

Collect and post communion prayer

Advent 1999 to Advent 2000	The Fourteenth Sunday after Trinity on p. 134
Advent 2002 to Advent 2003	
Advent 2005 to Advent 2006	Use the collect and post communion prayer for the Fifteenth Sunday after Trinity on p. 134

Sunday between 25 September 1 October

Proper 21

 ### Readings

Continuous

Esther 7.1-6,9-10;9.20-22

Queen Esther pleads for the life of her people. King Xerxes orders the death of Haman, the man responsible for so much of the suffering of the Jews. The Jewish people celebrate their salvation from their enemies (a tradition that is still celebrated today in the festival of Purim).

or Related

Numbers 11.4-6,10-16,24-29

The Israelites complain that they are receiving only a limited diet of manna. Moses prays to the Lord, who sends them quail to eat.

James 5.13-20

The letter of James ends with a focus upon prayer. Whether a person is in trouble or is content, they should remember to pray. The elders of the church also have a responsibility to pray for those in their church who are sick.

Mark 9.38-50

Jesus' disciples tell him that they noticed a man driving out demons in Jesus' name, even though he wasn't one of the Twelve. Jesus' view of discipleship is much more inclusive than theirs. He informs that that 'whoever is not against us is for us'. Jesus continues by warning against causing others to sin – especially those who are the smallest and are relatively insignificant. Even the smallest child is of infinite worth to God.

 ### Talk/address/ sermon

How do we recognize that someone belongs to Christ? We often wear different items so people can outwardly recognize us as belonging to a certain group or organization – whether it's a certain school, the Guides or Scouts, a football team or a company uniform. Explore the different symbols Christians use, such as the cross, fish, or peacock. What do these tell us about our own Christian faith? These are all outward signs of belonging to Christ, but how can we spot the more important 'inward' signs of faith?

 ### Congregational/ group activities

- The story of Esther is both dramatic and exciting. Act out the story in groups, using costumes or finger puppets for each of the main parts – Queen Esther, King Xerxes, Haman, Mordecai and the guards. As a background to this activity, learn as much as you can about the ways that Jewish people celebrate the festival of Purim

- Give each group a sheet with symbols (such as the hammer and sickle, badges of uniformed organizations, Christian symbols). What do we use symbols for? What do they tell us about those who wear  them? Make a display of the different organizations represented in the congregation. What are the signs of belonging to Jesus?

- Make a prayer card. Fold an A4 piece of card or stiff paper in half. Draw round your hand to make a praying hand-shaped card. Remember not to cut the fold.

- Discuss in groups: how can we recognize when someone is 'for Christ'? How do we feel a Christian should act? Draw up a list of ten important ways that a Christian should act. Which are the most important of these? Which do we find easy? Which are difficult for us, both as a congregation and as individuals?

 ## Prayers/ intercessions

Prayers for those who are sick or ill. It is especially good to have names of people who are known to the congregation as you pray:

For those who care for the sick – for doctors, nurses and hospital staff,
for district nurses and health nurses and health visitors,
for the families of those who are ill.

Use the following response:

Lord keep them close to you
And hear us as we pray.

Use the following prayer:

Dear God,
Thank you for the people who invented medicines,
like penicillin and vaccinations;
for all the medicines that stop you dying from things
like measles and smallpox and chickenpox.
Please allow people to make more medicines
until every single illness can be cured:
bacteria illnesses and virus illnesses.
I know you made all the amazing lovely universe
but I would like it if the dying rate could go down
very slowly, year by year. **Amen.**

Andrew Hood (age 6), taken from
Pocket Prayers for Children (p. 20)

 ## Stories and other resources

Christopher Herbert, *Pocket Prayers for Children*, NS/CHP, 1999

'Branch lines', from chapter 5, in *All Aboard!*

Steve Pearce and Diana Murrie, 'Belonging to God', 'Why we belong to God' and 'How we belong to God', in *Children and Holy Communion*, NS/CHP, 1997

'Queen Esther', in *In the Beginning*

'Jesus changes Simon's name', in *Instant Inspirations*

 ## Drama

Dave Hopwood, 'Prayer is like breathing', in *Acting Up*, NS/CHP, 1995

Michael Catchpool and Pat Lunt, 'A course on prayer', in *The Log in my Eye*, Kevin Mayhew, 1998

 ## Music

Father, lead me day by day (JP 43)

The journey of life (JP 468)

Travel on (CP 42)

Jesus, Jesus holy and anointed one (HON 271, SHP 78)

In the Lord I'll be ever thankful (HON 250)

Dear Lord and Father of mankind (HAMNS 115, HON 106, HTC 356, KSHF 76, MP 111)

Guide me, O thou great Jehovah (HAMNS 214, HON 188, HTC 538, KSHF 144, MP 201)

The price is paid (KSHF 528, MP 663)

Tell out my soul, the greatness of the Lord (HAMNS 422, HON 467, HTC 42, KSHF 498, MP 331)

Collect and post communion prayer

Advent 1999 to Advent 2000	**The Fifteenth Sunday after Trinity on p. 135**
Advent 2002 to Advent 2003	
Advent 2005 to Advent 2006	**The Sixteenth Sunday after Trinity on p. 135**

Sunday between 2 and 8 October

Proper 22

 ### Readings

Continuous

Job 1.1;2.1-10

Satan sets a second test for Job. This time he gives Job painful sores all over his body. Job not only suffers excruciating pain but also a wife who urges him to curse God so he can be left in peace to die.

or Related

Genesis 2.18-24

Man gives names to all the animals. The Lord creates woman with the divine purpose that together they should form an inseparable union.

Hebrews 1.1-4;2.5-12

The letter of Hebrews begins with seven descriptions of Christ. Each of these gives credence to Christ's superiority over all creation. He is the heir of all things, the radiance of God's glory who is far superior even to the angels themselves.

Mark 10.2-16

Some Pharisees test Jesus by asking him whether it is lawful for a man to divorce his wife. Jesus responds with a question of his own – what did Moses command them to do? Jesus continues by affirming the sanctity of marriage, as it was ordained by God at the beginning of creation.

Talk/address/ sermon

Although this Gospel is quite uncompromising in its message we do worship a God of love, a God who forgives and who, through Jesus, offers reconciliation with himself. We are human, we fail, but God's love is everlasting. The message is about human frailty, recognizing it in ourselves and in others. We need to be there for them. God is the judge, not us.

Ask the congregation to spot the seven marks of 'superiority' of Christ over creation, as listed in the Hebrews passage. Write these down on an overhead projector or whiteboard. What do they tell us about Christ? Does it change our view of Jesus when we read of descriptions of him as the sustainer of all things, through whom God created the worlds?

 ### Congregational/ group activities

- Create a large frieze for one of the walls of the church. Cut out pictures of animals from magazines and stick these together to make a collage. Write in large letters, 'God's creation'.

- In discussion groups ask people to think about the following questions:

    What happens when relationships break down?

    How can we support people in their relationships?

    How can the Church sometimes place people under pressure and how can this be avoided?

- Make a big book (similar to the one used in nursery and reception classes in schools). Collect eight large pieces of paper (A3 or A2) and staple together. On the cover write 'The story of creation'. On each of the pages depict what happened on each of the days of creation.

- Harvest is often celebrated at this point in the Christian year. Draw a large outline of a supermarket trolley on strong backing paper or card. Ensure you have plenty of empty cartons, containers or food labels. Help each person in the group to find their favourite foods and stick these onto the outline drawing of the trolley. Cut out large letters to spell 'THANK YOU' and add these to the top of the picture.

Dear Lord,
I would like to talk.
How do you become friends with someone
who doesn't like you particularly?
There is a girl in my class who likes all of my friends
but I get the impression she doesn't like me.
Should I feel hurt?
Should I talk to her?
Should I try to ignore it?
I don't know and I just thought you might know.
I know you will care and answer me. Amen.

Charlotte Dyer (age 9), taken from
Pocket Prayers for Children (p. 48)

- St Francis of Assisi is celebrated on 4 October. Use the dramatic story of his life as a starting point to discuss our need to care for creation and for the poor.

- Autumn leaves. On a leaf-shaped card or piece of paper, write or draw on one side what you think are your good qualities – a harvest of your talent. On the other side, you might write or draw your faults. Use signs or a code if you wish, so only God and you know what you have depicted.

 ## Prayers/intercessions

Use the following harvest prayers, with the trolley picture from the congregational/group activities:

Thank you, Lord, for harvest time, and for all that you provide for us. Thank you for (*the groups mention here the food that they added to the trolley*). Help us to share the things that we have with others. Help us not to be greedy and selfish, taking more than our share. Help us always to remember that you are the giver of all good gifts and to say thank you for them. Amen.

Thank God for all who love and care for us. Ask God to help us to be a help and support to others:

Versicle: God our loving Father
Response: **Hear your children's prayer**

Use the following prayer, that looks at problems we have with relationships:

 ## Stories and other resources

'St Francis of Assisi', in *Together for Festivals*

'Creation', in *In the Beginning*

'Creation', in *Livewires Live*

Taffy Davies, *Miles and the Screwdriver*, Scripture Union, 1985

Drama

'In the beginning', 'Arfur and the Big Blunder' and 'Harvest gifts', in *Acting Up*

Mark Niel, 'Bureaucracy Inaction', in *Oh No, Not the Nativity!*, Scripture Union, 1998

 ## Music

God who made the earth (JP 63)

Stand up, clap hands (JP 225)

Make me a channel of Your peace (JP 161, HON 328, MP 456)

God made the heavens and the earth (JU, p. 66)

Big blue planet, swinging through the universe (BBP 62)

I like the sunshine (BBP 70)

Father, Lord of all creation (HAMNS 356, HON 122)

Jesus, good above all other (HAMNS 378, HON 269, HTC 96)

The Lord's my shepherd, I'll not want (HAMNS 426, HON 490, HTC 591, MP660)

Collect and post communion prayer

Advent 1999 to Advent 2000	The Sixeenth Sunday after Trinity on p. 134
Advent 2002 to Advent 2003	
Advent 2005 to Advent 2006	Use the collect and post communion prayer for the Seventeenth Sunday after Trinity on p. 135

Sunday between 9 and 15 October

Proper 23

Readings

Continuous

Job 23.1-9,16-17

Job complains about his situation and demands a fair trial from God. He is cut off from a God who terrifies him, yet he refuses to give in to the darkness.

or Related

Amos 5.6-7,10-15

The choice for Israel is stark here – either to seek the Lord and live, or to be devoured and swept away. For Israel is guilty of terrible sins, including trampling upon the poor and oppressing the righteous.

Hebrews 4.12-16

The word of God is sharper than a double-edged sword and cuts through to the very soul and spirit. The writer then explains how Christ is not only our high priest in the heavens, but is also able to sympathize with all our weaknesses. For this reason we can approach God with confidence.

Mark 10.17-31

A rich man asks Jesus what he must do to inherit eternal life. Although the man has followed the laws devoutly all his life, Jesus knows what the man's main problem is – his devotion to his wealth. The man's decision to turn away shows his greater love for his possessions than for the offer of eternal life.

Talk/address/ sermon

What do we use our hands for? Compile a list. When we are little, grown-ups tell us what to do with our hands: 'Don't touch!', 'Wash your hands', 'Don't pick your nose' and so on. As we get older, we assume greater responsibility for what we do with our hands. We can choose to use them for good or bad things. The choice is ours. What are some of the difficult decisions that we have to make as children and as adults? Look at the story in Mark 10. The rich man was eager to follow Jesus and was obviously a devout follower of the Law, yet his love for his possessions ultimately prevented him from following Jesus. What can prevent us from following Christ today?

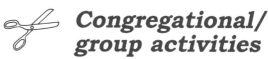 Congregational/ group activities

- It's not fair! This is one of the first sayings that we learn in life and one that we use frequently! What do we mean by 'fairness'? How does this compare with Job's situation?

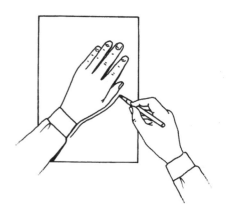

- Ask everyone to draw around their hands. Write on one side all the good things we can do with our hands and on the other side things it is not good to do.

- What objects or possessions are most important to you? Discuss this and draw pictures of these objects to use during prayers. Alternatively, ask people to bring in an object which means a lot to them. Why is it special to them? How does its 'sentimental' value differ from its relative money value? Think of creative ways that we can share in the Church. Perhaps we can be more welcoming of newcomers, invite someone for lunch, set up rotas to help with baby-sitting, etc.?

- Teresa of Avila is commemorated on 15 October. Find out as much as you can about her life. Write out one of her prayers (such as the one under the Prayers/intercessions section) on a piece of card. Draw around people's hands and cut out these shapes. Colour them in and stick them around the prayer.

- Draw a picture of the local priest. List all the duties that he/she is expected to perform. Do we often have too high an expectation of our own human priest? The next three Sundays from Hebrews focus on the similarities and differences between the earthly priest and Jesus, the 'heavenly' high priest. What does this teach us about how we should view our own priest and their work? What qualities do we expect from our priest?

- Wealth comparison. Read an interview with children from another country, such as Tanzania, about their expectations. What toys do they have? What is school like? What do they enjoy doing and what games do they like playing? Compare these to our own situation.

Prayers/ intercessions

Place drawings of possessions, or possessions brought in, on the floor. Use these as a meditation on possessions.

Use the hands from the previous congregational activities. Make a mobile or a big picture with them as intercession material.

Use this famous prayer of Teresa of Avila to reflect on our need to care for others:

> Christ has no body now on earth but yours,
> no hands but yours, no feet but yours;
> yours are the eyes
> through which to look with Christ's
> compassion on the world,
> yours are the feet
> with which he is to go about doing good,
> and yours are the hands
> with which he is to bless us now.

St Teresa of Avila (1515–82)

Focus on praying for those facing times of trial and for whom life doesn't seem fair:

> Lord Jesus,
> You suffered so much pain and cruelty on the cross
> But through it all, you held on to love.
> Be with us whenever life is very, very tough
> and keep us loving, no matter what happens –
> for that is your way,
> the way that leads to peace and truth.

Christopher Herbert, *Pocket Prayers for Children,* CHP.

Stories and other resources

Martin Wallace, 'St Patrick', in *The Celtic Resource Book*, NS/CHP, 1998

'In Love', in *Reign Dance*

'Gifts' and 'Creation', in *Pick and Mix*

'Love', in *Pick and Mix*

Drama

'The Adrian Puffin Show', in *A Fistful of Sketches*

Music

Come on, let's get up and go (JP 31)

Love, joy, peace (JP 425)

God is good, we sing and shout it (HON 168, MP 185)

God's love is deeper than the deepest ocean (JU, p. 90)

We thank you Lord (CP 136)

My God accept my heart this day (HAMNS 279, HON 341, HTC 551)

O thou who camest (HAMNS 233, HON 392, HTC 596, MP 525)

Thy kingdom come, O God (HAMNS 177, HON 519, HTC 334)

Collect and post communion prayer

Advent 1999 to Advent 2000	The Seventeenth Sunday after Trinity on p. 135
Advent 2002 to Advent 2003	
Advent 2005 to Advent 2006	Use the collect and post communion prayer for the Eighteenth Sunday after Trinity on p. 136

Sunday between 16 and 22 October

Proper 24

 ### Readings

Continuous

Job 38.1-7(34-41)

The Lord finally answers Job. God says nothing about Job's own suffering, nor about the problem of divine justice. However, neither does he condemn Job (which would have been the case if Job's counsellors had been correct in stating that Job suffered because of his guilt and sin). The Lord points towards his own omnipotence over all creation and over life itself.

or Related

Isaiah 53.4-12

This passage looks forward towards the coming Messiah, who will be crushed and suffer not for his own guilt but for the sin of us all. Although we have, like sheep, wandered away from God it is the Messiah who will be led as a lamb to be slaughtered.

Hebrews 5.1-10

The writer expounds how Christ is now our high priest in glory. An earthly high priest was 'selected from among men', but Jesus was chosen by his Father. An earthly priest would also be appointed to offer people's prayers and gifts and sacrifices for sins to God. Jesus offered these himself through his own suffering and has become the source itself of salvation.

Mark 10.35-45

This reading (following on so soon after that in Mark 9.33-37), shows how little the disciples have yet grasped about the true nature of the Gospel. James and John want Jesus to promise that they will be able to sit on his left and right hand in glory. Jesus warns them of the difficulties that lie ahead. He overturns the world's view of greatness by telling them that he has come to serve others. In the same way, they will be expected to follow his example and serve others rather than seek glory for themselves.

 ### Talk/address/ sermon

Dress up members of the congregation as some well-known heroes (if you can find costumes for these this would add to the impact, otherwise write out the names of the heroes on placards and place these around the people's necks). Ask what their main reasons for greatness are. Why do we think they are so heroic? Is it their strength, their fame, their money? Who are today's heroes (look back at Proper 20 for more material)? Dress up a member of the congregation as a Christian 'hero' such as Mother Teresa, William Wilberforce or Martin Luther King. What was heroic about their own life? How did it show Christ's teaching in practice?

Congregational/ group activities

- Interview members of the church about their past life (if possible find someone who has worked as a nurse, doctor or in another of the 'caring' professions). How do they care for people in their profession? Does it make any difference being Christian?

- There are many stories of heroes of the Christian faith, who have been famous not for their fame or money, but for their ultimate sacrifice – of giving their lives for others. Look at stories of modern martyrs such as Maximilian Kolbe or Oscar Romero.

- Are there any commemorative plaques, windows or artefacts in our church, given in memory of past members? Do any of the present congregation share their names? Why are people commemorated in this way? What would you give to your church in memory of you?

- Design a stained glass window using symbols of your life, or that of your group.

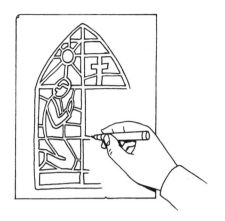

• What are the qualities we expect from a hero? Make a list. Is Jesus a hero and how can we become like him? Make a 'Rule of life' card, listing two or three things that you can try to do.

Prayers/ intercessions

Use the following prayer:

We pray to Jesus who is present with us to eternity, saying,
Jesus, Lord of life:
in your mercy, hear us.

Jesus, light of the world,
bring the light and peace of your gospel
to the nations . . .
Jesus, Lord of life:
in your mercy, hear us.

Jesus, bread of life,
give food to the hungry . . .
and nourish us all with your word.
Jesus, Lord of life:
in your mercy, hear us.

Jesus, our way, our truth, our life,
be with us and all who follow you in the way . . .
deepen our appreciation of your truth,
and fill us with your life.
Jesus, Lord of life:
in your mercy, hear us.

Jesus, Good Shepherd who gave your life for the sheep,
recover the straggler, bind up the injured, strengthen the sick
and lead the healthy and strong to play.
Jesus, Lord of life:
in your mercy, hear us.

Jesus, the resurrection and the life,
we give you thanks
for all who have lived and believed in you . . .
raise us with them to eternal life.
Jesus, Lord of life:
in your mercy, hear us,
accept our prayers, and be with us always. Amen.

Stories and other resources

Leslie Brandt, *Psalms Now*, Concordia, 1973

'Follow me', in *Livewires Live*

Brian Ogden, *Best Friends*, BRF, 1998

Drama

Michael Catchpool and Pat Lunt, 'Heaven's above', in *The Log In My Eye*, Kevin Mayhew, 1998

Music

Peace I give to you (JP 196, MP 553)

Make me a servant, Lord (JP 162)

If you see someone (JP 95)

From heaven you came (HON 148, MP 162)

Jesus is Lord! (HON 270, MP 367)

Christ is coming, Christ is coming (BBP 39)

Hail thou once-despised Jesus (HON 192, HTC 175, KSHF 145, MP 203)

I will sing the wondrous story (HON 237, HTC 212, KSHF 266, MP 315)

There is a green hill far away (HAMNS 137, HON 499, HTC 148, KSHF 532, MP 674)

Collect and post communion prayer

Advent 1999 to Advent 2000	The Seventeenth Sunday after Trinity on p. 136
Advent 2002 to Advent 2003	
Advent 2005 to Advent 2006	Use the collect and post communion prayer for the Nineteenth Sunday after Trinity on p. 136

Sunday between 23 and 29 October

Proper 25

Readings

Continuous

Job 42.1-6,10-17

After the Lord's long answer, Job responds by admitting his lack of understanding and unworthiness before the majesty of God. Job is restored to his former wealth and his family return to his home to comfort him.

or Related

Jeremiah 31.7-9

The Lord looks forward to a time in the future when the remnant of Israel will be gathered together and will return to him. They will return with weeping and praying to a God who will lead them beside streams of water, on a level path where they will not stumble.

Hebrews 7.23-28

Again, Jesus is compared with earthly priests. However, his is a permanent and eternal priesthood. Neither does he need to offer daily sacrifices to God, because his own sacrifice was 'once for all'.

Mark 10.46-52

Jesus and his disciples reach Jericho where a blind man, named Bartimaeus, is begging. He calls out for Jesus and asks for Jesus to heal him. Bartimaeus receives his sight and follows Jesus.

Talk/address/ sermon

Blindfold a 'volunteer' from the congregation and ask them to identify various objects (such as an orange or hairbrush) by feeling them. Then give them a drawing and see if they can tell you what it is. The last task is impossible to do. How could the blindfolded person be expected to see the drawing?

In the same way, many people feel it is impossible to know God, because we cannot see him. How can we know what he is like if we cannot see him?

 Congregational/ group activities

- Try to obtain a copy of a book in Braille in advance (your local library will help you to find a copy). How do people read using Braille? Ask children to try it in turn. Look at different forms of codes that we use to communicate. Write out a number of secret codes, using the braille form.

- Feely bags. Hide a number of different objects in a bag. Ask each person in the group to come up in turn and try to work out just by feel what these objects are. Give them only about ten seconds to do this. They then must go back and write down as many objects as they can remember.

- The life of Alfred the Great is commemorated on 26 October. He was not only famous for burning cakes, but also for establishing a time of considerable peace and fairness. Alfred's golden rule of life was very biblical: 'Do unto others as they should do unto you'. *Seasons and Saints for the Christian Year* provides several craft activities, such as making a scales of justice and a bookmark, that will help children to explore this theme of justice further.

- Draw up a list of kingly attributes. Make crowns and sceptres and orbs and any other symbols of kingship you can identify. If you were a king for a day what would you do?

- Following on from last week, what qualities do we expect a king to have – or a judge or a creator to have? God is all of these.

- If God was a bird, what kind of bird would he be? You can do lots of different comparisons, such as animal, flower, etc. It's important to stress that there are no right or wrong answers – just try to build up images or facets of God as people perceive him. You could make a collage picture to illustrate all that people have said.

 ## Prayers/ intercessions

Use the following response after each line:

We pray to you our God

Seek the Lord while he may be found: call on him while he is near . . .

Turn back to the Lord, who will have mercy: to our God who will richly pardon . . .

'For my thoughts are not your thoughts: neither are your ways my ways' says the Lord . . .

'As the heavens are higher than the earth: so are my ways higher than your ways and my thoughts higher than your thoughts . . .

As the rain and snow come down from heaven: and return not again but water the earth . . .

bringing forth life and giving growth: seed for sowing and bread to eat . . .

so is my word that goes out from my mouth: it does not return to me empty . . .

but it will accomplish my purpose: and succeed in the task I give' . . .

 ## Stories and other resources

Any missionary story, such as that of Gladys Aylward, in *Seasons and Saints for the Christian Year*

'Healing', in *Pattern of our Days*

'Healing', in *Pick and Mix*

God's Everywhere People, Church Mission Society, 1999

Talking Drum, Christian Aid/SCIAF, 1996

 ## Drama

Andrew Smith, 'The Perfect Sculpture', in *Much Ado About Something Else: 20 More Sketches*, CPAS, 1996

 ## Music

In everything I do (JP 391)

God is our guide (JP 56)

Give thanks to the Lord (JP 345)

The peace of the Lord be always with you (BBP 57)

He is the Lord (SHP 45)

We see Jesus (SHP 138)

God moves in a mysterious way (HAMNS 112, HON 173, KSHF 135, MP 193)

To God be the glory (HON 522, HTC 584, KSHF 559, MP 708)

Hills of the north, rejoice (HAMNS 470, HON 209)

Collect and post communion prayer

Advent 1999 to Advent 2000	Use the collect and post communion prayer for the Last Sunday after Trinity on p. 137
Advent 2002 to Advent 2003	
Advent 2005 to Advent 2006	

Bible Sunday

(Bible Sunday may be celebrated in preference to the provision for the Last Sunday after Trinity)

 ## Readings

Isaiah 55.1-11

The exiles are urged to return to God for healing and restoration. They must seek the Lord while he may still be found and call on him while he is still near. God's word is compared to the rain and the snow that fall from heaven and do not return to it without watering the earth and making it blossom and flourish.

2 Timothy 3.14–4.5

Paul affirms the authority of Scripture. It is useful for teaching, training and correcting behaviour. He tells Timothy that he should be prepared at all times to preach the word with patience and careful instruction.

John 5.36b-47

Jesus points out that Scripture itself is testifying to his authority and purpose. Yet the very people who study Scripture so diligently are unable to recognize the Messiah that it foretells will come.

Collect

> Blessed Lord,
> who caused all holy scriptures
>   to be written for our learning:
> help us so to hear them,
> to read, mark, learn and inwardly digest them
> that, through patience, and the comfort of your
>   holy word,
> we may embrace and for ever hold fast
>   the hope of everlasting life,
> which you have given us in our Saviour Jesus Christ,
> who is alive and reigns with you,
> in the unity of the Holy Spirit,
> one God, now and for ever.

 ## Talk/address/ sermon

The Bible is a library. All kinds of books are found there – adventure stories, sad stories, happy stories, books of rules, wise sayings, love stories and others. How have people tried to portray the Bible stories in the past, in an age when people couldn't read? Put up an overhead projector of a Celtic cross. What stories from the Bible have been shown? Why were these chosen out of all the stories of the Bible and what do they tell us about God?

Modern day: what are the best ways we can communicate the gospel? Look at different forms of modern technology and how they have been used to communicate the message.

 ## Congregational/ group activities

• What are people's favourite Bible stories? Play a game of charades using characters from the Bible. Ask people about their favourite characters in the Bible. Why are they their favourites? Members of the congregation dress as Bible characters. Others ask questions of them.

- Look at a specific passage in different translations. Ask a visitor from the Bible Society to explain how a translation of the Bible is put together.

- Ask the groups to act out a parable from different perspectives. What would the story of the prodigal son have been from the perspective of the two sons or the father?

- How can we send a message? Identify different ways: shout, write, phone, etc. How have people in the past tried to communicate the Bible stories? Draw the outline of a large Celtic cross on the largest sheet of paper possible. Ask groups to think about the most important stories from the Bible and to draw these and add them to the cross.

- Look at ways we can learn about Bible stories without using words. Make stained glass windows using coloured cellophane or waxed crayons on greaseproof paper.

 ## Prayers/ intercessions

Use the following response after each line:

We thank you and praise you Lord

For the opportunity to know and read your Word . . .

For the life and witness of all whose stories are found within its pages . . .

For the example, inspiration and hope it gives to all . . .

Use this alternative response with the following lines:

We pray to you O God

For those who are not free to read the Word . . .

For those who cannot meet to worship without fear . . .

For those who do not know about you or your Word . . .

 ## Stories and other resources

'Bible' and 'Buildings', in *Pick and Mix*

Chabert, Marvillier and Galli, *Tell Me the Bible,* Cassell, 1991

Chris Hudson, *Family Fortunes*, NS/CHP, 1999

Sheryl Herbert, *Get into the Bible*, Bible Reading Fellowship, 1998

Drama

Dave Hopwood, 'The Good Ol' Book', in *Playing Up,* NS/CHP, 1998

 ## Music

He's got the whole wide world (JP 78)

Tell me the stories of Jesus (JP 228, MP 629)

Search me, O God (JP 212, MP 587)

The best book to read (JP 234)

The word of God (JP 474)

God be in my head (HAMNS 236, HON 166, HTC 543)

Immortal, invisible, God only wise (HAMNS 199, HON 242, HTC 21, KSHF 210, MP 327)

The heavens declare thy glory, Lord (HAMNS 168, HTC 254)

Post communion prayer

God of all grace,
your Son Jesus Christ fed the hungry
with the bread of his life
and the word of his kingdom:
renew your people with your heavenly grace,
and in all our weakness
sustain us by your true and living bread;
who is alive and reigns, now and for ever.

Dedication Festival

The first Sunday in October or Last Sunday After Trinity

 ## Readings

Genesis 28.11-18

Jacob has a dream of a stairway reaching from earth to heaven. He sees angels descending and ascending to heaven. The Lord reiterates the covenant with Jacob that he made with Abraham. Jacob names the place where he had his vision 'Bethel' (meaning house of God).

or

Revelation 21.9-14

John has a vision of the holy city, Jerusalem, coming down out of heaven from God. It shines with the glory of God and on the twelve foundations of the walls of the city are written the names of the twelve apostles of the Lamb.

1 Peter 2.1-10

Christ is the living stone, who has been rejected by men but chosen by God. We also are like living stones who are being built into God's spiritual house.

John 10.22-29

Jesus is in Jerusalem for the Feast of Dedication. Some Jews question him over his claims to be the Christ. It is Jesus' claim that 'I and the Father are one' that causes them to try and stone him to death.

Collect

Almighty God,
to whose glory we celebrate the dedication
  of this house of prayer:
we praise you for the many blessings
you have given to those who worship you here:
and we pray that all who seek you in this place
  may find you,
and, being filled with the Holy Spirit,
may become a living temple acceptable to you;
through Jesus Christ your Son our Lord,
who is alive and reigns with you,
in the unity of the Holy Spirit,
one God, now and for ever.

Talk/address/sermon

What makes a church? What do we need? Compile a list: altar, spire, stained glass windows, etc. What is important about our church building? How do we keep the building in good repair? If the church fell down or became unsafe, or burnt down, what would happen? Would that be the end of the church? The church is really us – the living stones. What do we need to do to keep a 'living stones' church in good repair?

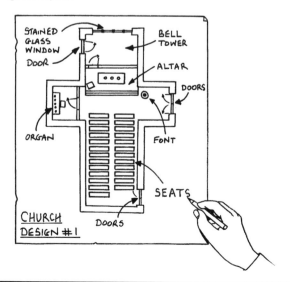

Have a roll of vinyl wallpaper unrolled down the centre aisle or in some suitable position in the church. Draw stepping stones on it. Get some people to move along the rolled-out paper from stepping stone to stepping stone as you talk about what we can be doing to prepare ourselves as God's church for Christ's coming.

Congregational/ group activities

- Design a church building from scratch. What would be the main focus? How would the walls be decorated? Where should the altar/font/seats/organ, etc. be placed? Why are they placed as they are at the moment in your church?

- Living stones graffiti wall: ask the congregation to add a prayer and their names to each brick and use these prayers in the time of intercession.

- Learn the actions to the song 'I am the church'.

- How could our church be made more welcoming to visitors? What changes could we make to ensure that all are welcome?

- Invite the headteacher or a teacher from the local school to come to the service. How could we help in preparing for a visit from school children to the church? How could the church support the school – in prayer, in visiting the school and financially?

- Look at place names in your locality. What do they mean and where do they originate? Look at the meaning of Bible names, of people, towns and cities. What do they tell us about the people and where they lived and the importance of their faith?

- Living stones: ask people in advance to bring in a photo of themselves. Cut out pieces of card in brick shapes and stick on their photo. Build up a large wall from these images.

Prayers/ intercessions

We pray that Christ may be seen in the life of the Church, saying:

Jesus, Lord of the Church:
in your mercy, hear us.

You have called us into the family
of those who are the children of God.
May our love for our brothers and sisters in Christ
be strengthened by your grace.
Jesus, Lord of the Church:
in your mercy, hear us.

You have called us to be a temple
where the Holy Spirit can dwell.
Give us clean hands and pure hearts

so that our lives will reflect your holiness.
Jesus, Lord of the Church:
in your mercy, hear us.

You have called us to be members of your body,
so that when one suffers, all suffer together.
We ask for your comfort and healing power
to bring hope to those in distress.
Jesus, Lord of the Church:
hear our prayer,
and make us one in heart and mind
to serve you with joy for ever. Amen.

Adapted from *Patterns for Worship* (pp. 80–1)

Stories and other resources

Patterns for Worship (pp. 80–1)

'Solomon's Temple', in *In the Beginning*

John Ryan, *Mabel and the Tower of Babel,* Wayland, 1993

Music

A new commandment (JP 303, MP 1)

I hear the sound (JP 100)

I am the church! (JU, p. 24)

God has put a circle round us (BBP 46)

There's no veil (SHP 130)

Be thou my vision (HAMNS 343, HON 56, HTC 545, MP 51, SHP 38)

God is here! As we his people (HAMNS 464, HTC 560)

How firm a foundation (HON 216, HTC 430, MP 243)

Post communion prayer

Father in heaven,
whose Church on earth is a sign of your heavenly peace,
an image of the new and eternal Jerusalem:
grant to us in the days of our pilgrimage
that, fed with the living bread of heaven,
and united in the body of your Son,
we may be the temple of your presence,
the place of your glory on earth,
and a sign of your peace in the world;
through Jesus Christ our Lord.

All Saints' Sunday

Sunday between 30 October and 5 November (also The Fourth Sunday Before Advent)

All Saints' Day is celebrated on the Sunday between 30 October and 5 November, or if this is not kept as All Saints' Sunday on 1 November itself. If you wish to use the collect and readings for the Fourth Sunday before Advent these can be found in *The Christian Year: Calendar, Lectionary and Collects*.

 ## Readings

Wisdom 3.1-9

Those who have trusted God in this life are under his protection even after death. God has tested them and found them to be worthy even when tried by suffering. So he will reward them for their faithfulness. They will live for ever in his presence.

or

Isaiah 25.6-9

On the day of the Lord, God will give a feast for his people whom he has delivered. He will swallow up death for ever and wipe away all tears. His people will joyfully declare all that he has done.

Revelation 21.1-6

Here is a vision of a new heaven and a new earth and the new Jerusalem. God now makes his home with us. There will be no more death, tears or pain; all is made new. God will refresh those who thirst with living water.

John 11.32-44

This is the story of the raising of Lazarus. Mary blames Jesus for not coming sooner to prevent the death of her brother Lazarus. Four days dead, he lies in a tomb. Jesus deeply moved weeps at his grave. He orders the stone at the entrance to be removed despite Mary's sister Martha's protests. He prays to his Father and declares they will see the glory of God. Then Jesus summons Lazarus. To the amazement of all Lazarus still wrapped in grave clothes comes out of the tomb.

Collect

Almighty God,
you have knit together your elect
in one communion and fellowship
   in the mystical body of your Son Christ our
   Lord:
grant us grace so to follow your blessed saints
in all virtuous and godly living
that we may come to those inexpressible joys
that you have prepared for those who truly love
   you;
through Jesus Christ your Son our Lord,
who is alive and reigns with you,
in the unity of the Holy Spirit,
one God, now and for ever.

 ## Talk/address/ sermon

How do we react to sad news? Invite responses from the congregation and write them up on a flip chart or overhead projector if available. Sometimes newspapers or the television carry stories of delayed reactions to emergency calls and their tragic results. How would we feel as a relative if this happened to a loved one? Add responses to flip chart (responses might include grief, tears, anger, frustration, being let down and possibly guilt).

 ## Congregational/ group activities

- Make a local book of remembrance. Using a loose-leaf folder or scrapbook decorate the cover with a suitable illuminated text from one of today's readings together with the name of your church. Ask older members of the congregation to suggest the names of former worshippers to be included in the book and to look for memorabilia, e.g. photos, or newspaper or magazine cuttings about them. Originals could be photocopied. The children or young people could tape record reminiscences to be transcribed later. Sensitivity of course needs to be exercised, particularly with the newly bereaved. This is a project you can develop over a month.

- Divide the congregation into groups: Marthas and Marys, Lazarus's, onlookers and disciples. Re-read the passage. Explore in each group their characters' reaction to Jesus' behaviour and words in the story for about five to ten minutes. Reform into new groups ensuring that there is at least one Martha and Mary, Lazarus, onlooker and disciple in each group. Allow each character to put their point of view to the others. Write up reactions and display them. Alternatively devise an impromptu drama based on the story incorporating each character's viewpoint on the lines indicated above

- On a large sheet of paper make two columns headed 'Sad' and 'Glad'. Look at the readings and list the sad and glad things under the appropriate heading. Alternatively younger children can make sad and glad faces on paper plates and older ones can write the appropriate text underneath.

Prayers/intercessions

The following prayer is based on today's Gospel:

Lord, Mary poured out her anger on Jesus because she felt he had let her down. Help us to show understanding to those who are hurting and distressed. (In the silence we remember . . ..)

Lord, hear us
Lord, graciously hear us

Lord, Jesus wept at Lazarus' grave. Help us not to be ashamed of expressing our pain when sad things happen in our world. (In the silence we remember . . ..)

Lord hear us
Lord, graciously hear us

Lord, Jesus was blamed for not really caring about his friend. Help us not to answer back when we are misunderstood by others. (In the silence we remember . . ..)

Lord, hear us
Lord, graciously hear us

Lord, Jesus prayed that those at the grave might have faith to see the glory of God. Be with those who doubt your goodness. (In the silence we remember . . ..)

Lord, hear us
Lord, graciously hear us

Lord, Jesus called back Lazarus from death. Help us to see that his faithful people are safe within his hands. (In the silence we remember . . ..)

Lord, hear us
Lord graciously hear us

Stories and other resources

Robert Atwell, *Celebrating the Saints* (p. 399), Canterbury Press, 1998

'All Saints', in *Seasons and Saints for the Christian Year* (p. 95)

Meryl Doney, *The Very Worried Sparrow*, Lion, 1993

'All Saints', in *Seasons, Saints and Sticky Tape*

Lesley Francis and Nicola Slee, *Autumn: Betsy Bear Learns about Death*, NCEC, 1996

Mary Hathaway, *A Word for all Seasons*, Kevin Mayhew, 1997

C.S. Lewis, 'Further up and Farther in' (especially p. 157ff), in *The Last Battle*, Lion, 1980

Drama

Derek Haylock, 'A grave business', in *Sketches from Scripture*, NS/CHP, 1992

'Lazarus', in *Playing Up*

Music

Mighty in victory (JP 430)

I'm not ashamed to own my Lord (HON 240, MP 323)

O Lord, all the world belongs to you (HON 378)

How deep the Father's love (SHP 54)

I am the bread of life (HON 222, MP 261, SHF 182)

Jerusalem the golden (HON 259, HTC 573)

Post communion prayer

God, the source of all holiness
    and giver of all good things:
may we who have shared at this table
    as strangers and pilgrims here on earth
be welcomed with all your saints
    to the heavenly feast on the day of your kingdom;
through Jesus Christ our Lord.

The Third Sunday Before Advent

Sunday between 6 and 12 November

 ### Readings

Jonah 3.1-5,10

Jonah the prophet now obeys God and goes to Nineveh to warn the people that their great city will soon be destroyed. The Ninevites believe God and turn away from their wrongdoing. God has pity on them and spares them.

Hebrews 9.24-28

Hebrews was probably written to a group of Christians tempted to return to observing Jewish religious practices and thus escape persecution for being Christians. The sacrificial ritual of high priests in the Temple had to be repeated annually to gain only limited access to God. Christ's sacrificial death was all that was necessary to do away with sin once and for all. Consequently he has opened up for us the way into the presence of God. He will come again to save those who eagerly await him.

Mark 1.14-20

After the imprisonment of John the Baptist Jesus begins his ministry in Galilee. His message is 'Repent and believe the good news'. He calls the fishermen Simon and Andrew, James and John to come with him and catch men. They immediately follow him.

Collect

Almighty Father,
whose will is to restore all things
in your beloved Son, the king of all:
govern the hearts and minds of those in authority,
and bring the families of the nations,
divided and torn apart by the ravages of sin,
to be subject to his just and gentle rule;
who is alive and reigns with you,
in the unity of the Holy Spirit,
one God, now and for ever.

 ### Talk/address/ sermon

Give the congregation a piece of paper and ask them to draw or briefly describe in a sentence their picture of God. These need not be shown to anyone else. Get them to reflect on this exercise for a short time.

A boy was once asked to draw a picture of God. He drew a picture of a burglar complete with a bag labelled swag. Underneath he wrote: 'God made bad people too'. Jonah had a problem with this viewpoint. If we read the rest of the story he wanted the people of Nineveh to be punished for their evil deeds. But what about him, wasn't he bad too?

God made bad people too

In the Gospel Jesus picks some very flawed people to be his disciples. Simon Peter denied him, James and John quarrelled continually about their importance, Judas betrayed him. Look also at the background and behaviour of some of the others, e.g. Matthew and Simon the Zealot, Thomas and Mary Magdalen.

Of course, God wants people to change (repent), but he offers us the good news that he can help us change. Do we need to change our picture of God?

Congregational/ group activities

- Continue work on your remembrance book. You might like to add some less than perfect people whom God has changed. Suggestions might include the dying thief in Luke's Gospel, St Paul, the persecutor turned apostle, and John Newton, the slave trader.

- Read younger ones the story of Burglar Bill. Talk about why he and Burglar Betty changed.

- Make a chart of the story of Peter through Mark's Gospel. Note his failures and his high points (ref. Mark 1.16-18, 8.27-30, 31-33, 9.2-7, 14.29-31, 14.66-72, 16.4-7).

- Look at the story of Jonah and tell it in cartoon form, e.g. his first call, the storm at sea, being swallowed by the big fish, preaching in Nineveh, the people of Nineveh at prayer, etc.

- Share stories about the changes that following Jesus has made to our lives. Turn them into thank you prayers that you can offer later in the service.

Prayers/ intercessions

Play a recording quietly of John Newton's hymn 'Amazing grace' inviting the congregation to offer their thank you prayers to God while the music is playing.

*R*ead this story:

A child was taken to see a sculptor at work. He watched him wielding the hammer and chisel and the chips of stone flying this way and that. But he could see no recognizable shape, because work on this particular block of stone had only just begun.

A few weeks later he was taken to the workshop again. The child stared in amazement: 'How did you know there was a lion in there?'

Jesus sees the rock in Simon Peter while he is still a fisherman. He also sees the lion inside us. Invite the congregation to spend some time thinking about this, then end with this prayer:

> O Christ, the Master Carpenter
> Who, at the last, through wood and nails
> Purchased our whole salvation,
> Wield well your tools in the workshop of your world,
> So that we, who come rough-hewn to your bench,
> May here be fashioned to a truer beauty of your hand.
> We ask it for your own name's sake.

Arthur Gray, *Iona Community Worship Book* (p. 98)

Stories and other resources

Janet and Allan Ahlberg, *Burglar Bill,* Picture Lions, 1979

Nick Fawcett, 'Following Jesus', in *Prayers for all Seasons*, Kevin Mayhew, 1995

Michael Forster, 'Having a whale of a time', in *The Word for all Age Worship*, Kevin Mayhew, 1995 (p. 60)

Francis Dewar, *Live for a Change*, Darton, Longman and Todd, 1988 (p. 71)

Jan Godfrey, 'Jesus' Friends', in *Praise, Play and Paint!*, NS/CHP, 1995 (p. 96)

Drama

Dave Hopwood, 'Wet fish and stomach acid', *A Fistful of Sketches,* NS/CHP, 1996

Dave and Lynn Hopwood, 'Jonah and the whale', in *Telling Tales,* CPAS, 1997

Music

I will make you fishers of men (JP 123)

Big man (JP 16)

Peter and James and John (JP 197)

O happy day! (HON 369, MP 499)

James and Andrew, Peter and John (HON 257)

Jesus, take me as I am (MP 382)

Jesus, you are changing me (MP 389)

Glory be to Jesus (HAMNS 66, HON 159, HTC 126, KSHF 125)

God has spoken – by his prophets (HTC 248)

Join all the glorious names (HTC 214, MP 392)

Post communion prayer

God of peace,
whose Son Jesus Christ proclaimed the kingdom
and restored the broken to wholeness of life:
look with compassion on the anguish of the world,
and by your healing power
make whole both people and nations;
through our Lord and Saviour Jesus Christ.

The Second Sunday Before Advent

Sunday between 13 and 19 November inclusive

 ### Readings

Daniel 12.1-3

In times of persecution and darkness God's people need the hope and assurance that God has not abandoned them. Daniel's message is that at the end God will deliver his people and demonstrate his justice.

Hebrews 10.11-14(15-18),19-25

The context of Hebrews as we saw last week is the pressure of persecution. Accordingly the writer urges them not to return to the old ways for Christ's sacrificial death has opened up a new way to God. Now we have confidence to enter God's presence. Draw near to him, hold on to hope, and encourage one another to act lovingly. In no way neglect meeting with one another regularly for worship as we eagerly await God's day.

Mark 13.1-8

Jesus tells his disciples that the impressive temple buildings they are admiring will be razed to the ground. Jesus warns them that there will be false Messiahs, wars, rumours, famines and earthquakes, but the end is yet to come.

Collect

Heavenly Father,
whose blessed Son was revealed
  to destroy the works of the devil
and to make us the children of God and heirs of
  eternal life:
grant that we, having this hope,
may purify ourselves even as he is pure;
that when he shall appear in power and great glory
we may be made like him
  in his eternal and glorious kingdom;
where he is alive and reigns with you,
in the unity of the Holy Spirit,
one God, now and for ever.

 ### Talk/address/ sermon

'Lord, give me patience, but hurry up!' is a prayer we can readily identify with. Few people like waiting even for pleasant things. Waiting is something that we all have to do and often endure. Explore with the congregation the things we have to wait for both good and bad.

So how do we wait? Expectantly? Hopefully? Fearfully? Anxiously? Resignedly? Prayerfully? Or simply by filling in time?

But what if you are suffering or in pain? A wit remarked that we call people in hospital or doctor's and dentist's waiting rooms 'patients' because they often have to be! What if you are being persecuted or tortured or imprisoned for your beliefs as still happens today in the world. What would help you? Invite suggestions. Write them on a flip chart or overhead projector. One thing that helped early Christians wait was their hope in the day of the Lord. On that day God would bring justice and vindication to those who suffered for him and show that they were not forgotten.

Congregational/ group activities

- In the Second World War the government employed Winston Churchill lookalikes to deceive the enemy. For more sinister reasons Shift, the ape in C.S. Lewis' *The Last Battle* dresses up poor Puzzle the donkey in a lion's skin to fool others into believing he is Aslan, Lord of Narnia. He then uses Aslan's name and reputation in a bid for power. Some people have to distinguish between fakes and genuine articles as part of their job. If you have someone in the congregation who is an antique dealer, a bank cashier, a detective, a trading standards' officer or vehicle inspector, etc., ask about how they would go about this. Make a list of questions to ask.

- Play a truth game. Ask someone to bring one or two genuine articles and some imitations/fakes/copies, e.g. real and cosmetic jewellery, fashion clothing and cheap imitations, or branded foods or toys and imitations. Devise some tests to distinguish the genuine from the fake.

- Jesus warns us in today's Gospel about the dangers of deception. There are those who seek to mislead or deceive us about faith matters. How might the exercises we have done help us in testing for truth? Make a list of the tests we might use. Or read the parable in Francis Dewar's *Live for a Change* (p. 9).

- Find out about those who are persecuted today. Material can be gained from a number of agencies including The Barnabas Fund (The Old Rectory, River Street, Pewsey, Wiltshire SN9 5DB) or Amnesty International. Perhaps you might make this a regular monthly intercession feature and display information on your notice board.

- Add to your remembrance book the names and short stories of those who suffered in war from persecution. These can be either locally known 'saints' or national or international figures. Edith Cavell, Maximilian Kolbe, Janani Luwum, Oscar Romero, Corrie Ten Boon and Martin Luther King are some possibilities. Their stories and others can be found in some of the resource books listed below.

Prayers/ intercessions

Either pray for the persecuted: you could adapt the prayer 'The God of Columba' (p. 89) in *The Iona Community Worship Book* to include your own list of the persecuted. Other useful prayers can be found in the *Lion Prayer Collection* in the section headed 'World poverty and oppression' (p. 233).

Or if you have explored the theme of 'waiting' in the service there is a helpful litany entitled 'You keep us waiting' in *The Iona Community Worship Book* (p. 80).

Stories and other resources

Mary Batchelor, *Lion Prayer Collection*, Lion Publishing, 1992

Ted Burge, *Lord for all Seasons*, Canterbury Press, 1998

Francis Dewar, *Live for a Change*, Darton Longman and Todd, 1988

Geoffrey Hanks, *70 Great Christians*, Christian Focus Publications, 1992

'The God of Columba', in *The Iona Community Worship Book*

C.S. Lewis, *The Last Battle*, Lions, 1980 (pp. 7–37)

Cleodie Mackinnon, *Stories of Courage*, Oxford Children's Reference Library, OUP, 1974

 Music

Be bold, be strong (JP 14, MP 49)

I walk by faith (SHP 61)

Purify my heart (SHP 112)

Do not be afraid (MP 115)

Hallelujah, my Father (KSHF 149, MP 206)

When I needed a neighbour (HAMNS 433, HON 548, JP 275)

Crown him with many crowns (HAMNS 147, HON 103, HTC 174, MP 109, SHF 75)

Holy Spirit, Truth divine (HTC 235)

The head that once was crowned with thorns (HAMNS 141, HON 480, HTC 182, KSHF 508, MP 647)

Forth in thy name, O Lord (HAMNS 239, HON 143, HTC 306, MP 159)

Post communion prayer

Gracious Lord,
in this holy sacrament
you give substance to our hope:
bring us at the last
to that fullness of life for which we long;
through Jesus Christ our Saviour.

Christ the King

Sunday between 20 and 26 November inclusive (also The Sunday Next Before Advent)

 ### Readings

Daniel 7.9-10,13-14

The Jews are in exile and need reassurance that God has not abandoned them. Daniel records a vision of the heavenly court in session. The books of judgement are opened. Then one like a Son of Man coming in glory enters the throne room. He is given supreme authority for ever by the Ancient of Days.

Revelation 1.4b-8

A vision of Christ in glory intended to encourage a suffering and persecuted Church. Christ is surely coming. He will finally vindicate his people. He will not come in obscurity, rather every eye will behold him. Those who caused his death will see his scars. All will bow down before him.

John 18.33-37

At the trial of Jesus Pilate questions him regarding the nature of his kingship. Jesus has been charged with the political crime of rebellion against Rome. However, Jesus emphatically denies any designs for political power or military conquest. While he accepts the title of king, Jesus prefers to see his identity as a witness to the truth. His genuine subjects are those who listen to him.

Collect

Eternal Father,
whose Son Jesus Christ ascended to the throne
   of heaven that he might rule over all things as
   Lord and King:
keep the Church in the unity of the Spirit
and in the bond of peace,
and bring the whole created order to worship at
   his feet;
who is alive and reigns with you,
in the unity of the Holy Spirit,
one God, now and for ever.

 ### Talk/address/ sermon

Show a picture of Christ in glory on which the scars of his crucifixion are visible. (You may be fortunate in having a stained glass window that depicts this, but a large reproduction of Graham Sutherland's *Coventry Cathedral Tapestry* would also be suitable. Point out that Christian artists who portray Christ in glory consistently show the marks of his suffering. In this they are following the tradition of Scripture, for instance the Suffering Servant raised to glory found in Isaiah 53 and elsewhere in the Bible. John in his Gospel sees the moment of Christ's glory in his being lifted up on the cross to die (John 12.31,32). In Revelation when the Lion of Judah is announced they see a lamb looking as if had been slain (Rev 5.5,6).

If Jesus is only shown as the man on the cross then those who suffer may feel a sense of despair – so that's the fate of the good and innocent. If he is portrayed unmarked by suffering then those who suffer may well think – he does not speak to us, he cannot understand. A victorious king on the other hand who bears the scars of his suffering gives them reason for hope in the darkness.

Congregational/ group activities

- Make a banner that depicts both aspects of Christ's kingship, his suffering and his glory. Graham Kendrick's hymns, 'Meekness and majesty', or 'The Servant King (From heaven you came)' may supply you with useful images. You could display your banner at a final procession at the end of the service.

- Make bunting in the method suggested in *Seasons and Saints for the Christian Year* (p. 96), but use pictures or symbols associated with Jesus, e.g. king, lion, lamb, shepherd, light of the world, bread of life, the vine, the carpenter, teacher, healer, saviour, prophet, etc. Display in the church or use to decorate an Advent Jesse tree.

- Complete your book of remembrance. Use the names written in your book in your intercessions and place it on display in the church.
- Read the last few paragraphs of C.S. Lewis' *The Last Battle* (p. 171 to end) to your group and reflect on them. He speaks of eternal life as 'Chapter One of the Great Stories which no one on earth has read which goes on for ever; in which every chapter is better than the one before' (p. 172). How helpful do we find this?

Prayers/ intercessions

Praise and thanksgiving for the reign of Christ are the theme of our worship today so our prayers should reflect this. The Te Deum provides an excellent framework for prayer especially if we have been making a book of remembrance this month. (The biddings in brackets are suggestions, please feel free to adapt.)

Leader: You are God and we praise you:
you are the Lord and we acclaim you;
you are the eternal Father:
all creation worships you.
To you all angels all the powers of heaven:
cherubim and seraphim sing in endless praise,
Holy holy holy Lord God of power and might:
heaven and earth are full of your glory.
Especially we praise you for . . .
(*the wonder and beauty of creation*)

All: **You are God and we praise you:
you are the Lord and we acclaim you.**

Leader: The glorious company of apostles praise you:
the noble fellowship of prophets praise you
the white-robed army of martyrs praise you.
Throughout the world the holy Church acclaims you:
Father of majesty unbounded;
your true and only Son worthy of all worship:
and the Holy Spirit advocate and guide.
Especially we give thanks for your grace shown in the lives of . . . (*here mention names from your book of remembrance or past members of the church, patron saints etc.*)

All: **You are God and we praise you:
you are the Lord and we acclaim you.**

Leader: You Christ are the King of glory:
the eternal Son of the Father.
When you took our flesh to set us free:
you did not abhor the Virgin's womb.
You overcame the sting of death:
and opened the kingdom of heaven to all believers.

(*Thank you for coming among us and giving your life for us so we might live.*)

All: **You are God and we praise you:
you are the Lord and we acclaim you.**

Leader: You are seated at God's right hand in glory:
we believe that you will come and be our judge.
Come then Lord and help your people:
bought with the price of your own blood;
and bring us with your saints:
to glory everlasting.
(*Honour those who suffer persecution, comfort those who mourn and bring us to reign with you in glory.*)

All: **You are God and we praise you:
you are the Lord and we acclaim you.**

Adapted from the Te Deum (ICET)

Stories and other resources

C.S. Lewis, *The Last Battle*, chapter 16, Lions, 1980

'Ascension', in *Pick and Mix*

Stuart Thomas, *Come to the Feast Book 1*, Kevin Mayhew, 1997 (pp. 117–19)

Seasons and Saints for the Christian Year (p. 96)

 # Music

You are the King of glory (JP 296)

Who's the king of the jungle? (JP 289)

King of kings and Lord of lords (JP 148)

Jesus is king (MP 366, SHP 76)

The King is among us (MP 650)

Christ is the King! O friends rejoice (HAMNS 345)

Let all the world in every corner sing (HAMNS 202, HON 296, HTC 342, MP 404)

The Kingdom is upon you! (HAMNS 512)

O worship the King all glorious above (HAMNS 101, HON 393, HTC 24, MP 528)

Post communion prayer

Stir up, O Lord,
the wills of your faithful people;
that they, plenteously bringing forth the fruit of good works,
may by you be plenteously rewarded;
through Jesus Christ our Lord.

Christ the King

Appendix A

Collects and Post Communion Prayers
Ordinary Time (Before Lent)

The following prayers will be used with the Proper 1, 2 or 3 services. Please see the tables on these Sundays to match the collects and post communion prayers with the correct services.

The Fifth Sunday Before Lent

Collect

Almighty God,
by whose grace alone we are accepted
    and called to your service:
strengthen us by your Holy Spirit
and make us worthy of our calling;
through Jesus Christ your Son our Lord,
who is alive and reigns with you,
in the unity of the Holy Spirit,
one God, now and for ever.

Post communion prayer

God of truth,
we have seen with our eyes
    and touched with our hands the bread of life:
strengthen our faith
that we may grow in love for you and for each other;
through Jesus Christ our Lord.

The Fourth Sunday Before Lent

Collect

O God,
you know us to be set
in the midst of so many and great dangers,
that by reason of the fraility of our nature
we cannot always stand upright:
grant to us such strength and protection
as may support us in all dangers
and carry us through all temptations;
through Jesus Christ your Son our Lord,
who is alive and reigns with you,
in the unity of the Holy Spirit,
one God, now and for ever.

Post communion prayer

Go before us, Lord, in all we do
with your most gracious favour,
and guide us with your continual help,
that in all our works
begun, continued and ended in you,
we may glorify your holy name,
and finally by your mercy receive everlasting life;
through Jesus Christ our Lord.

The Third Sunday Before Lent

Collect

Almighty God,
who alone can bring order
to the unruly wills and passions of sinful humanity:
give your people grace
so to love what you command
and to desire what you promise,
that, among the many changes of this world,
our hearts may surely there be fixed
where true joys are to be found;
through Jesus Christ your Son our Lord,
who is alive and reigns with you,
in the unity of the Holy Spirit,
one God, now and for ever.

Post communion prayer

Merciful Father,
who gave Jesus Christ to be for us the bread of life,
that those who come to him should never hunger:
draw us to the Lord in faith and love,
that we may eat and drink with him
at his table in the kingdom,
where he is alive and reigns, now and for ever.

Appendix B

Collects and Post Communion Prayers
Ordinary Time
(After Trinity and Before Advent)

The First Sunday After Trinity

Collect

O God,
the strength of all those who put their trust in you,
mercifully accept our prayers
and, because through the weakness of our mortal
    nature
we can do no good thing without you,
grant us the help of your grace,
that in the keeping of your commandments
we may please you both in will and deed;
through Jesus Christ your Son our Lord,
who is alive and reigns with you,
in the unity of the Holy Spirit,
one God, now and for ever.

Post communion prayer

Eternal Father,
we thank you for nourishing us
with these heavenly gifts:
may our communion strengthen us in faith,
build us up in hope,
and make us grow in love;
for the sake of Jesus Christ our Lord.

The Second Sunday After Trinity

Collect

Lord, you have taught us
that all our doings without love are nothing worth:
send your Holy Spirit
and pour into our hearts that most excellent gift of
    love,
the true bond of peace and of all virtues,
without which whoever lives is counted dead before
    you.
Grant this for your only Son Jesus Christ's sake,
who is alive and reigns with you,
in the unity of the Holy Spirit,
one God, now and for ever.

Post communion prayer

Loving Father,
we thank you for feeding us at the supper of your Son:
sustain us with your Spirit,
that we may serve you here on earth
until our joy is complete in heaven,
and we share in the eternal banquet
with Jesus Christ our Lord.

The Third Sunday After Trinity

Collect

Almighty God,
you have broken the tyranny of sin
and have sent the Spirit of your Son into our hearts
    whereby we call you Father:
give us grace to dedicate our freedom to your service,
that we and all creation may be brought
    to the glorious liberty of the children of God;
through Jesus Christ your Son our Lord,
who is alive and reigns with you,
in the unity of the Holy Spirit,
one God, now and for ever.

Post communion prayer

O God, whose beauty is beyond our imagining
and whose power we cannot comprehend:
show us your glory as far as we can grasp it,
and shield us from knowing more than we can bear
until we may look upon you without fear;
through Jesus Christ our Saviour.

The Fourth Sunday After Trinity

Collect

O God, the protector of all who trust in you,
without whom nothing is strong, nothing is holy:
increase and multiply upon us your mercy;
that with you as our ruler and guide
we may so pass through things temporal
that we lose not our hold on things eternal;
grant this, heavenly Father,
for our Lord Jesus Christ's sake,
who is alive and reigns with you,
in the unity of the Holy Spirit,
one God, now and for ever.

Post communion prayer

Eternal God,
comfort of the afflicted and healer of the broken,
you have fed us at the table of life and hope:
teach us the ways of gentleness and peace,
that all the world may acknowledge
the kingdom of your Son Jesus Christ our Lord.

The Fifth Sunday After Trinity

Collect

Almighty and everlasting God,
by whose Spirit the whole body of the Church
    is governed and sanctified:
hear our prayer which we offer for all your faithful people,
that in their vocation and ministry
they may serve you in holiness and truth
to the glory of your name;
through our Lord and Saviour Jesus Christ,
who is alive and reigns with you,
in the unity of the Holy Spirit,
one God, now and for ever.

Post communion prayer

Grant, O Lord, we beseech you,
that the course of this world may be so peaceably
    ordered by your governance,
that your Church may joyfully serve you
    in all godly quietness;
through Jesus Christ our Lord.

The Sixth Sunday After Trinity

Collect

Merciful God,
you have prepared for those who love you
such good things as pass our understanding:
pour into our hearts such love toward you
that we, loving you in all things and above all things,
may obtain your promises,
which exceed all that we can desire;
through Jesus Christ your Son our Lord,
who is alive and reigns with you,
in the unity of the Holy Spirit,
one God, now and for ever.

Post communion prayer

God of our pilgrimage,
you have led us to the living water:
refresh and sustain us
as we go forward on our journey,
in the name of Jesus Christ our Lord.

The Seventh Sunday After Trinity

Collect

Lord of all power and might,
the author and giver of all good things:
graft in our hearts the love of your name,
increase in us true religion,
nourish us with all goodness,
and of your great mercy keep us in the same;
through Jesus Christ your Son our Lord,
who is alive and reigns with you,
in the unity of the Holy Spirit,
one God, now and for ever.

Post communion prayer

Lord God, whose Son is the true vine and the source
    of life,
ever giving himself that the world may live:
may we so receive within ourselves
    the power of his death and passion
that, in his saving cup,
    we may share his glory and be made perfect in his
    love;
for he is alive and reigns, now and for ever.

The Eighth Sunday After Trinity

Collect

Almighty Lord and everlasting God,
we beseech you to direct, sanctify and govern
    both our hearts and bodies
in the ways of your laws
    and the works of your commandments;
that through your most mighty protection, both here
    and ever,
we may be preserved in body and soul;
through our Lord and Saviour Jesus Christ,
who is alive and reigns with you,
in the unity of the Holy Spirit,
one God, now and for ever.

Post communion prayer

Strengthen for service, Lord,
the hands that have taken holy things;
may the ears which have heard your word
    be deaf to clamour and dispute;
may the tongues which have sung your praise
    be free from deceit;
may the eyes which have seen the tokens of your love
    shine with the light of hope;
and may the bodies which have been fed with your
    body
    be refreshed with the fullness of your life;
glory to you for ever.

The Ninth Sunday After Trinity

Collect

Almighty God,
who sent your Holy Spirit
to be the life and light of your Church:
open our hearts to the riches of your grace,
that we may bring forth the fruit of the Spirit
in love and joy and peace;
through Jesus Christ your Son our Lord,
who is alive and reigns with you,
in the unity of the Holy Spirit,
one God, now and for ever.

Post communion prayer

Holy Father,
who gathered us here around the table of your Son
to share this meal with the whole household of God:
in that new world
    where you reveal the fullness of your peace,
gather people of every race and language
    to share in the eternal banquet
    of Jesus Christ our Lord.

The Tenth Sunday After Trinity

Collect

Let your merciful ears, O Lord,
be open to the prayers of your humble servants;
and that they may obtain their petitions
make them to ask such things as shall please you;
through Jesus Christ your Son our Lord,
who is alive and reigns with you,
in the unity of the Holy Spirit,
one God, now and for ever.

Post communion prayer

God of our pilgrimage,
you have willed that the gate of mercy
should stand open for those who trust in you:
look upon us with your favour
that we who follow the path of your will
may never wander from the way of life;
through Jesus Christ our Lord.

The Eleventh Sunday After Trinity

Collect

O God, you declare your almighty power
most chiefly in showing mercy and pity:
mercifully grant to us such a measure of your grace,
that we, running the way of your commandments,
may receive your gracious promises,
and be made partakers of your heavenly treasure;
through Jesus Christ your Son our Lord,
who is alive and reigns with you,
in the unity of the Holy Spirit,
one God, now and for ever.

Post communion prayer

Lord of all mercy,
we your faithful people have celebrated that one true
    sacrifice
    which takes away our sins and brings pardon and
    peace:
by our communion
keep us firm on the foundation of the gospel
and preserve us from all sin;
through Jesus Christ our Lord.

The Twelfth Sunday After Trinity

Collect

Almighty and everlasting God,
you are always more ready to hear than we to pray
and to give more than either we desire or deserve:
pour down upon us the abundance of your mercy,
forgiving us those things of which our conscience is
   afraid
and giving us those good things
   which we are not worthy to ask
but through the merits and mediation
of Jesus Christ your Son our Lord,
who is alive and reigns with you,
in the unity of the Holy Spirit,
one God, now and for ever.

Post communion prayer

God of all mercy,
in this eucharist you have set aside our sins
and given us your healing:
grant that we who are made whole in Christ
may bring that healing to this broken world,
in the name of Jesus Christ our Lord.

The Thirteenth Sunday After Trinity

Collect

Almighty God,
who called your Church to bear witness
that you were in Christ reconciling the world to yourself:
help us to proclaim the good news of your love,
that all who hear it may be drawn to you;
through him who was lifted up on the cross,
and reigns with you in the unity of the Holy Spirit,
one God, now and for ever.

Post communion prayer

God our creator,
you feed your children with the true manna,
the living bread from heaven:
let this holy food sustain us through our earthly pilgrimage
until we come to that place
   where hunger and thirst are no more;
through Jesus Christ our Lord.

The Fourteenth Sunday After Trinity

Collect

Almighty God,
whose only Son has opened for us
a new and living way into your presence:
give us pure hearts and steadfast wills
to worship you in spirit and in truth;
through Jesus Christ your Son our Lord,
who is alive and reigns with you,
in the unity of the Holy Spirit,
one God, now and for ever.

Post communion prayer

Lord God, the source of truth and love,
keep us faithful to the apostles' teaching
   and fellowship,
united in prayer and the breaking of bread,
and one in joy and simplicity of heart,
in Jesus Christ our Lord.

The Fifteenth Sunday After Trinity

Collect

God, who in generous mercy sent the Holy Spirit
    upon your Church in the burning fire of your love:
grant that your people may be fervent
    in the fellowship of the gospel
that, always abiding in you,
they may be found steadfast in faith and active in ser-
    vice;
through Jesus Christ your Son our Lord,
who is alive and reigns with you,
in the unity of the Holy Spirit,
one God, now and for ever.

Post communion prayer

Keep, O Lord, your Church,
    with your perpetual mercy;
and, because without you our human frailty cannot but
    fall,
keep us ever by your help from all things hurtful,
and lead us to all things profitable to our salvation;
through Jesus Christ our Lord.

The Sixteenth Sunday After Trinity

Collect

O Lord, we beseech you mercifully to hear the prayers
    of your people who call upon you;
and grant that they may both perceive and know
    what things they ought to do,
and also may have grace and power
    faithfully to fulfil them;
through Jesus Christ your Son our Lord,
who is alive and reigns with you,
in the unity of the Holy Spirit,
one God, now and for ever.

Post communion prayer

Almighty God,
you have taught us through your Son
that love is the fulfilling of the law:
grant that we may love you with our whole heart
and our neighbours as ourselves;
through Jesus Christ our Lord.

The Seventeenth Sunday After Trinity

Collect

Almighty God,
you have made us for yourself,
and our hearts are restless till they find their rest in
    you:
pour your love into our hearts and draw us to yourself,
and so bring us at last to your heavenly city
where we shall see you face to face;
through Jesus Christ your Son our Lord,
who is alive and reigns with you,
in the unity of the Holy Spirit,
one God, now and for ever.

Post communion prayer

Lord, we pray that your grace
    may always precede and follow us,
and make us continually to be given to all good works;
through Jesus Christ our Lord.

The Eighteenth Sunday After Trinity

Collect

Almighty and everlasting God,
increase in us your gift of faith
that, forsaking what lies behind
and reaching out to that which is before,
we may run the way of your commandments
and win the crown of everlasting joy;
through Jesus Christ your Son our Lord,
who is alive and reigns with you,
in the unity of the Holy Spirit,
one God, now and for ever.

Post communion prayer

We praise and thank you, O Christ, for this sacred
    feast:
for here we receive you,
here the memory of your passion is renewed,
here our minds are filled with grace,
and here a pledge of future glory is given,
when we shall feast at that table where you reign
with all your saints for ever.

The Nineteenth Sunday After Trinity

Collect

O God, forasmuch as without you
we are not able to please you;
mercifully grant that your Holy Spirit
may in all things direct and rule our hearts;
through Jesus Christ your Son our Lord,
who is alive and reigns with you,
in the unity of the Holy Spirit,
one God, now and for ever.

Post communion prayer

Holy and blessed God,
you have fed us with the body and blood of your Son
and filled us with your Holy Spirit:
may we honour you,
not only with our lips
but in lives dedicated to the service
    of Jesus Christ our Lord.

The Twentieth Sunday After Trinity

Collect

God, the giver of life,
whose Holy Spirit wells up within your Church:
by the Spirit's gifts equip us to live the gospel of Christ
    and make us eager to do your will,
that we may share with the whole creation
    the joys of eternal life;
through Jesus Christ your Son our Lord,
who is alive and reigns with you,
in the unity of the Holy Spirit,
one God, now and for ever.

Post communion prayer

God our Father,
whose Son, the light unfailing,
has come from heaven to deliver the world
    from the darkness of ignorance:
let these holy mysteries open the eyes of our under-
    standing
that we may know the way of life,
and walk in it without stumbling;
through Jesus Christ our Lord.

The Twenty-First Sunday After Trinity

Collect

Grant, we beseech you, merciful Lord,
to your faithful people pardon and peace,
that they may be cleansed from all their sins
and serve you with a quiet mind;
through Jesus Christ your Son our Lord,
who is alive and reigns with you,
in the unity of the Holy Spirit,
one God, now and for ever.

Post communion prayer

Father of light,
in whom is no change or shadow of turning,
you give us every good and perfect gift
and have brought us to birth by your word of truth:
may we be a living sign of that kingdom
where your whole creation will be made perfect
   in Jesus Christ our Lord.

The Last Sunday After Trinity

Collect

Blessed Lord,
who caused all holy scriptures
   to be written for our learning:
help us so to hear them,
to read, mark, learn and inwardly digest them
that, through patience, and the comfort of your holy
   word,
we may embrace and for ever hold fast
   the hope of everlasting life,
which you have given us in our Saviour Jesus Christ,
who is alive and reigns with you,
in the unity of the Holy Spirit,
one God, now and for ever.

Post communion prayer

God of all grace,
your Son Jesus Christ fed the hungry
with the bread of his life
and the word of his kingdom:
renew your people with your heavenly grace,
and in all our weakness
sustain us by your true and living bread;
who is alive and reigns, now and for ever.

Music and drama books from National Society/ Church House Publishing

Acting Up
Dave Hopwood

This selection of 27 raps, narrated mimes, response stories, entertaining monologues and dialogue sketches is specially written for performance to or by children.   £5.95   ISBN 0 7151 4866 4

Feeling Good!
Peter Churchill

Thirty delightful songs specially written for younger children to sing in church, school or at home.   £5.95   ISBN 0 7151 4850 8

A Fistful of Sketches
Dave Hopwood

This collection of 27 narrated mimes, mimes to well-known pieces of popular music, sketches, raps, performance poems and prayers are designed for young people to perform or enjoy.

£5.95   ISBN 0 7151 4869 9

Jump Up If You're Wearing Red

Fifty brand-new or well-loved traditional songs are included in this book, with helpful diagrams and simple explanations of the easy-to-follow, fun action. The songs are ideal for singing with youngsters aged 3–9 in church children's groups, nursery and primary schools, family services and at home.   £11.95   ISBN 0 7151 4868 0

Playing Up
Dave Hopwood

Thirty witty and thought-provoking sketches specially written for use with children in family services, school assemblies or as street theatre, which bring to life all the action, adventure and excitement of a range of Bible stories.   £6.95   ISBN 0 7151 4895 8

Plays for all Seasons
Derek Haylock

Twenty-one drama pieces about the special days and seasons of the Christian year – from Advent and Christmas to Harvest and All Saints' Day.   £6.95   ISBN 0 7151 4884 2